A QUESTION OF PRIVILEGE

CAROLYN GOSSAGE

A QUESTION OF PRIVILEGE

CANADA'S INDEPENDENT SCHOOLS

PETER MARTIN
ASSOCIATES LIMITED

Canadian Cataloguing in Publication Data

Gossage, Carolyn, 1933-
    A question of privilege

Bibliography: p.
Includes index.
ISBN 0 88778-156-X

1. Private schools – Canada – History.   I. Title.
LC51.G68   371'.02'0971   C77-001253-1

Design: Michael Solomon

PETER MARTIN ASSOCIATES LIMITED
280 Bloor Street West, Toronto, Canada M5S 1W1

United Kingdom: Books Canada, 1 Bedford Road, London N2, England

ACKNOWLEDGEMENTS

Much of the research for this book was made possible through grants from the Canada Council Explorations Program and the Ontario Council for the Arts. In addition, the cooperation of the member schools of both the Canadian Headmasters' Association and the Canadian Association of Principals of Independent Schools for Girls was invaluable. Almost without exception the assistance I received from these schools and from individual staff members went far beyond the bounds of basic courtesy. The contents of their archives, yearbooks, scrapbooks, old letters, diaries and documents were made available, pictures and photographs were removed from walls, interviews were arranged, working space provided. In short, nothing was too much trouble, and I am most grateful.

Beyond this there are countless friends, relatives, colleagues and even total strangers who have been extraordinarily helpful and supportive, to say nothing of my long-suffering family.

To Margaret Wente I owe a special debt for her efforts with the editing of the manuscript. Her interest and enthusiasm were truly gratifying.

Among the many others to whom I am particularly indebted for advice and encouragement are Miss Katharine Lamont, Dr. Stephen Penton, Alison Prentice and the late Dr. Hilda Neatby. I would also like to thank Lynn Corrigan, Shirley Stewart and Mr. and Mrs. H. Swinkin for the typing and transcription of the manuscript and other material and to Peter Secor for his technical assistance with the photographs and enlargements.

My appreciation is also extended to the many artists and photographers, known and unknown, amateur and professional, whose original efforts made possible the illustrations —illustrations which were obtained from such a wide variety of sources that individual acknowledgement is virtually impossible.

Much useful information was also made available to me through the following institutions, organizations and governmental departments: Archives of the City of Vancouver; Archives of the Province of Nova Scotia; Association of Independent Colleges and Schools in Alberta; Department of Education of British Columbia; Department of Education of Manitoba;

Department of Education of Nova Scotia; Department of Education of Saskatchewan; Independent Schools Association of British Columbia; Manitoba Provincial Archives; New Brunswick Provincial Archives; Newfoundland Provincial Archives; Ontario Ministry of Education (with particular thanks to Mr. George Mills and Mrs. Helen Gorman); Saskatchewan Archives Board. The permission of the above-mentioned individuals and institutions to quote excerpts is much appreciated.

Finally I would like to acknowledge gratefully the "blessing" of the National Ballet School and its Director and Principal, Betty Oliphant, who made it possible for me to take an extended leave of absence from the school, a privilege which, I might add, was granted without question.

For E. Gordon Waugh,
a scholar by choice,
an educator by example . . .
unforgettable and unforgotten.

CONTENTS

In the image of middle-class equality that Canadians have of their society . . . the private school does not belong. It is something associated with aristocratic societies of Europe and is rarely if ever thought of as being a significant feature of Canadian life.
— John Porter, *The Vertical Mosaic*

They [Independent Schools] are no longer the preserves of the "privileged"—although those fortunate enough to attend them are privileged in the exact sense of the word. The progressive educationalist will tell you that "the whole child" goes to school; the Independent School, as we know it in Canada, ministers to the whole child in all aspects of his being.
— The Right Hon. Vincent Massey, C.H.,
"What's Past is Prologue . . . "

A QUESTION OF PRIVILEGE

Private schools have been called undemocratic, elitist, anachronistic. They themselves claim to be a valid and increasingly valuable alternative to a state-sponsored system of education. There is justification for both opinions.

In Canada, as elsewhere, the term "private school" has come to embrace a variety of concepts. In its broadest sense, it includes any educational institution that operates outside the public sphere: parochial schools, bilingual schools, free schools, pre-schools. The list is endless. Yet the kind of schools most people think of as "private schools" are more properly known as "independent schools", a designation given to those schools that belong to one of two associations, the Canadian Headmasters' Association (CHA) and the Canadian Association of Principals of Independent Schools for Girls (CAPISG). These member schools are privately supported, non-profit institutions that offer university preparatory courses and often elementary education as well. They are the schools that for generations have been regarded in the public mind as the cradle of the Establishment, home of the Old School Tie and the infamous Old Boy Network. It is these schools—and more particularly their origins, character, and development—with which this book is concerned.

The formal association of these independent schools dates back to the 1930s, with the founding of the Canadian Headmistresses' Association in 1931 and its male counterpart, the Canadian Headmasters' Association, four years later. (The Headmistresses' Association has since been re-christened the Canadian Association of Principals of Independent Schools for Girls, a more unwieldy but non-sexist term that became necessary because of a recent embarrassment of "headmatresses"—male heads of girls' schools.) The designation "independent school" was adopted by the associations more than twenty-five years ago, but despite its egalitarian ring, it has done little to change a

1

persistent image of aristocracy. And, like the now familiar expression WASP (White Anglo-Saxon Protestant), coined in the
1950s at Phillips Exeter Academy, one of New England's oldest
prep schools, the term "independent school" is also an American
import.

Currently there are fifty schools in Canada that belong to one
or both of the independent school associations. They have a
combined enrolment of close to 17,000 students, more than half
of whom are girls. This total represents only about two per cent
of Canada's primary and secondary school population. Of these
fifty schools, fifteen are essentially boarding schools, eighteen
are day schools and seventeen admit both boarders and day
students, although here the number of resident students is limited to fewer than thirty per cent of the total enrolment. The
number of students in each school ranges from seventy to more
than 800.

Geographically, the location of the independent schools follows national patterns of population and prosperity. Ontario,
the heartland of Big Business and the Establishment, harbours
the lion's share, twenty, while Quebec and British Columbia
have twelve and ten respectively. From there the numbers dwin-
dle. In Nova Scotia we find three, in New Brunswick and Manitoba two, and in Alberta only one. The remaining provinces are
unrepresented, although this has not always been the case.

Included in the combined membership of the CHA and the
CAPISG are twenty-three schools for girls. Twenty are classified
as boys' schools and seven are totally co-educational. There are,
however, a few grey areas in that certain boys' schools accept a
limited number of girls at the senior level and several others
operate on a coordinate or cooperative basis with neighbouring
schools for girls. In fact, of the twenty-six schools included in the
Headmasters' Association, half are co-educational to some degree.

By definition, an independent school belonging to either the
CAPISG or the Headmasters' Association must offer courses
designed to prepare its students for university entrance. It must
also be a non-profit, self-sustaining corporation, although provincial grants are available to accredited private schools in both
Alberta and Quebec. The fate of the school rests essentially with
its Board of Governors, trustees, or directors, a body whose duty

it is to set financial and educational policy and whose members are recruited almost exclusively from the ranks of former students, parents, and friends of the school. There is a notable absence of female Governors on the boards of most boys' schools, while the Boards of most co-educational and girls' schools continue to be predominantly male. Women, presumably, have not advanced sufficiently in the ways of the business world to be of much value, unless of course they happen to be independently wealthy or excessively wise.

Not only is the Board charged with the responsibility of keeping the school afloat financially, it must also appoint a headmaster or headmistress who will carry out school policy to the satisfaction of the Board and who can, in turn, harness the support of the staff, the parents, the Old Boys or Girls, the students, and the community at large. Like board members, most heads are themselves products of the private school system, but demands made on them are at once more practical and more complex. It was once suggested (by a veteran headmistress) that any prospective head should possess, as minimal qualifications: the education of a college president, the executive ability of a financier, the humility of a deacon, the adaptability of a chameleon, the hope of an optimist, the wisdom of a serpent, the courage of a hero, the gentleness of a dove, the patience of Job, the grace of God, and the persistence of the Devil. In short, the ideal head is a sort of Superman or Wonder Woman in an academic gown, who can move mountains, find pots of gold at the end of the rainbow, and keep everyone smiling. It is no disadvantage, either, to be able to wield a hammer or patch up leaky plumbing. If there has been a high turnover of headmasters and headmistresses at many of these schools in recent years, it is scarcely to be wondered at.

Although all independent schools are technically non-denominational, at least half of them were founded as church-affiliated schools. The majority retain ties with one church or another, a fact borne out in many cases by their names. The saints are well represented, as are a host of prominent churchmen. St. George is the most popular of the blessed (there are schools bearing his name in Toronto, Montreal, and Vancouver); and St. Margaret, St. Clement, St. Andrew, and St. John have also been favoured. Several bishops of various denominations are honoured, among them Bishop Strachan (the first

Anglican bishop of Toronto), Bishop Mountain (Bishop's College School, Lennoxville), Bishop Ridley (Ridley College, St. Catharines), and Bishop Albert Carman (Albert College, Belleville). The early religious affiliation of a school often had considerable bearing on its basic orientation. If a school's roots were Anglican—and this was the case for roughly two-thirds of them—it was almost certain to be well-steeped in British traditions of private education, and usually imported many of those features so widely associated in most people's minds with the private school: the house and prefect systems, the strong emphasis on sports and games, and so on. But if its origins were Baptist, Methodist, or almost anything else, its distinguishing features were probably somewhat different. It would have been more likely to stress religious education rather than sports and character development; and was more often intended to train future missionaries and clergymen than "gentlemen of business". Most important, in Canada the Anglican faith has traditionally been the religion of the well-to-do and influential. Because of this, for generations many of the "principal people" (a term coined by Lord Simcoe)—the elite and those concerned with social one-upmanship—have chosen to send their young to schools with Church of England ties and a British public school flavour. And, in turn, it is a small handful of these schools that have gradually become bastions of privilege, at least in the minds of the public and the social analysts.

Yet curiously the schools themselves perceive their role in a vastly different way. The legacy that the private school has inherited from the church is its duty not only to foster academic excellence, but to attend also to the formation and development of the child's moral fibre. Fifty years ago the strong-minded Montreal headmistress Maude C. Edgar stated flatly, "The building of Character is the whole aim and end of any school worthy of its name." Though contemporary ideas of what constitutes "character" may be somewhat different, particularly when it comes to traditional religious piety, nearly all independent schools continue to make a conscientious effort to perpetuate and instill a particular code of ethics and set of values. It is the cornerstone of their purpose and function.

These values are not, however, the values of an aristocracy or an elite ruling class. The ideals most esteemed by these schools could not be more universally middle-class: integrity, fair play, service, and above all, responsibility. John Evans, president of the University of Toronto, pressed home the point in a recent address to the boys of Upper Canada College. "You are a privileged group," he said. "With privilege must go responsibility . . . . You will be expected to yield higher than average returns, and returns which can be measured in terms of service to others. If you fulfill these expectations, there is no justification for society to begrudge you the advantages which you have enjoyed . . . . But remember, the hazard of choking is much greater for those born with a silver spoon in their mouth."

It could be argued that the values that the independent school seeks to perpetuate are a truer reflection of the attitudes of those who teach there than of those who send their children there. As James McLachlan pointed out in his recent historical study, *American Boarding Schools*:

> Most boarding school headmasters were not rich Americans, but middle-income intellectuals, moralists and clergymen who would have blanched at the sight of an "upper-class value" . . . . These schools have consciously educated their students to avoid, abjure and despise most of what are traditionally thought to be aristocratic or upper-class values and styles of life. They have worked instead to *prevent* the development of aristocratic attitudes.

In general, these observations apply to Canadian independent schools equally well. A contemporary headmaster asserts that since the boys in his school are destined to become leaders, the school will do its level best to make them wise ones:

> We confront our students with the enormous importance of leadership and responsibility. Discrimination and leadership are the essence of our training. It is not enough for a student to emerge as the effective leader of his group. He has to prove to us that his natural leadership is tempered by scruples: a sharp sense of right and wrong, a deep sense of justice, a keen application of intelligence, a fearless realism, a proper compassion and humility.

If not all graduates live up to this demanding idea, it is not for lack of effort (or rhetoric) on the part of the schools.

The ethos of the independent schools is mirrored in their mottoes: "Dare to be Wise", "Not For Ourselves Alone", "Keep

Well the Road", "Simplicity, Sincerity, Service", "Serve Ye Bravely", and the ever-popular "A Sound Mind in a Sound Body" (once used by three boys' schools simultaneously, but never adopted by any of the girls' schools). It is a generally accepted principle that mottoes acquire added dignity when preserved in another tongue. The emblems of Canadian schools are adorned with Latin inscriptions, French inscriptions, even Gaelic inscriptions, but rarely English ones. And while it is doubtful whether these wise and pious exhortations have ever had the least effect on the conduct of the students, they have supplied generations of headmasters, headmistresses, and guest speakers with a ready source of inspiration for Prize Day addresses. Like the school emblem or crest, the school uniform (complete with tie, sash, badges and pins), the school song, hymn and prayer, even the school flower, the school motto is enshrined in tradition—and at the independent school, tradition still matters. It is part of the bonding process.

The independent school, then, has defended its role by claiming that its function is to train those already privileged by virtue of talent or birth to social responsibility. Its detractors, on the other hand, claim that its more fundamental role is to perpetuate that privileged elite by the deliberate exclusion of outsiders. Two Queen's University sociologists, Ioan Davies and Kathleen Herman, write:

> [The graduates of independent schools] are disproportionately represented, not only in the upper echelons of government, but of business and other major institutions . . . . Access is rigorously controlled, drawing from a pool of potential recruits that is confined to a small segment of society . . . . The social distance that separates private school members from the world is deliberately contrived and carefully managed: fear of pollution and taboos to protect purity are strong.
>
> (*Social Space, Canadian Perspectives*, New Press, 1971)

Following these rather startling observations to their logical end, one could only conclude that these schools are a blot on the land, perhaps part and parcel of a devious conspiracy, designed by Professor John Porter's "British Charter Group" to create an artificial aristocracy in the midst of our meritocratic North American paradise. Yet it is no conspiracy that keeps the independent schools so exclusive. It is something far less sinister and at the same time much more difficult to remedy: the inexorable balance-sheet.

While it is true that private alternative schools continue to exist in virtually every democratic country in the world, in Canada for those in the middle-income bracket the cost barrier has long since placed a private school education well beyond easy accessibility. It now costs anywhere from $800 to $2,800 a year for day school tuition, and a year at one of the costlier boarding schools may amount to more than $5,000. It is an irony that becomes apparent when the origins of these schools are examined, for in North America, if not elsewhere, most of them were originally established to provide a superior type of pre-university education at a price almost anyone could afford. Yet these astronomic fees are no conspiracy to restrict the schools' clientele. Unsupplemented by state subsidies, they are barely enough to keep the schools afloat.

Today, the bursaries and scholarships that do exist are generally limited to fewer than one student in twenty. With spiralling inflation and costs-of-living, the dollar value of original bequests and donations has diminished so much that often the amount available barely covers the cost of a school uniform and a few pieces of sports equipment. This applies most particularly to girls' schools, which tend to be much less generously supported by their alumnae than the boys' schools. And while the school prospectus, like the glossy travel brochures it often resembles, carries enticing pictures of expansive playing fields and happy smiling faces, it conveniently omits mention of cracking plaster, inedible food, leaky roofs, rats in the basement, or bats in the attic. A good half of Canada's independent schools are housed in antiquated buildings, including a century-old castle, a former sanitorium, and a sizable collection of mouldering mansions. More than one school has closed because it did not have the funds to make renovations that would satisfy the building inspector.

In fact, the history of virtually every independent school in the country has been a continuing saga of insolvency, prompting endless variations on the following plaint (uttered in 1919) that echo down through the years:

The School never forgets her sons, but follows them with loving interest. She rejoices in their successes, glories in

their honours and is always ready to welcome them when
they return. . . .

It goes without saying that if the outstretched palms of welcome
happen to be crossed with silver, the rejoicing is all the more
heartfelt.

Maintaining the interest and support of former students is a
problem with which all these schools have struggled from the
outset. As early as the 1890s at least two of them had a salaried
bagman to solicit donations on the school's behalf. Today some
employ "executive secretaries", often Old Boys who act as public
relations men and fund-raisers. A popular vehicle for maintaining contact with graduates and, it is hoped, for sustaining their
interest, is the newsletter to the members of the "school family"
(which is sent whether or not the Old Boys' or Girls' association
dues are outstanding). In some cases these publications are
issued two or even three times a year and are quite elaborate,
with photographs, reports, interviews, and lengthy lists of births,
deaths and marriages. At the very least, the newsletter serves as a
reminder (welcome or not) of the school's continuing existence.
But here again it is evident that on the whole the girls' schools are
at a disadvantage, not only because they usually have less money
to spend on such an enterprise, but also because it is far more
difficult to maintain contact with Old Girls, most of whom have
acquired a new surname and many of whom are highly indiffer-
ent to the fate of their old school once they have closed the doors
behind them.

But while windfalls from the private money tree are few and
far between, every surviving school has its share, however small,
of faithful benefactors—often several generations of them—on
whom it depends to rise to the occasion in times of crisis, be it
fire, flood, or crumbling walls. Sometimes the bequests are
rather unconventional ones. There is, for example, the story of
the headmaster of a country boarding school who struck up a
cordial friendship with a local widow of department store
wealth, occasionally calling on her on a Sunday afternoon to
engage in pleasant conversation. Her interest in the fortunes of
his school became increasingly evident and when her chauffeur
arrived at the headmaster's door shortly before Christmas, bearing a large and obviously weighty parcel, he found it difficult to
contain himself. A donation of rare books for the school library

was more than he could have hoped for. In eager anticipation he opened the box to find a copy of the widow's autobiography . . . and another . . . and another . . . accompanied by a gracious note indicating that she thought perhaps the school might be able to make use of some of her extra copies.

Principals and governors of Canadian schools, like their American counterparts, have grown increasingly conscious of the need to avoid insularity by opening their doors to a greater cross-section of the population. They are genuinely concerned that their schools will become inaccessible to all but the richest of the rich—not to protect the havens of the privileged, but simply because of the economic facts of life. In Canada, however, the solutions are harder to find, for in contrast to the many old and munificently endowed prep schools of the United States, the financial position of most Canadian schools borders on bankruptcy. The independent school may be a much-needed alternative to state-administered education, but it is becoming an alarmingly costly one. The popular belief that such schools are the exclusive domain of the wealthy may soon become an incontestable truth.

Apart from money, when it comes to attracting a wider spectrum of students, there are other obstacles. Even if the schools could afford to fling open their gates to every boy or girl who qualified academically, they must contend with their own image as snob factories, an image that repels more often than it attracts. The singular virtues and advantages of the independent school are often less than inviting to potential recruits, who are loath to leave the comfortable security of their local high school, where increasingly most demands are self-imposed and practically nothing is compulsory. Nor is the prospect of having to don a uniform or jacket and tie every morning an appealing thought or, for that matter, the prospect of the sex-segregated classroom. And it is partly owing to the pressures of the students themselves that so many independent schools have, in the last few years, begun to admit members of the opposite sex, or even attempted mergers with nearby sister- or brother-schools. It is a matter of conjecture whether or not this movement towards co-education has come about because of a burning desire on the part of school administrators to move with the times, or whether it is a change born of economic necessity. Most of the newly co-educational independent schools hasten to reject the suggestion that they have been forced into trying out the "two minuses equal a plus" theory in order to survive, yet there is every evidence that the cost factor—and the need to attract students—have enhanced the cause of co-education.

Yet even as many schools struggle to diversify their student bodies, the very myth of the private school as an elitist strong-hold continues to attract some parents. And it is difficult to deny that there is a good deal of truth in the theory advanced by sociologist Mary Percival Maxwell (herself a graduate of Haver-gal College) that "having attended and particularly having graduated from a Canadian private school appears to be a pass-port into local elites across the country". As Evelyn Waugh once said, "They may kick you out but they never let you down."

Probably there will always be parents who insist that their sons and daughters attend these schools in order to rub shoulders with the offspring of the affluent and the influential, and in turn to improve their chances of making "good" marriages or suc-cessful careers. One mother admitted quite freely that she sent her daughter to Bishop Strachan School because she didn't want her to marry a plumber—"not because he plumbs, you under-stand, but because his background, upbringing, ideals for the present and future would be too different. He would simply have nothing in common with her." She was blissfully unaware that one of her darling daughter's schoolmates at the time was in fact a plumber's daughter.

Attitudes of this sort have prompted more than one headmas-ter or headmistress to grumble about parents who send their children to the right school for the wrong reasons. While it would be ludicrous to suggest that independent schools churn out nothing but clear-eyed, clean-cut paragons of Christian vir-tue, if and when snobbery does exist it is almost never because of the school, but in spite of it. People who believe that private schools take nice, wholesome youngsters and tranform them into self-important and offensive snobs forget that snobbery, like charity, begins at home.

Yet the schools themselves have done little to counteract their unfortunate public image. Over the years, some have presented an incredibly smug and self-congratulatory aspect to the outside world. Partly out of a basic conservatism, partly as a defense mechansim, the majority have deliberately maintained a rather cloistered, inner-sanctum air. Until fairly recently, public scrutiny was something to be avoided, since, in the schools' view, it would probably lead only to misunderstanding, misrepresentation, or both. Few actively sought publicity; and most schools confined their public exposure to carefully-worded advertisements in a few select magazines and newspapers.

If the schools themselves have been reticent, their alumni have been even more so. Once they have left the hallowed halls of their former schools, surprisingly few graduates advertise or even acknowledge the fact that they were ever near the place. Most likely they would reject Jane Austen's suggestion that one does not love a place the less for having suffered in it. Or perhaps, having entered the mainstream of life, they have simply been reluctant to appear different or privileged—an awkward condition at the best of times, most particularly for those involved in politics. More than a few federal MPs with an independent school background neglected to mention that fact in their official biographies for the 1973-74 Parliamentary Guide. In a recent *Globe and Mail* article on private schools Clay Powell, Ontario's assistant attorney general, is said to have physically winced when he was once introduced as a former Upper Canada College student. "I felt I had to apologize for it." he said *(Globe and Mail,* June 10, 1976).

In an effort to counter adverse public opinion and attract private and corporate interest ("The Canadian business community has a strong and yet often unrecognized ally in Independent Schools"), the Canadian Headmasters' Association recently issued a pamphlet outlining the "special advantages" of an independent school education. It featured a variety of testimonials, including one from the Ontario Ministry of Education's chief inspector of independent schools, and concluded with a lengthy list (admittedly incomplete) of prominent graduates in business, politics, government, law, the church, the armed services, the arts, and the academic world. The names left off the list perhaps tell as much about the "image" the Association was trying to project as the names that were included.

The presidents of Bell Telephone, Abitibi, and the Royal Bank of Canada are included on the list, but John A. "Bud" McDougald, identified in Peter Newman's book *The Canadian*

Establishment as the most powerful man in the Canadian business world, is not (he was asked to leave Upper Canada College after playing a prank on the headmaster). There is no mention of the Eatons or Bassets. The politicians mentioned include Premier Richard Hatfield of New Brunswick and Premier Frank Moores of Newfoundland; Robert Stanfield; and several present and former cabinet ministers, including Walter Gordon, John Turner, James Richardson, Donald MacDonald, and Alistair Gillespie—but not NDP MP Terry Grier. Activist Toronto alderman Dan Heap is not mentioned either, nor is William Kilbourn. The late Vincent Massey, former Governor-General of Canada, Senator John Aird, and a variety of ambassadors and diplomats are on the list, as well as six judges and a few bishops. Names from the armed services include Admiral R.H. Leir, General Bruce Matthews, and Sir Edwin Leather, Governor-General of Bermuda. Tom Symons, former president of Trent University, and Rocke Robertson of McGill are two representatives from the academic world.

When it comes to the arts, however, the Headmasters' Association is a good deal more circumspect. Robertson Davies, Raymond Massey, and Hume Cronyn are worthy of mention, but Galt McDermott, the composer of the rock musical "Hair"; novelist John Glassco, writer Scott Symons, and Bill Glassco, founder of Toronto's Tarragon Theatre, are not. Neither sports nor science is mentioned, and there is no special category for the media, omissions that exclude Hockey Night in Canada's famous father-and-son team Foster and Bill Hewitt, broadcaster Peter Gzowski, journalist Charles Taylor, theatre critic John Fraser, and *Maclean's* editor and chronicler of the ways of the elite, Peter C. Newman. Other well-known graduates of private schools include Canada's best-known publisher, Jack McClelland; Casey Baldwin, the first Canadian to fly an aircraft; Dr. Joe MacInnis, underwater research scientist who recently masterminded a successful dive at the North Pole; the photographer John Reeves; and Dan Gibson, a leading wildlife photographer and filmmaker.

Since the brochure was a Canadian Headmasters' Association venture, aimed primarily at the business community, the names of well-known Canadian women were not included. If there were such a list, it would include such people as Senator Carine

Wilson; Emily Ferguson, the first woman police magistrate in the British Commonwealth; Jean Sutherland-Boggs, first woman director of the National Gallery; actresses Kate Reid, Margot Kidder and Jackie Burroughs; comedienne Barbara Hamilton; Veronica Tennant, principal dancer with the National Ballet of Canada; Patricia Beatty, dancer-choreographer and founder of the Toronto Dance Theatre; Ann Southam, composer of electronic music; veteran actress, Dora Mavor Moore; writers Phyllis Brett Young and Isabel Le Bourdais, and a score of others.

While this brief enumeration lends some evidence to the contention that the private school system contributes disproportionately to the boardrooms of the nation, it also proves that private school graduates can be found everywhere in Canadian society. Some can even be found doing battle against the very system that educated them.

Another aspect of the public view of these private institutions is the collection of persistent myths pertaining chiefly to boarding rather than day schools. There is an impression that most boarding schools are like something from an Evelyn Waugh novel—glorified reform schools and hotbeds of homosexuality that are little more than repositories for unwanted young incorrigibles whose wealthy parents are divorced, alcoholic or otherwise unfit or unwilling to cope with child-rearing. The picture, though exaggerated, is not entirely false. A few schools have openly accepted a proportionate number of "misfits" and "problem children" and made every effort to help them adapt and adjust to life. But most have chosen to concentrate their efforts on more certain prospects. Today, even when a school is extremely hard-pressed financially, it is reluctant to take on a student with behavioral or psychological difficulties—or, for that matter, any boy or girl who appears more than minimally reluctant to live away from home. The day-to-day operation of a residential school is complex enough without deliberately jeopardizing the delicate balance of student and staff morale.

Yet another point of dispute, of equally long standing, is the quality of education at both boarding and day schools. Just as it is often accepted as a truism that the students at these schools are dullards, semi-delinquents, and over-indulged brats, it is also assumed that the teaching staff are a collection of oddball reactionaries, non-conformists and rejects from the public schools or the British Isles, eccentric and mildewed pedagogues who are underpaid and uncertified if not downright incompetent. Vivid images are conjured up of dowdy maiden ladies with pursed lips and pinched noses tramping about in sensible shoes and hair-styles to match. The schoolmasters, for their part, are generally pictured as Canada's own Mr. Chips—tweedy, down-at-the heel, lost in a perpetual cloud of pipe smoke. These are images that have been immortalized both in literature and on film, and in the not-so-distant past there were undoubtedly enough examples of both to lend credence to these flights of fancy. But it would be a challenge to find many of them in Canadian schools today.

Given the premise that the quality of teaching is inferior, it would be mysterious if not miraculous that the independent schools have consistently managed to prepare a higher propor-tion of students for university entrance than the public high schools. For what they are worth, current statistics indicate that seventy-five per cent of today's male high school graduates and thirty-five percent of the females will continue their education at the post-secondary level. The independent schools claim that their average hovers around ninety per cent for both sexes. Of course, it is not the schools alone that prepare these students for university; often it has been assumed from the day they were born that a university education will be as much a part of their lives as braces and summer camp.

It can be argued that independent schools are in a position to pick and choose their students not only for their affluence but also for their academic potential, and that they can discard non-achievers and troublemakers at will. In 1971 St. Andrew's College under Dr. J.R. Coulter announced in its prospectus that "if at any time a boy's influence is considered harmful or if his presence in the school is regarded as undesirable, the Board reserves for the Headmaster the right to request his immediate withdrawal". Such an intimidating statement of school policy undoubtedly struck fear into the hearts of both boys and their parents, who stood to forfeit the balance of the school fees for the year if their son should be invited to remove himself from the premises. A sobering thought at today's tuition fees.

Most independent school students have at least a minimal respect for order and authority, although not everyone is "reached" to the same degree. For those who consistently refuse

to abide by the "rules of membership" (a term used by one
Ontario boarding school for boys), the chances are good that
their stay at the school will be brief. Attitude—something that in
earlier days might have been called "character"—counts for a
great deal. Good manners and self-control are expected as a
matter of course, and since a school's students are readily
identifiable by their uniforms, they are constantly reminded of
the need to "uphold the reputation of the school" at all times in
all places.

In terms of academic achievement, the high success rate of the
independent schools has been attributed, at least in part, to their
well-ordered climate of discipline and control. The average
pupil-teacher ratio of ten to one for boarding schools and twelve
to one for day schools is also bound to have a salutory effect on
any school's academic record. Without question one of the major
advantages of the independent school is its size. Most are small
enough for the teachers and students to know (if not to like) one
another on an individual basis, and it is this fact that makes these
schools such an attractive alternative to the vast, bureaucratic,
and depersonalized public schools. The same intimacy and opportunity for innovation that students and their parents find so
appealing also attract numbers of dedicated teachers, despite
the generally lower salary scale. The independent school is free
to experiment in a way that the public school is not: to alter or
expand, to hire and to fire with relative impunity. This almost
total freedom from government-imposed restrictions, quotas
and controls is at the root of a spirit of innovation and experimentation that has often become as much a part of a school's
identity as the more visible trappings of tradition. Long before
most state-funded schools had conspired to purloin monies
from the public purse for such "frivolities" as field trips, after-
school programs and "enrichment" activities, many educators
within the independent school community had recognized the
value of curriculum flexibility and the importance of fostering
individual talents whenever and wherever possible. "The
justification of the independent school," said Joseph McCulley,
former headmaster of Pickering College, "is not that it is better
than public schools . . . nor worse . . . but that it is different . . .
with substantial qualities and merits of its own. Uniformity
should not and cannot be the aim of life in a democracy."

In 1963 the late Kim Beattie, compiler of a two-volume history of Ridley College, one of Canada's more venerable private schools, observed: "Canadians still do not understand the role of independent schools and have a shamefully inadequate estimate of the contribution they have made to Canada in the creation and production of well-educated, well-balanced citizens." This book is intended to help bridge that chasm of misunderstanding, by examining the roots and origins of a representative number of independent schools, and by recounting something of the lives of the often extraordinary men and women who left their mark on the schools and on generations of students. Nearly all of the schools belonging to the two independent school associations are discussed, with the exception of some fairly recent arrivals. Some of the schools that have failed are covered as well, either because their stories are memorable or because the reasons for their failure are illuminating.

To depict the history of any school from its beginnings is an awesome task. Certain restrictions are both necessary and inevitable, as are omissions and generalizations. The most one can hope for is to capture the essence, the prevailing qualities of a school, or, in this case, a specific group of schools. How and why did they and others like them develop? What sort of people were involved? What were they trying to achieve? What did these schools have in common, and how did they differ from one another? Why did some survive, wile others wilted and died?

The short histories that follow are not intended as a Michelin Guide to the independent schools of Canada. There are no recommendations, evaluations, or prescriptions about which are "best" for a child, and it would be folly to attempt them. Children differ far too widely in their needs and responses. Nonetheless, the history and impressions recorded here will undoubtedly be interpreted according to personal persuasion. To some, this book will appear as a vain attempt to justify the continuing existence of private alternative schools. Others may find it unfair or unfounded. I would like to think of it as something approaching a factual record, that will find its usefulness in providing a long-needed historical perspective. While the issues of the present are difficult to ignore, before any further value judgments are made or pronouncements pronounced, the past should be given its due.

Education by Denomination
1788-1850

PROBABLY the most outstanding feature of Canadian education is its diversity. The British North America Act entrusted each province with the responsibility of educating its children, and so today educational policy is set by ten separate government authorities, each with its own administrative structure and even its own terminology. Terms such as "college", "separate school", and even the word "education" itself are subject to regional interpretation. Much of this disparity can be attributed to the simple geographical vastness of the country, and to the fact that the provinces undertook their separate responsibilities over a considerable span of time. At Confederation in 1867 the new Dominion comprised only four provinces, Upper Canada, Lower Canada, Nova Scotia, and New Brunswick. In the eighty-two years that elapsed before Newfoundland finally joined the union, there occurred unprecedented changes in educational needs and expectations.

Long before Confederation, however, historical and ideological forces were at work that would shape the pattern of education in this country through the nineteenth century and beyond. The most significant of these—and the source of the greatest conflicts—were religious.

For nearly two centuries, virtually all formal education in the new colony was a denominational by-product. Canada's first schools were established in Quebec in the early seventeenth century by the Recollects and Jesuits, their primary purpose to convert the native population to Catholicism. Later, under British rule, the Society for the Preservation of the Gospel, a Church of England missionary organization, established schools in New Brunswick, Nova Scotia, and Newfoundland—in the fervent hope of redeeming a few Catholics, as well as any other stray or uncommitted souls. Yet until the nineteenth century there were very few Protestant clergy to be found anywhere in the colony, nor was there any church with the resources to establish the control over education that the Roman Catholic church had exercised in Quebec from the beginning.

As a result, the majority of English-speaking Protestant colonists were left to their own devices. It was this vacuum that led to the later battle among the Methodists, Baptists, Anglicans, and others over the redemption of these uncommitted souls in the early nineteenth century and laid the groundwork for the arch-denominationalism that followed. In the forefront of "salvation" was education of the young. Most churches, of whatever denomination, claimed the historic right to supervise the education of their members, and the religious factionalism that subsequently developed often manifested itself in the establishment of rival schools. Education was the ideal vehicle for propagating the faith, not only among the "faithful", but occasionally among the misguided adherents of other doctrines, even the dreaded "Romanism". Early in the 1800s, for instance, a Baptist school in Lower Canada proudly advertised the number of converts from Catholicism it had claimed in the course of the preceding year.

In Upper Canada, the war was waged less between Protestantism and Romanism than among the Protestants themselves. At first the Anglican clergy were far outnumbered by Baptist and Methodist preachers. The Methodists, with their circuit-riding, frontier-style religion imported from the United States, acquired a considerable following; whereas the Anglican church, with uncertain financial resources, found lack of funds a major obstacle in its efforts to strengthen its position. The system of Clergy Reserves later provided a partial solution to the Anglicans' dilemma, but it also succeeded in fanning the flames of interdenominational jealousies and resentments, and eventually gave rise to a bitter conflict between church and state over the control of education—a conflict which has continued to confound Ontario's educators and politicians to this day.

Denominationalism was not the only source of the bewildering diversity that characterized nineteenth-century education in Canada. Until the middle of the century and beyond, education was basically a local affair, and the responsibility for schooling largely a family matter. The diversity that resulted was often essentially a matter of funding—or the lack of it.

In a predominantly rural society, education was not a particularly high priority. It was a luxury limited by local resources and by the seasonal demands of ploughing and harvesting. In rural districts a group of families might together hire an itinerant schoolmaster to teach for five or six months of the year, negotiating the wages and tuition fees. In the cities and towns, education within the home was relatively common in many middle- and upper-class families. Upper Canadian newspapers carried frequent advertisements for governesses and tutors—especially for those who would value a warm home atmosphere above a large salary. Quite often, too, a clergyman's wife would take on a few select pupils.

As they became more settled, many rural areas organized formal elementary grammar schools which were eligible for financial aid from the provincial government and which were required to report regularly to the Legislature. But there also existed perhaps an equal number of non-aided schools that were supported entirely by subscribers. In urban areas with populations sufficient to support such ventures, an increasing number of private schools were opened. A good many of these were schools designed to turn a profit or at least to provide a living for their entrepreneurial educators. Between 1815 and 1846 there are records of fifty-eight privately operated schools in Toronto alone. They must not have fulfilled the expectations of their founders, for most did not survive beyond a year or so. Although some of these schools were small, exclusive—and expensive—a number of them were very inexpensive, designed to educate quantities of children from less provident families. It was a case of prestige versus volume, though both types of school operated in the name of profit.

Whether government-aided or not, nearly all of these day schools charged tuition fees. For those unable to attend day school, the most accessible path to literacy was the Sunday School, where at least the pupils were taught to read their hymnaries and passages from the Bible.

Prior to Confederation, however, the availability of schools which provided education beyond the elementary level was extremely limited. It should come as no surprise that the schools which filled this educational void, especially for those middle-class families who did not have the resources for private tutoring, were almost all denominational ventures. (It might surprise some people to learn, however, that the Bishop Strachan School in Toronto [1867] was established as a boarding and day school at a time when the only educational alternatives available to the parents of Anglican girls were Catholic convents or high-priced private finishing schools. Bishop Strachan, like the other schools that will be examined in the following chapters, was originally intended not only for the well-to-do but for middle-class families who wished to educate their children beyond the elementary level.)

The influx of refugee Loyalists from the United States

school on the side. Nor has this accountability to a higher authority always been an altogether attractive arrangement from the feeder schools' point of view. In the long run, the advantages of independence have been found to outweigh the benefits of university affiliation.

The number of university-affiliated preparatory schools which are now defunct tends to bear this out. Both academies operating in conjunction with Mount Allison university in New Brunswick have closed. In Ontario, Woodstock College and Moulton Ladies' College, Baptist schools jointly controlled by McMaster University, are long gone. Regina College, a Methodist undertaking in Saskatchewan which began as a residential school, was eventually absorbed by the University there. The disparate interests of a preparatory school and a university almost preclude the possibility of any successful long-term association, and most schools have found autonomy to be basic to their survival.

Without question the schools that have survived the test of time—and there were many that did not—owe their continued existence to a combination of circumstance, good fortune, and good management. But the essential key to their survival has been an unremitting sense of destiny, which has prevailed through fires, financial crises, internal squabbles, and external pressures. In the final analysis, an unwavering faith in their own purpose is the one true constant in the histories of the schools that follow.

King's College School

Nova Scotia

1788

In Nova Scotia, as in other parts of British North America, problems of survival had first claim on new arrivals to the colony. Most of the 400 souls who comprised the British population of Nova Scotia after 1763 were militiamen posted at Canso and Annapolis to secure the newly-won colony. It is not difficult to imagine the boredom and loneliness they must have experienced in the name of King and Country, and soon a number of them had made arrangements for their wives and children to join them in their misery.

As the settlement grew from a military outpost to a community the matter of education came to the fore, as it does wherever there are children. Since the community had no ready-made teachers, a request was sent to the Home Government in England in an effort to remedy the situation. The British government, preoccupied with more pressing concerns, passed the problem along to the Church of England, and in consequence—when help did arrive—it came from a rather unexpected source. The Society for the Propagation of the Gospel in Foreign Lands, the branch of the Church of England that promoted missionary work, eventually dispatched several missionaries and teachers to bring light into the Nova Scotian darkness. At that time a schoolmaster (schoolmistresses were unheard of until much later) was required to be a deacon of the church, but since deacons were in short supply, this stringent restriction was withdrawn almost immediately, and educators continued to trickle from England into the colony.

It was not until the American Revolution that education became established on a more formal basis. The arrival of over eighteen thousand United Empire Loyalists from across the border produced an immediate demand for more adequate schooling. Backwoods methods were no longer acceptable. The impetus provided by the arrival of the Loyalists was to have a profound effect on education in British North America, and its immediate result was the founding of the "Mother of independent schools in Canada".

King's College School in Windsor, Nova Scotia was the first residential school for boys, not just in English Canada, but in all of Britain's overseas empire. Its creation, however, was first proposed in New York City, at a meeting of Loyalist clergy, before the American Revolution. One of the key figures at this gathering was the Irish-born Charles Inglis, a clergyman of the Church of England who later fled the new-born country and returned to England in 1784. In 1787 he was on his way back to North America to serve as the Bishop of Nova Scotia, the first missionary bishop of the Church of England anywhere in the world. The extent of his domain was staggering: it included not only Nova Scotia, New Brunswick, Newfoundland and Prince Edward Island, but Upper and Lower Canada and Bermuda into the bargain.

One of Inglis' first concerns when he arrived in Nova Scotia was the establishment of an academy or collegiate school for boys as the first stage in an ambitious educational plan that was to culminate in the founding of King's College. On All Saints' Day, November 1, 1788, King's Academy opened its doors in Windsor, Nova Scotia. The site chosen for the school afforded a magnificent view over the surrounding countryside and the Annapolis Valley. Tuition was set at four pounds a year for the Latin school and three pounds for the English and mathematics school—the price of Latin scholarship evidently came high. Arrangements were made for the boys to be "furnished with Diet, Lodging and Washing", and the official announcement for the school's opening noted that "the strictest attention will be paid to the Morals, Health, Tuition and Manners of the Students". The fond hope was also expressed that the Academy would prove "highly beneficial to the Youth of Nova Scotia and inferior to no similar Institution in the Colonies".

But securing the services of a suitable and properly qualified man to take charge of the new venture proved to be a considerable problem. The Archbishop of Canterbury, when solicited for his advice, was "much chagrined" at being unable to come forward with any suggestions. In the end it was the Bishop's own nephew, Archibald Inglis, who rather grudgingly agreed to uphold the family honour and fill the breach until the right man could be found. Still another Inglis, the Bishop's eleven-year-old son, John, was among the Academy's first students. (He later followed in his father's steps to become the third Bishop of Nova Scotia.)

The opening exercises of the Academy reflected its founder's weighty sense of purpose. It was an affair of truly marathon proportions. There were prayers, a lengthy Latin oration and an "earnest address" to the tutors and their seventeen students on the subject of their respective duties. This was followed by a full-blown discourse in praise of the worthy Bishop and the wisdom of the Sovereign in having appointed "a Divine possessed of every virtue and qualification". The Bishop, in his inevitable reply, was then given the opportunity to say a few words on the subject of Morality. Evidently the Devil had already infiltrated the new colony, for the local magistrate was urged to enforce rigorously the laws against drunkenness, profanation of the Lord's Day, swearing and "other vices" that the students might not be injured by bad example.

In light of the ongoing debate over discipline in modern schools, some of the original regulations of King's Academy may have a surprisingly familiar ring. Regulation Thirteen, for example, declared that "children should be treated as rational beings, and, therefore, persuasion and arguments adapted to their understanding should be employed to promote application and good behaviour among the students". It should be noted, however, that the "arguments and persuasions" included confinement, extra tasks, a system of fines, and, of course, corporal punishment.

The implementation of these regulations fell to its headmaster, who did his best to perform his duty to God, the school, and his uncle, Bishop Inglis. Within a year, however, a suitable replacement was found in William Cochran, another Irishman who, like the Bishop, was a graduate of Trinity College, Dublin.

Henceforth it would be Cochran's responsibility to uphold the lofty ideals on which the Academy had been founded. In an age when the interests of the church and the state were considered by most as inseparable, his prime concern would be to educate the young men of the province in "the true religion of the Church of England, as well as to provide them with first-rate scholastic education". One of the King's Academy's distinguished sons from this early period in its history was the brilliant and witty Thomas Chandler Haliburton, whose book about the caustic Yankee, Sam Slick, once rivalled the works of Charles Dickens in sales and popularity.

In time, a substantial three-story stone building was erected for the school, and it became referred to, for the first time, as the Collegiate School. But despite its auspicious beginnings both it and the university continued to fall upon hard times until, in 1835, there were only three students at King's College and four at the Collegiate School. Eventually, under more dynamic leadership the situation improved and enrolment gradually began to increase, but when the Society for the Propagation of the Gospel, long a faithful supporter, decided to withdraw its annual grant in the mid-1800s, the fate of the school was left hanging in the balance once again.

It was at this point that the school's Old Boys rallied with their support, forming an alumni association and agreeing to raise funds annually to replace the SPG grants and add to the school's endowments. The association also exerted enough influence to bring about sweeping changes in the composition of the school's Board of Governors and its curriculum. This revitalization had scarcely begun when the entire school building was destroyed by fire. (No boys' boarding school of any repute seems to have escaped at least one fire sometime in its past.) During the next two years the school limped on in temporary quarters, then closed altogether in 1875.

The Board of King's Collegiate School, however, was not content to let the school pass into oblivion without making some attempt to revive it. Temporary classrooms and residences were arranged through the university and by 1882 a new building had been erected. In the interval, the original tone of the school seems to have changed very little. A directive issued by the Board in 1891 declared that "All boarders, at all times except during play hours, within the school bounds, are to wear the College cap with a red tassel. Neglect of this regulation shall be sufficient reason for the removal of the boy's name from the books of the school." It appears that "sundry evils" had crept into the school in former years, but parents were assured that these had been "gradually, but effectively eradicated" and that the school was again confidently commended as a "wholesome place".

With the growing interest in the arts and physical culture that characterized Victorian concern with moulding a boy's overall character, several new staff members were added – among them a drill-sergeant who doubled as a fencing-master and also provided instruction in the piccolo and flute, a male violin teacher, and three maiden ladies who were responsible for such frivolities as singing, dancing, and piano playing. The drill-sergeant's arrival heralded the beginning of the school Cadet Corps, one of the few that has survived to this day. With these new and exciting features to recommend it, boarders were attracted to the school not just from the Atlantic provinces, but from the West Indies and the United States as well. Upper Canada College in Toronto (founded 1829) was finally persuaded to relinquish its widely advertised claim to the title of "Canada's oldest residential school", and since 1910 King's College School has made good use of the same phrase in its own publicity.

When King's College University's main building was destroyed by fire in 1920 the university was moved to Halifax, and it seemed only logical and practical for the board of King's College School to declare itself an independent body. In 1929 the school inherited the grounds and remaining buildings of the university which included fifty-two acres of land, five residences, and a chapel. It has since added several modern additions to the existing buildings. But in the interval, through the Depression, the war years and beyond, KCS has undergone no radical transformation of philosophy. Today, despite its recent amalgamation with Edgehill School for Girls, it continues to maintain its efforts to uphold past traditions and instill the qualities of "Manhood, Gentleness, and Learning" to which its founders ascribed.

Stanstead College

Stanstead, Quebec

1817

The American War of Independence was an indirect factor in the establishment of at least one other existing independent school in Canada. The war left in its wake many British Loyalists who, subjected to persecution and abuse in their homeland, chose to accept the British government's open invitation to free land grants in Nova Scotia, New Brunswick, Ontario (Upper Canada), and the Eastern Townships of the province of Quebec (Lower Canada). Dismissed by the French as too remote and inaccessible, the Townships region southeast of Montreal became under British rule "wastelands of the Crown". After the State of Vermont decided in 1791 to join the United States instead of Canada, increasing numbers of colonists began crossing the Vermont-Quebec border to settle in the Townships and take advantage of the land grants there. The Township of Stanstead was among the first to be settled. To all intents and purposes it was a Yankee community, and so most of the students at Stanstead's first school, erected in 1817, were American-born and good Congregationalists into the bargain.

Like King's College School in Nova Scotia, which received an annual stipend from the Society for the Preservation of the Gospel, the little enterprise at Stanstead was also externally funded. In Quebec, as elsewhere, the clergy and the lay community shouldered most of the responsibility for education, with only sporadic government assistance. Attempts to create a government-supported educational system bore little fruit until the introduction into Lower Canada of "Royal Schools" in 1807. The concept of government-controlled education, already well established in Europe, was just beginning to gain acceptance in

North America, but the Roman Catholic clergy of Lower Canada regarded the concept as a dangerous attempt at assimilation. The Royal Schools, therefore, received their greatest support in areas such as Stanstead where there was a Protestant majority.

The Stanstead Royal School, as it was first known, was supported by the Royal Institution for the Advancement of Learning, the same body which later provided funds for the creation of McGill University. But despite Stanstead's grand title, in actual fact the little red brick schoolhouse, which still stands on its original site, represented nothing so much as the New England Puritan ethic from which it had sprung. Its first teacher, recruited by the Royal Institution, was a clergyman, Thaddeus Osgoode, and like most of his students he was American-born and a Congregationalist. Under his hand the little school thrived and grew until the school trustees, impatient with the Royal Institution's penny-pinching, decided to apply for a grant from Quebec's Provincial Assembly to erect a bigger and better school. Thus, with considerable fanfare, the Stanstead Seminary opened in 1829 as a boarding and day school. However, the government's allotment, although generous, proved insufficient to the need, and the slack had to be taken up by substantial private donations from within the community. Unlike Upper Canada College, which opened the same year and aroused local resentment almost from the day it opened, the school in Stanstead has maintained a singularly harmonious relationship with the community, perhaps because more than most schools it has depended on that community's good will.

From the start the Seminary welcomed "Young Ladies" as well as "Gentlemen" and offered an ambitiously full curriculum which included natural and moral philosophy, mathematics, chemistry, astronomy, French, drawing, music, and orthography. At one stage it even experimented with a twelve-month school year with a few days' holiday between each of four terms. Even in those days, however, the idea met with a less than enthusiastic response. In the end it was conceded that there were pleasanter ways to while away lazy summer afternoons, and the plan was dropped.

About the time of Confederation, the trustees of the Stanstead Seminary began discussing the possibility of renovating and restructuring the school. At the same time they heard that the Methodist Church in Canada was planning to establish a residential college in Quebec. By committing themselves to raise $25,000 privately, the Stanstead trustees swept aside all competition from neighboring communities. By 1873 the charter of the new Stanstead Wesleyan College had been granted by the province and a handsome five-storey building was erected on land donated by a benevolent Stanstead citizen, the same land on which the school's buildings now stand. A revised curriculum included the first two years in a degree course recognized by McGill University, as well as a teachers' preparatory course and a commercial course. The latter, offered to young men only, promised "as thorough a preparation for business life as school or college can impart . . . a great advantage at the outset of a business career." It was hoped that this new curriculum would bring the school "into greater harmony with the plans of the Protestant Board of Education, providing more perfectly for the scholastic needs of the youth of our country, and realizing, it is hoped, more fully the ideal of the projectors of this Institution; 'a real People's College'." As a courtesy to its American students it also offered substitute courses in American history and geography.

In keeping with its objectives as "a real People's College" Stanstead offered outstanding education at bargain prices. A year's tuition was fixed at twenty dollars and weekly room and board could be arranged for an additional three dollars. This, however, did not include bed-linen, towels, and table napkins (which had to be provided by the boarders), nor did it include fuel for the wood-burning fireplaces in each room. The problem of heat and comfort was left to the occupants. It was not a fee structure designed for profit and before long the College was experiencing the usual financial difficulty. By 1900, however, through the concerted efforts of its trustees and principal, the College's financial position had improved considerably and it had acquired several new buildings, again largely through local philanthropy. The Eastern Townships Conservatory of Music was incorporated into the school, and the College took on the responsibility of educating all local Protestant children of elementary school age—an obligation which it fulfilled for the next fifty years.

Since 1958 Stanstead has been operated as a boys' school and its enrolment has become necessarily more cosmopolitan, but even today the long-standing support which it has received from the surrounding community remains an inherited tradition which few other independent schools can claim. In all probability this local support has helped to ensure its survival.

St. John's-Ravenscourt

Winnipeg, Manitoba

1820

While the refugee Loyalists from the United States played an essential part in the establishment of both King's College School and Stanstead in the east, the influence they exerted west of Ontario was marginal. In the west, the earliest private education schools were founded as part of the struggle by various Protestant denominations to gain congregations. In the process, it was again the clergy that broke new ground in the interest of education.

The origins of Canada's third-oldest English-speaking school —by far the oldest in western Canada—can be traced to a little log mission school on the banks of the Red River. The Reverend John West, sent out by the Church of England in 1820 to perform "Good and Godly" works in the new settlement of Fort Garry, began at once to direct his energies toward the establishment of a mission school there. With the help of the church missionary society, his little school was launched in 1820. Before long it attracted the interest of local Hudson's Bay Company officials as well as of members of Selkirk's Scottish settlement. Within two years the little log house had become a substantial building, "with apartments for the Schoolmaster, accommodation for the Indian children, and a day school for the children of the settlers".

The mission school was continued for several years under the direction of Rev. D. T. Jones, West's successor, but he soon ventured forth on his own. His school opened privately in 1833 on the site of the original mission school. The Red River Academy, as it was impressively christened, was designed to provide boarding accommodation for the children of Hudson's Bay Company factors from remote posts in the northwest, and to this day among the school's guiding principles is the education of youngsters from far-flung communities where educational facilities are limited. In the course of its reorganization, the new Academy became less concerned with Indian education and concentrated its efforts on meeting the needs of the white population. With the support of Sir George Simpson, governor of the Hudson's Bay Company, the success of the new Academy at Red River was virtually guaranteed.

The term "academy" by this time had acquired a certain prestige. By the early 1800s, there were almost 1,000 incorporated academies in the United States alone. It is difficult to establish with any degree of certainty the origins of the academy, but it appears to have been a product of an eighteenth-century nonconformist movement in England. Whether Reverend Jones, an Englishman, chose the term because of its British origin or simply because it had become a fashionable and prestigious nomenclature in the United States is not clear.

Jones' successor as headmaster, a dour Scotsman who was also an iron-rod disciplinarian, held the school together until his death in 1849. His demise coincided exactly with the arrival of the first Anglican bishop of Rupertsland, who immediately arranged for the church missionary society to take the Academy under its wing once again as a diocesan school. The school was renamed St. John's College and was endowed with the motto "In thy light shall we see light". But its fortunes under church sponsorship waxed and waned until still another Anglican archbishop, Robert Machray, re-established the school as St. John's College School. For over thirty years he served as its headmaster and chief promoter, and it is possible that his dedication stemmed from the hope that from his school he could create a university, much as King's College had followed upon King's College School. Some time during this period a small number of girls were admitted to St. John's as students, although their stay was relatively short-lived, and it was not until 1971 that girls, grades 10 through 12, once again became part of the school.

A letter written by a pupil at the College during Archbishop Machray's time may provide a measure of comfort to those who deplore the modern child's ignorance of the three R's:

November 18, 1874

My dear mama,

> I was gated for Latin and Arithmetic on monday and I
> onely finished my apple on Wedensday. The workmen
> fixed the Ginnasin on Tusday with a horintial bar. Parrelel
> bars, Indian clubs & some other things. Be sure and send
> me a plume cake and some mony I was expecting you on
> Tusday. I forgot my belt at Frazers that morning and am
> going for it tomorrow. I hope you and Barney and cousin
> Vic are quite well. I ame quite well. if you send me 2 dollars I
> could buy a fine pair of skats from one of the boys. I send
> my love to you. Barney and Vic. I must say goodby. ore else
> I wont have a chance to send it. I send this picture to barney.
> I remain
>
> My Dear Mama
> Yours loving son
> Frank.

Although Archbishop Machray may not have succeeded in instil-
ling literacy into all of his students, the College's move to new
quarters in 1890 was due almost entirely to his efforts. The
school that arose on Main Street at Anderson in Winnipeg was
constructed from clay bricks baked in a kiln right on the spot.
For the next sixty years, St. John's stood at this location,
flourishing and fading according to the times until the sale of the
property in 1950, the year of the great Winnipeg flood. The
demolition of the old building's towers and chimneys brought
the history of St. John's to an abrupt halt, and its amalgamation
with Ravenscourt School for Boys (founded in 1929) marked the
beginning of a new, successful enterprise. The history of
Ravenscourt School is shorter than that of St. John's by more
than a century. Ravenscourt's initial success as a country day
school was largely due to its backers' confidence in the man they
had chosen as its first headmaster, the youthful Norman Young,
a native Manitoban and Rhodes Scholar recently returned from
a teaching post at a school for boys in Africa.

The school opened in the autumn of 1929, with an enrolment
of twenty-four boys, in the magnificent old mansion from which
it took its name. To tie in with the name of its new home the

raven was chosen as the school emblem; the school's motto was "Steadfastness, Courage and Friendship". Ravenscourt was operated as a country day school: the boys lunched at school, had games in the sunny part of the day, and studied in the late afternoon. Ravenscourt thrived and before long faced the age-old problem of finding larger quarters. The school found a large house, vacant for twenty years and reputed to be haunted. Haunted or not, the Thompson House made an ideal new home, and it remains a familiar landmark on the grounds of the present amalgamated school, overlooking the Red River. On the new property the woods were cleared and an orchard planted. Each boy was allotted his own tree to plant and to care for, and on frosty nights it was not uncommon to see school sweaters wrapped cosily around the trunks of several little fruit trees.

While life at Ravenscourt was perhaps happy and uncomplicated, the rest of the world was preparing for war. In 1939 Norman Young and his regiment, the Queen's Own Cameron Highlanders, left for overseas duty. His farewell message to the boys testified to his devotion both to the school he had helped to establish and the country he was about to serve. "Work with all your heart and strength for Canada—for your home and for your 'company of comrades'—your school. Be loyal to these and you will help win this war against evil." Many of the young "Ravens" who followed their headmaster overseas failed to return, and Norman Young himself was killed on the beach at Dieppe. The school carried on under the direction of Percy Wykes until 1949.

By 1950 Ravenscourt, like St. John's, was in deep financial difficulty and in danger of closing. As enrolment continued to fall off, discussions about amalgamation dragged on for nearly two years. The issue was further complicated by St. John's ties with the Anglican Church, whose designates appeared content to sell the building and let the school die. Their failure to act to keep St. John's alive was sharply criticized at the time as a "breach of faith". In the end the old boys and governors of St. John's and Ravenscourt (Johnians and Ravens) took the matter into their own hands and negotiated a trial amalgamation which eventually became permanent. St. John's moved to the Ravenscourt site and within three years an extensive and ambitious building program was underway. Regenerated, St. John's-Ravenscourt was well on its way to becoming one of western Canada's finest boarding and day schools.

Its new headmaster, R. L. (Dick) Gordon, an Old Boy and ex-paratrooper, was determined that the school should attract outstanding all-around students with a rich diversity of background from across Canada, regardless of their social position or ability to pay the fees. To achieve this end the Red River Scholarship Plan was introduced, financed by a substantial endowment fund built up through gifts from alumni and friends of the school. Twelve annual scholarships for both boys and girls provide amounts ranging from relatively small sums to the full fee.

As well as producing its fair share of Rhodes scholars, St. John's-Ravenscourt has sent forth no fewer than fourteen National Hockey League players. It is a school with an open and distinctively western flavour and a willingness to chop and change with the times. It now welcomes girls, and has abolished the school cadet corps and uniforms for the upper school. But while on the surface life may have become more relaxed, competition, both academically and athletically, has never been absent from the school's atmosphere and today is as keen as at any time in SJR's history.

Upper Canada College

Toronto, Ontario

1829

In terms of prestige and reputation, Upper Canada College has stood head and shoulders above the majority of other Canadian schools for boys for generations. From time to time its supremacy has been challenged from one quarter or another, but the fact remains that in the minds of a great many people Upper Canada College is the preeminent independent school in Canada, the school that more than any other is regarded as the cradle of the Canadian Establishment.

In 1829, the year that the school opened, Upper Canadian society was still in its infancy, yet education had already become a matter of both public and private concern. The colony's first governor, John Graves Simcoe, considered it a matter of utmost importance "that seats of learning be established, not only to begin but to complete the education of the children of the Principal People of the country". Simcoe himself offered a hundred pounds a year to "any respectable man" who could be persuaded to become a schoolmaster in Upper Canada.

But it was not until the arrival of the young and ambitious John Strachan that an educational program suited for the training of sons of the Principal People became established in Upper Canada. When the young Scottish schoolmaster John Strachan first arrived in Upper Canada in 1800, he was appalled at the incredibly backward state of education in the colony, and he saw this as a likely area in which to make his influence and ideas felt. After working as a private tutor in Kingston he was ordained as a member of the Anglican clergy in Cornwall, where in 1803 he set up a small parish school. Within a few years of its establishment a good many sons of Upper Canada's Principal People—Jarvises and Ridouts from York, Cartwrights, Macaulays, and Bethunes from Kingston—were being dispatched to Strachan's Academy.

Strachan had chosen the designation "academy" in preference to "school" on the grounds that an academy was much more than a simple grammar school. The term also implied a slightly less classical emphasis in the curriculum, a point of some significance in Strachan's mind, for he realized almost at once that his educational program, if it was to succeed, must be adapted to the colony's practical needs. Strachan was, above all things, a practical man. While directing the affairs of both his parish and his Academy he also published his own mathematics text. Surely he had his own students in mind, for it included introductory lessons on the buying and selling of stocks, land surveying, and business forms. Strachan obviously believed that while it was all very well to produce gentlemen, it was even more important to produce "Gentlemen of Business".

In 1812 the capital city of York was a muddy town of 800 citizens and 120 homes. Strachan's move there was greeted with delight by the people who had been sending their sons to faraway Cornwall. General Brock had offered to Strachan the chaplaincy to his troops in addition to the parish and school at York, a combination too attractive for Strachan to refuse. Strachan's new school, the Home District Grammar School, came to be known as the Blue School after Reverend Strachan donated the paint for the building's exterior from the proceeds of a lecture series. There the sons of York continued to be educated along reasonably practical lines, probably with the aid of Strachan's own mathematics text, the first to be printed in Canada.

Like Simcoe before him, Strachan grew increasingly concerned about the fact that there was as yet no institution of higher learning in the colony. His sense of urgency was shared by Sir John Colborne, the newly arrived Lieutenant Governor of Upper Canada (afterwards, Field Marshall Lord Seaton). Sir John, however, believed that the establishment of a first-rate preparatory institution—a "Minor College"—was a more pressing need than a full-fledged university. He sent a request to the Vice-Chancellor of Oxford University for "a cargo of masters" to supply the planned school. When they arrived, the new masters found themselves in primitive quarters until the new College's imposing buildings on King Street were completed.

In establishing the Royal Grammar School (later Upper Canada College), Colborne was fulfilling a desire to re-create in Upper Canada all that he considered worthwhile in the British public school system. The choice of British masters for the new school merely reflected this concern. They had to be men of scholarship, but more important, they had to be the sort of men who would encourage and stimulate among the boys a love of "healthy and manly games" and develop a spirit of self-reliance and good sportsmanship.

Even in the beginning, the College stood in the shadow of controversy. First, there was its location in York's extreme west end, "an inconvenient distance" from the more populated eastern and central parts of the town. To add to this, although the College was technically unaffiliated with any church, its headmaster was an Anglican clergyman and its staff, with one exception, were of the same faith. The apparent blessing of John Strachan, the Anglican Bishop of York, only exacerbated the animosity on the part of those of a different religious persuasion. The increasingly powerful Bishop's popularity even then was anything but universal. There was as well, resentment in other Upper Canadian communities over the expenditure of public money on an exclusive classical college in York—money which, some felt, could have been put to far better use in endeavours closer to home. The fact that the school's fees were in the beginning so modest that only the poorest of the poor could not afford them failed to impress its critics. Alarmed by its exclusive nature and by the fact that it was in his view "most extravagantly endowed", Upper Canada's chief rabble-rouser William Lyon Mackenzie vehemently denounced it and the Family Compact that supported it. "The College," he claimed, "was never intended for the people, that all classes may apply to the Fountain of Knowledge."

Sir John Colborne had imported for the new school not only well-trained English masters, but the traditional English emphasis on classical studies. The College's classical curriculum—a model of the type subsequently imposed on every one-room schoolhouse in the province—proved to be a major bone of contention. To most people it seemed infinitely more important for their children to learn the laws of nature and commerce than the various Latin declensions. Even the wealthier professionals—Upper Canada's ruling minority—questioned the value of such a curriculum, and Bishop Strachan himself, although he supported the College in principle, failed to find much merit in the College's classical stance. Its English "birch rod" style of discipline also engendered discontent.

Yet in the face of all opposition Sir John Colborne's "indulged and privileged child" forged ahead, heedless of its critics, and managed to set new standards of scholarship in the colony. At the wish of the superintendent of Indian affairs, it even undertook the responsibility of educating the sons of several Indian chiefs. Regrettably there remains no record of the effectiveness of its attempts to expand its influence to include the colony's original inhabitants.

Within ten years of its founding, the administration of the College was turned over to the council of the University of King's College. Then in 1853 control passed to the Senate of the University of Toronto, and hence the school came under the watchful eye of the Ministry of Education. Finally, in 1900, largely through the efforts of Upper Canada Old Boys, the university relinquished control and the College appointed its own independent governing body. During these years of growth and change the College continued to suffer periods of disrepute. There were complaints that it stood on a main thoroughfare where it was impossible to keep the boys out of mischief. At that time the school was located on one of King Street's notorious Four Corners, nicknamed Education, Legislation, Salvation, and Damnation after, respectively, the school, Government House, St. Andrew's Church, and a tavern. The province's first auditor-general was reputed to have found Upper Canada College "the worst school I have ever seen or heard of". Another critic rated it "a bastard among our educational institutions, born of fraud, and nurtured by spoliation—reaping where it has not sowed and gathering where it has not strewed", and declared that "this illegitimate offspring of Sir John Colborne's scheming brain should be called to strict account". Others were more favourably inclined. Sir George W. Ross, Ontario's minister of education and later its premier, in laying the cornerstone of the new Upper

Canada College in the northern suburb of Deer Park, praised it expansively and dedicated himself to its preservation: "Anything wrong that should happen to such a college, with such a career, would be nothing short of calamity."

The relocation of the College in 1891 to a thirty-acre site at the crest of the Avenue Road hill came as the result of a compromise with the university. The old site at the Four Corners had become commercially valuable but educationally unsuitable. The university realized a good portion of the proceeds when the property was sold, whereas the College, for its trouble, was awarded a new building and land by the provincial legislature. As it turned out, the architect chosen by the province not only exceeded his allotment for the building by a hundred thousand dollars but produced a jerry-built edifice that proved to be so structurally unsound that it had to be torn down sixty years later.

St. Clair Avenue at the turn of the century was still a dirt road bordered with pine trees. An apple orchard lay to the west of the College, and except for a few houses it was surrounded by open fields. The old streetcar line on Avenue Road stopped several blocks away at Dupont, and it was a long, cold climb up the plank sidewalks on wintry mornings to the College gates.

Although the meals were reportedly abundant, few schoolboys are without a sweet tooth. "Auntie" Harrison, a woman of obvious foresight, followed the College north and opened a small shop close by where for five cents a boy could purchase a pyramid (a chocolate cream confection), a sticky bun and a bottle of pop. For a "new boy", however, life could be full of unpleasant vicissitudes: "running the gauntlet" between two long lines of boys armed with switches or paddles, or having to sing a song or eat soap on demand. The British tradition of fagging was still very much alive, and the water jugs of senior boys had to be filled with hot water and their boots—including the soles—shined to a fine polish.

Even in its new location the College did not escape criticism. When the city wanted to extend Avenue Road northward, several votes were cast in favour of running the new road right through the College grounds instead of off to the side. In the end, however, sanity and charity prevailed. The College clock tower remains a familiar landmark at the top of the hill, although the present clock cannot claim the nickname of its forerunner, "the four-faced liar', whose accuracy depended on the number of pigeons that chose to roost on its hands at any given time.

From the outset, Upper Canada College has strived to maintain the highest of standards, both intellectual and moral. Just as any other school, it has produced its share of barflies and bounders as well as of honoured sons, but in the business of making soldiers, scholars and men of business it has been notoriously successful. Its alumni are found in boardrooms across the nation. Perhaps Upper Canada College will never be universally acknowledged as the "blessing and ornament to the Province" that its founder intended it to be. For some it continues to represent all that is worst about Canada's class structure, a perpetuation of power among a small, privileged group that discourages outsiders. Yet it is undeniable that Upper Canada College has achieved a significant measure of excellence.

As for the making of gentlemen, let us leave the last word to Stephen Leacock, an Old Boy of the King Street era and later a master at the College's Deer Park location. In 1941 he contributed an essay to the first issue of the school's Old Boys' publication, *Old Times*, that is worth reprinting in its entirety.

A MEMORY OF THE OLD SCHOOL ON KING STREET
THE STRUGGLE TO MAKE US GENTLEMEN

It seems that there is a good deal of alarm just now in England over the idea that "gentlemen" may be dying out. In an old civilisation things come and go. Knighthood came and went: it was in the flower, then in the pod and then it all went to seed. Now it seems to be gentlemen that are going. It appears that the upper classes are being so depressed and the lower classes so pushed up, and both slipping sideways so fast, that you simply can't distinguish an upper birth from a lower. In fact it is hard to make up their births at all.

I wasn't meaning to write on that topic. The thing is too big. Everyone admits that if gentlemen go, then Heaven only knows what will happen to England. But then Heaven only ever did. But the point here is that the question has got mixed up with the fate of the public schools. I mean of course in the English sense, the one the public can't get into. The best solution, it is generally admitted,—in fact a solution "definitely in sight"—is in the idea that if you throw the big board schools into the public schools and then throw the small private schools into both of them, then you so mix up your gentlemen with your others that they all turn into gentlemen. Of course, you can't face this all at once; a whole nation of gentlemen is a *goal* rather than—well I mean to say it takes time. Meantime if it is "definitely in sight," that's the place where the genius of England likes to leave it. It can roost there and go fast asleep along with Dominion Status for India and the Disestablishment of the Church.

But, bless me that was only the introduction of what I meant to write about. This talk of "Gentlemen" in England started way back at our old Upper Canada College on King St., sixty years ago, and the desperate struggle there to make us gentlemen. We didn't understand for a while just what they were trying to do to us. But gradually we began to catch on to it, and feel that it was no good. There was a kindly old oratorical principal I will not name, but whom the affection of old boys will easily recall, a kindly principal, I say, with a beautiful sonorous voice that used to echo through the "Prayer Hall" in exaltation of this topic. "This school I insist," he would declaim, "must be a school of *"gentlemen."* We used to sit as janitors all thinking, "This is going to be a tight shove. I'll never make it." But presently we learned to take it more easily. We noticed that the Gentlemen question generally broke out after a theft of school books, or the disappearance of small change foolishly left in reach. Not being yet gentlemen we made a distinction between "stealing" a thing and hooking it. A gentleman, you see classes both together. He'd just as soon steal a thing as hook it.

But, bit by bit, and gradually, we were led towards the idea. We were often told by oratorical visitors that Upper Canada College was founded as a "school for gentlemen". When I entered the school there were still a few old, very old, boys around, who belonged to the early generations of the foundation. We felt that the school had been fooled on some of them.

Personally, however, I got by on a side issue. In those days there was none of the elaborate registration, the card-index stuff, that all the schools have now. Any information they wanted about us they got *viva voce* on the spot, by calling us up in front of the class and asking for it. So there came a day soon after I entered when old Mr. Martland (Gentle) called me to be questioned and a junior master wrote down the answers. "What," he asked, "is your father's occupation". I hesitated quite a while and then I said, "He doesn't do anything." Mr. Martland bent over towards the junior who was writing and said in an impressive voice—*"A *gentleman*". A sort of awe spread round the room at my high status. But really why I hesitated was because I didn't exactly know what to say. You see I knew that at that moment my father was probably along on King St. having a Tom-and-Jerry in the Dog and Duck, or at Clancey's, — but whether to call that his occupation was a nice question.

Slowly we learned the qualification of a gentleman and saw that the thing was hopeless. A gentleman it seemed would take a bath (once a week on bath night) and never try to dodge it. A gentleman would not imitate Bishop Dumoulin or chew gum in St. George's. A gentleman, it seemed, *couldn't* tell a lie: not wouldn't, just *couldn't*. Limitations like these cut such a swath through our numbers, that in time we simply gave up. There was no use in it. Mind, don't misunderstand me. Of course we could *behave* like gentlemen, oh, certainly, *look* like gentlemen. At first sight you'd mistake us for it. But we knew all the time that we weren't.

I suppose you have the same problems still in what we call the new school, and even in the newest parts of it. But remember, where we failed, you may succeed. That school was founded to make gentlemen. Stick at it. You'll get there.

Stephen Leacock

Bishop's College School

Lennoxville, Quebec

1836

Bishop's College School, another school of this "early" period, was founded just one year before Queen Victoria's accession to the throne. Like Upper Canada College, its reputation as a first-rank school is well established, but its origin probably has more in common with Reverend John West's little log school on the Red River that became St. John's. When Lucius Doolittle, a Vermont-born clergyman of the Episcopal Church, set out to establish a classical school at Lennoxville, he was literally building in the wilderness. Its first boarders, lying huddled in their beds, could often hear wolves howling at the outskirts of the village. Like so many eastern Townships communities, Lennoxville was a Loyalist sanctuary, and after the War of 1812 it also attracted a number of retired army officers and other English gentlemen. The Archbishop of Lower Canada, George Jehoshaphat Mountain, remarked of Doolittle's school that "such has been the accession of respectable families of late to this neighbourhood, that I think I have nowhere seen in America such a collection of right English-looking youths of gentlemanly stamp."

There is some evidence that Doolittle's school, like King's College School in Nova Scotia and others, was partly funded by the Society for the Preservation of the Gospel. In any case, after five successful years, direction of the school was undertaken by Edward Capsman, a Cambridge man and a scholar of some reputation. The Lennoxville School had by now become a personal concern of Bishop Mountain's, and when in 1845 the University of Bishop's College in Lennoxville received its charter the grammar school became a "subordinate feature of the undertaking".

By 1854, the grammar school had ceased to be even subordinate and had closed altogether, like other schools in similar situations a victim of lack of attention on the part of the university whose precursor it was. But it reopened within a few years, again as a "junior department" of the university. Before long it was filled to overflowing and some boarders had to be put up with local families, an arrangement often adopted by the early academies in the eastern United States. Soon a handsome Gothic building was raised on the university campus and the problem of accommodation was solved, for the moment.

There is every indication that the grammar school was successful in its efforts to maintain a distinctly British tone. A member of Governor-General Lord Monk's party, visiting the school in 1864, observed that "the boys are more like English boys than any that I have seen out here and pride themselves on their English cheer. . . . They seem to have the same respect and love for their College as Eton boys have for Eton. . . . Lennoxville is the Eton of Canada—a charming and civilized place."

It was during this same period, however, that the school was infused with some blood and thunder from the South. The arrival of the "Rebs" following the Confederate defeat in the United States Civil War created a welcome diversion. Among this group of new arrivals to Bishop's College Grammar School was the son of Jefferson Davis, the ex-president of the Confederacy, who had settled into exile in Lennoxville. Some of these young southern "gentlemen" were hell-raisers as well. One of them, J. H. Stotesbury, many years later recorded some of his memories of those times:

> I remember a trip several of us took to Sherbrooke in an open sleigh on a cold winter afternoon. Arriving in Sherbrooke we thought a drink of hot port wine would warm us up. We took more than was good for us. Next morning we were hailed before the Rector [headmaster], a late arrival from England. He seemed more concerned over what we had been drinking than over our escapades. We told him it was port wine. He asked, "Don't you know that you can get *no* good port wine outside of England?" Our punishment was to be kept in bounds for a week or ten days, but as "bounds" covered a thousand acres or more, we did not feel severely punished. We always had our huts in the woods to visit and our squirrel and muskrat traps to look after.

Mr. Stotesbury also recalled an episode which took place shortly after the "Rebs' " arrival:

> During my time the boys used to march in a body to attend Sunday morning services in the village church. My brothers and I had got hold of a lot of Confederate bills and we conceived the idea of putting them on the collection plate. So we divided them with the other boys and when the plate came around each boy contributed his share. When the plates reached the altar they were overflowing with bills. The minister must have thought it a good joke for I do not remember that anything was said about it.

But if the southerners imported some foreign pranks, their sense of honour was in the best British tradition. Stotesbury continues:

> A fine thing I remember about the school was the sense of honour and fair play that prevailed. No matter how grave the offense, every boy was always ready to own up and take his punishment. There was no such thing as a big boy bullying a smaller one. The big boys were always ready to take the part of the smaller ones and see that they had fair play. We had what was called being "placed in chancery", and woe to the boy who did anything mean or contemptible. In chancery he was completely ostracized, and none of the other boys was allowed to speak to him for a stated period.

Life at Bishop's was possibly far more benevolent than at many contemporary British public schools, where despite Dr. Thomas Arnold's humanizing influence bullying and fagging were still a way of life.

For Sir John A. Macdonald, Stotesbury has nothing but praise. When he and his brothers had arrived in Lennoxville late in December, 1865, the school had already broken up for the holidays and the outlook for their own Christmas was dreary. "Imagine, therefore, our surprise on awakening Christmas morning to find at the foot of our bed, a pair of skates and a beautiful red sled for each boy, the gift, we learned later, of Sir John Macdonald. How he knew of these forlorn boys I do not know." Stotesbury and his brothers would also have witnessed the formation of Canada's oldest existing cadet corps. Although Upper Canada College has also claimed the title, the Bishop's College School corps predates Upper Canada College's original

Rifle Corps and won its battle honours in defence of the Eastern Townships during a Fenian raid on June 7, 1866.

The rector referred to in Stotesbury's reminiscences was not only headmaster of the grammar school, but also vice principal of the College. It was thought that this dual office would help cement closer ties between the two institutions, from which both would benefit academically and financially. But a widening gap developed between the two bodies, and the situation was not improved by the.fact that within this small scholastic community there were no less than four deliberative bodies: the Corporation, the Executive Committee of the Trustees, the College Council, and the School Council. At Corporation meetings there were rumblings about the inadequacy of the masters' salaries, the lack of heat, the danger of fire, the shortage of space and the chronic shortage of water; the state of the dwellings and the state of the playing fields, to say nothing of primitive sanitary fixtures. Then, in 1874, the school was demolished by fire.

Within two years a new school building had been erected and the school once again thrived, until 1891, when it was once more completely destroyed by fire. Again the Corporation sprang into action and a new building, "in almost every respect superior to the one destroyed", was soon underway.

Still, a gnawing antagonism persisted between Bishop's University and its junior division, Bishop's College School. Divided loyalties and misplaced priorities only widened the rift. Finally, in 1920 the formal ties were at last severed and Bishop's College School moved from the university campus. The BCS preparatory school, which had opened in 1904, was the first to absent itself, moving just across the St. Francis River (and still within sight of the university) into two large new buildings. These buildings represented the first stage in a master plan concocted during World War I by Commander J.K.L. Ross, a wealthy Montreal sportsman and disgruntled former board member of Bishop's College, whose dream was to create his own school in Lennoxville. Ross, incidentally, was the owner of Sir Barton, in 1919 the first Canadian horse in racing history to win the Triple Crown. Ross' luck ran out, however, and the elaborate scheme he had devised to create his own school never materialized. Handsome brass door handles bearing the letters L. S. are still in use at BCS, a legacy of Ross' fond dream and empty pocketbook.

The upper school followed the preparatory school across the river the following year, and Bishop's College School settled into its new surroundings, a cordial but totally autonomous neighbour to the university which had alternately nurtured it and tolerated it.

In the autumn of 1972 Bishop's College School, like an increasing number of American preparatory schools, expanded its enrolment policy to include girls as well as boys. It was a radical departure from some entrenched points of view, born of economic necessity but also from a desire to move with the times. In announcing its decision, the Board of the school observed that

> Boys and girls are entering a vastly different world from that of ten or fifteen years ago. When our two schools (BCS and King's Hall, Compton) were founded they reflected the society in which they flourished. Boys were trained for an all-male business world; girls were being prepared for the accepted role of homemakers. All this has changed and it is up to us to prepare our boys and girls for a society in which there is greater equality of the sexes.

Pickering College

Newmarket, Ontario

1842

At the Quaker-founded Pickering College north of Toronto, equality of the sexes was a basic educational tenet from the beginning. Among the Quakers, it has always been a matter of principle that girls should receive the same opportunities as boys. Thus it seemed only natural that they should be included in plans for the establishment of a Society of Friends school.

As early as 1801, forty Quaker families had settled on lands near Newmarket granted to them by royal charter. By 1842 the area was one of the main centres of Quakerism in Upper Canada. It was at the urging of John Joseph Gurney, a brother of Elizabeth Fry, that the community agreed to establish a school. Until then, those Quakers who wanted something more than the rudiments of learning for their children had had to send them far away to a school in New York State. This meant a long separation from home, to say nothing of the expense. In Gurney's view, the new school would provide a combination of "a sound cultural education with practical activities, suited to life in the country". There is every reason to believe that the school did just that. The boys' and girls' divisions, however, were at first totally separate, not co-educational but coordinate.

The Westlake Boarding School, Pickering College's forerunner, opened in 1842 near Picton, Ontario. In accordance with the Quakers' very practical views on education, manual labour was an integral part of the curriculum. After twenty-five years of moderately successful operation, however, the school closed, possibly because of its poor location but also because of lack of funds. The property was sold and the money used to purchase a new site, which the Friends considered more suitable. When the

Friends' school re-opened in Pickering, Ontario, it operated on an entirely co-educational basis, with an academic program designed to fit more closely into the Ontario system of education. It did retain, though, the Quaker emphasis on moral and spiritual values and the importance of work and mental discipline. But unlike other private schools, it did not encourage competition among the students. "None but concerned students, those willing to work, are invited to attend. There are no prizes ... no marking system nor any inducement held out to students to work and study, except the satisfying of their sense of duty and the pleasure which comes to those who endeavour to acquire knowledge for its own sake."

Eventually, a growing difference of opinion on several matters, including the introduction of art and music into the curriculum, led to a "separation" within the Society of Friends and the temporary closing of the school in 1885. When it re-opened, the factions must have been reconciled, for the school's reputation within the educational community mounted steadily and it continued to operate successfully until 1905, when a disastrous fire gutted the main building. Undaunted, a committee immediately began making plans for a new school, but it was decided that Newmarket might be a more suitable location. The name Pickering College, however, was retained despite the move.

When the new school at Newmarket was complete, its benefactors must have been well pleased with their investment—a handsome Georgian building, set on a height of land not far from the original Friends' meeting place. But although it had a fine new building, Pickering College continued to have its share of problems. As society at large drifted towards increasing secularism, the demand for the type of education Pickering could provide diminished. The religious atmosphere of the school began to decline, and towards the end of World War I the federal government took over the premises for use as a military convalescent hospital.

For the next ten years the Pickering buildings served in this capacity. The Friends had mixed feelings about re-opening the school once again, but finally they agreed that the school should resume operation as a residential school for boys only. The mixed blessings of co-education, with all its inherent complexities, were sidestepped for the moment.

Pickering College re-opened in 1927 as a single-sex school, but one that differed greatly from the majority of other Canadian boys' boarding schools. During the next twenty years it became known for its open-minded and experimental approach to education under its new headmaster, Joseph McCulley. For the times, his approach to the matter of discipline was unorthodox, even permissive. Although not a Quaker himself, McCulley held fast to the liberal ideals on which the school had been founded, and although he was a product of the Ontario school system, he was not content to reproduce it. It was his belief that within a well-ordered structure there was still plenty of room for individual freedom. His contribution to Pickering during those years was invaluable. He is revered as well as remembered.

One of the outstanding men who worked in cooperation with McCulley was Taylor Statten, Pickering's director of character education and its first guidance counsellor, possibly the first at any school in Canada. Taylor Statten's interest in progressive methods of education may have stemmed from his acquaintance with the highly controversial child psychologist Dr. W. E. Blatz, whose philosophy of the individuality of each child and belief in the dangers of competitiveness (hence, of marks and report cards) were to have a profound influence on the future of education in Ontario. At Blatz's Institute of Child Study, which still operates under the wing of the University of Toronto, his child-rearing theories have been put into practice for fifty years. Anyone who is familiar with Blatzian doctrine and manages to sift through the Hall-Dennis Report on education in Ontario will recognize the fine hand of Blatz at almost every turn of the page. It would probably amuse him to know that what was once considered heresy was more in the nature of prophecy.

Today Pickering College is no longer considered a "progressive school" in the same sense as it was in the McCulley era, but to a degree it still differs from most other independent boys' schools. Written entrance examinations are considered a poor substitute for a personal interview with the boy and his family. The school's current headmaster, Harry Beer, a former student and a member of the Society of Friends, believes that "these examinations, written under pressure in an artificial situation, generally reveal very little about a boy's real ability or potential".

The Quaker roots of the school are reflected in a philosophy which places great emphasis on the importance of tolerance and service to mankind. Again in keeping with Quaker tradition, the relationship between student and teacher has always been friendly. Caning, a means of discipline in the best British public school tradition, has never found adherents in the Society of Friends, and in this respect most if not all other boys' schools in the country have followed Pickering's lead in recent years.

The boys at Pickering come from a variety of backgrounds. It is definitely not an "exclusive" sort of school, nor does it pretend to be. "We have boys from two-salary homes and we also have boys from the Children's Aid — boys who have had quite a difficult time, because they haven't had homes or families," the headmaster points out. "A boy without parents can come to a place like this where there is, I hope, love and affection and supervision and he can accept it." Pickering was also among the first schools to accept non-Christian and non-white students, "without any quota". Direct and personal involvement of all students in the day-to-day operation of the school has become a tradition. Here, as in all other aspects of education at Pickering, the emphasis is on the rights and privileges of "the other fellow". Perhaps this, more than anything else, has been the goal of the school from its inception: to develop in all its students a sincere concern for others.

The March of Intellect
1850-1900

ST HELENS SCHOOL
DUNHAM RD.

Overleaf: St. Helen's School, Dunham, P.Q.

B Y the mid-nineteenth century the idea of universal public education had begun to take hold. In Upper Canada the Common School Act of 1841 had introduced a property tax to fund public education. Though it was badly drafted and impractical, it reflected the prevailing belief that support of public education was a collective responsibility. Schooling had become far too important a matter to be left to individual and local initiative.

Before long, universal education came to be regarded as the ultimate panacea for the social, political, and moral problems of the age. Conservatives saw it as the best defense against radicalism; liberals saw it as the best means of achieving political reform and social justice. In 1831 William Lyon Mackenzie wrote, "All reforms in government must begin by enlightening the people themselves. . . . Therefore, my friends, encourage Education in every township, and seek not to put off the teacher of skill, talent and moral character, but reward him liberally." Clearly, public education was the surest means to instil respect for authority and Christian morality in people at all levels of society.

On the other hand, the birth of the public school system served to undermine the traditional character of education in Canada. It effectively ended parental control over the selection of both teachers and curriculum. The school became the instrument not of the family, but of the state and of society at large. The numbers of private non-aided schools catering to the needs of the less wealthy declined as larger government grants and an improved central administrative system brought them under the public umbrella. Sooner or later most of the small grammar schools and academies came under state control, mainly because they could never have found the funds to become truly self-supporting on their own.

It was not until the consolidation of the public school system that the term "private schooling" began to take on a new meaning. No longer did it denote a broad spectrum of alternatives, from city schools for children of the poor, to rural schools operated seasonally for farmers' sons, to the more familiar preparatory institutions. The private schools that survived constituted, instead, a conscious (and often expensive) rejection of the new state system by parents who sought for their children denominational education, superior or more specialized teaching,

59

a healthier environment, or a combination of all of those features—in short, those advantages that the emerging state schools did not or could not offer.

By the second half of the century the problem of survival was no longer the central concern of the various Protestant denominations of the Dominion, and nearly all could afford to undertake ambitious academic enterprises. The churches, too, supported the March of Intellect, and while each denomination marched to its own drummer all sought to expand their intellectual and academic spheres of influence. In a reaction against the increasing dominance of the Anglican Church in higher education other denominations had begun to establish their own institutions of higher learning. Upper Canada Academy (later Victoria College, University of Toronto) opened in Cobourg, Ontario under Methodist sponsorship in 1836. Presbyterians chose Kingston as the site for Queen's University in 1840, and in New Brunswick Mount Allison University grew from the Mount Allison Wesleyan Academy established in 1843.

In the field of secondary education for both boys and girls, the interdenominational competition was even keener. The Methodist-Episcopalians established Albert and Alma Colleges, while the Baptists established Woodstock and Moulton. The Presbyterians were responsible for Halifax Ladies' College, among others. Not to be outdone, the High Anglicans founded Trinity College School and its sister school, Bishop Strachan, as well as two other girls' schools that have not survived (Bishop Hellmuth College in London, Ontario and Bishop Bethune in Oshawa), while the Anglican Evangelicals sponsored Havergal and Ridley.

The common view of these schools was that they were reflections of a colonial mentality and little more than imitations of British models. And indeed, a good many schools possessed all the trappings of their British counterparts, such as prefects and their emphasis on sports and games. Many of their staff and heads had gained their teaching experience in England or Scotland. But after Confederation an emerging spirit of nationalism often led to an emphatic rejection of things British, and schoolmasters and mistresses, when they could not be found locally, were even imported from below the border rather than from across the Atlantic. American domination of the faculty at one independent school was so overwhelming, in fact, that it led the new headmaster to voice an all-too-familiar lament about cultural imperialism.

In emulation of both the British and American systems, many private boarding schools were established not in centres of population but in small-town or country surroundings; possibly because land was easier to obtain, but certainly also because a rural environment was universally acknowledged to be far healthier for the rearing and education of children than the city with its many diversions. The pastoral ideal was a recurrent theme of the Victorian age, and it was a strong selling point for many schools. Stanstead College's prospectus of 1885 pointed out: "The quietness of the village and surrounding countryside invites to studiousness, while the absence of many temptations peculiar to large towns and cities renders the place eminently safe for the residence of students removed from the watchful guardianship of home." Schools in suburbs or small towns close to cities stressed their wholesome environments while at the same time advertising the ready availability—close but not too close—of "cultural advantages". Peaceful rural isolation promoted one of the primary functions of the private school, which was to be "as nearly as possible *parental*". The private school was seen as a substitute family, often with the headmaster's wife serving as surrogate mother, that would impart family values in an atmosphere more homogeneous, less pluralistic, and certainly less distracting than that offered by the emerging co-educational public schools.

One of the attractions of the country school was its promise of a great deal of healthy outdoor activity, an aspect of the Victorian belief in Muscular Christianity, which encouraged games and sports as instruments of character formation and morality. To its adherents, athleticism was a central part of the educational process. As good sportsmanship and fair play became part of the standard training of the well-educated boy cries of "play up and play the game" were to echo through the latter part of the nineteenth century, and well beyond. The belief that participation in team sports was instrumental in the moulding of a boy's character was inherited directly from the British public school system, where athleticism had been fostered as a means of discouraging such undesirable pursuits as hounds and hares and poaching, by channelling a boy's energies into more positive outlets. Manly and muscular pastimes soon became indispensable in the making of the truly "Christian Gentleman". Most churchmen, as well as others involved in founding or directing private schools, wholeheartedly advocated the belief that through athleticism, Christian attitudes and virtues would be bound to develop. Although it has diminished to a certain degree, the emphasis on games has remained a prominent feature of the independent school. It is still, at any rate, considered a very practical way of keeping the young actively involved in school life and effectively "out of mischief".

For the Christian Gentlewoman, on the other hand, the development of social refinement was often more important than either athletic skills or team spirit. Although advanced courses in music and art were offered in addition to the regular academic curriculum, it was not until the 1890s or later that organized competitive sports for girls were introduced. According to the image of Victorian womanhood, anything much more strenuous than croquet was frowned upon. Physical education for genteel maidens with upswept hair and voluminous skirts as often as not consisted of swinging Indian clubs in unison on a spacious lawn. At one eastern Canadian girls' school the prescribed attire for these calisthenics was "a plain black skirt (no drapery), short, reaching just above the ankle; a scarlet blouse waist, with loose sleeves and black collar and cuffs; black stockings and bloomers. Also a warm loose underwaist to replace corset."

The education of women had begun to gain footholds, though it was still an outrageous concept to a good many people. At mid-century the general opinion was that girls' secondary education was a non-essential frill, if not an outright danger. Education for women was best confined to normal school training, after which feminine talents could be put to excellent practical use in the grammar schools of the state. Virtually no provision was made for the higher education of women from the public purse. It was only through private effort and generosity that anything at all was done to further the educational interests of women.

It was the pioneering effort of Miss Buss and Miss Beale, two of Britain's leading protagonists in the fight for women's rights to quality education, that helped pave the way for the establishment of several Canadian girls' schools. Frances M. Buss was only twenty-three when she opened her day school, North London Collegiate School, in 1850. It became the model for countless girls' high schools throughout England, and later Canada. Dorothea Beale, principal of Cheltenham Ladies' College for nearly fifty years and the founder of St. Hilda's College, Oxford, also left an indelible mark. With unflagging determination both these women fought to combat the prejudices of the day and devoted their lives to the creation of a new educational climate for women—one in which girls would be adequately prepared to sit the same university entrance exams and eventually attain the same university degrees as boys. It was an uphill battle. Cambridge University was the first to capitulate when it permanently accepted female students in 1867, although it waited until 1948 to grant them degrees. Oxford University, on the other hand, took another ten years to make up its mind to admit women as students, but by 1920 was granting them degrees. Despite their efforts on behalf of women's education in Britain, Miss Buss and Miss Beale achieved a reputation that is commemorated in this oft-quoted ditty:

> Miss Buss and Miss Beale
> Cupid's darts do not feel.
> How different from us,
> Miss Beale and Miss Buss.

In Canada, the idea of preparing girls for university developed at about the same time as in England. Professor Van Norman of Victoria University in Cobourg, Ontario was among the first to actively encourage female education. In his view it had "a more important bearing upon the improvement and well-being of Society than that of the other sex; and therefore young ladies should enjoy the facilities for acquiring an intellectual and moral education, in some degree proportionate to those afforded young gentlemen." His Cobourg Ladies' Seminary opened in 1845 but a year later, unable to find a building in Cobourg that was large enough, he moved the school to Burlington, where it became the Burlington Ladies' Academy. Van Norman's efforts were the leading edge of a flood of ladies' colleges and seminaries that sprang up across the country as the century advanced.

Although the idea of female education met with somewhat less prejudice in Canada than it did in Britain, there was a "finishing school" aspect to many Canadian girls' schools which would linger on well into the twentieth century. Although many of the Ladies' Colleges proudly advertised the singular educational advantages available within their sheltering walls, more often than not these advantages tended to be social and cultural ltural—ornamental rather than academic. In sharp contrast to the boys' schools, until nearly the end of the century the majority of the Ladies' Colleges were intended not as preparation for university work but as terminal institutions. They were finishing schools in more than one sense, designed both to complete a girl's necessary education and to apply a permanent veneer of social grace and Christian propriety.

In the education of young women, manners and deportment were at least as important as English literature and Latin. While her brothers, if not being prepared for university courses, might be receiving practical instruction in business procedures, the young gentlewoman's waking hours were devoted to instruction in such vital matters as

> exercise, exposure, eating, sleeping and sitting, walking, dress, and room; domestic matters, table manners, schoolroom manners, hotel and railroad manners; street manners; manners in public assemblies,—as in church, concert, parties and parlors; manners towards kindred and friends; manners in intercourse with other ladies; manners and intercourse with gentlemen. In short, no pains will be spared . . . so to regulate the daily deportment of each pupil as to make easy and habitual all the graces and proprieties of refined and accomplished womanhood. (Stanstead College Calendar, 1885-6)

The likelihood that a girl would receive far more instruction in manners than in matter was greatly increased if she attended a co-educational school (which was inevitably administered entirely by men), or a girls' school whose Board was composed of men, as nearly all of them were. On the other hand, many of the teachers themselves were educated, independent, and strong-minded women—often extraordinarily liberated, and almost always spinsters. As unmarried women they were free to offer their undivided attention to the intellectual advancement of their pupils; but in general, they lacked the authority to guide school policy itself. School policies were determined by Boards of Governors, and those governors wanted their daughters to be trained not for intellectual independence but for Victorian womanhood—in other words, wife- and motherhood. An education such as her brother received would not only be useless to a girl, but could possibly be dangerous, certainly inappropriate. In a country where the University of Toronto did not admit its first woman student until the 1880s, it was not until the end of the century, and perhaps even later, that attitudes changed sufficiently to render the "finishing school" ideal something less than elegant and desirable.

In due course a few girls' schools began to place a more vigorous emphasis on university preparation, and at the same time their students began lobbying for more active and competitive sports. By the turn of the century croquet hoops and "Swedish drill" were starting to give way to cricket, basketball, ice and ground hockey, and even lacrosse. Female muscularity was becoming less unbecoming—so long as it was Christian in tone, for a Christian education remained as important as it ever had been, perhaps even more so. The avowed promise of the church-affiliated schools to inculcate in children a sense of morality, duty, and piety was as attractive to parents as it ever had been.

As female education gained ground, advocates of co-education continued preaching their own gospel. "Not that co-education is best for every girl," declared the Reverend Alexander Burns, governor and principal of Ontario's first Ladies' College, Hamilton Wesleyan, founded in 1861, "or that it is likely even to become universal, but because it is practically the only hope the multitudes can ever have of securing a higher education. No one that has ever become acquainted with the system under fair trial," he continued, "will hesitate for a moment to admit that GIRLS can hold their own in every part of the curriculum. . . .There can be no possible objection to co-education on the grounds of intellectual inequality, nor is the girl's health more likely to suffer than her brother's." The founders of at least two mid-nineteenth-century boarding schools, Albert College, and Woodstock College, evidently espoused this enlightened point of view. Although both schools opened the same year, it is doubtful whether either institution took notice of the other's progress. It is true that they shared the ever-present problems of building, money raising, and staffing, and both welcomed "persons of all grades and opinions without restriction". But there were marked differences in the development of the two schools, differences which in the end led to the survivial of one and the disintegration of the other.

Many schools founded during this period in fervent hope and enthusiasm were destined to disappear. The Baptist colleges, Woodstock and Moulton, fell victim to administrative decisions in which they and their supporters had no voice. The Anglican King's Hall Compton and St. Helen's, along with a host of other church-sponsored ladies' colleges such as Bishop Bethune, Bishop Hellmuth, the Hamilton Wesleyan College, the Ottawa Ladies' College and its Presbyterian sister Brantford Ladies' College, have vanished as well. Little by little religion and education went their separate ways. At the same time that society began to distinguish more sharply between the two, the churches, too, concluded that their own funds would be more profitably directed to endeavours other than secular education. Although many private schools continue to be church-supported, the support is only spiritual, not financial. Those schools that could not find other resources did not survive.

Near the end of the century, as well, the denominational schools began to face competition from another quarter: the revitalized private venture school, often highly successful, that operated without benefit of church support. The individual men and women who founded these new private venture schools were determined to create institutions that would be truly independent—of stockholders and governing bodies as well as of church influence or interference. Indeed, they would run their own show with a sense of personal commitment that equalled and perhaps even surpassed the churches' earlier ventures into education.

Albert College

Belleville, Ontario

1857

First known as the Belleville Seminary, Albert College now bears the Christian name of its former principal and guiding light, Bishop Albert Carman of the Methodist-Episcopalian Church. Like the Baptists and the Congregationalists, the Methodist-Episcopalians were staunch believers in the total separation of church and state—a position which endeared them not at all to the intrepid champions of the common school, Dr. Egerton Ryerson and his band of disciples at the Ontario Ministry of Education. While Ryerson firmly believed that piety was necessary to the public good, he favoured a brand of nondenominational Protestantism in the public school system. The clergy of the lower churches, however, such as the founders of the Belleville Seminary, were equally ill-disposed to accept the views of the Anglicans and the Roman Catholics. If there was anyone they despised more than Ryerson it was "Johnny Strachan—the Divine" and the "Romans". The philosophical rock upon which Albert College was founded was none other than denominationalism at its righteous best.

Just after the mid-century mark, a subscription campaign was launched for a Methodist-Episcopalian school which would include its own theological department. The circuit riders were dispatched to gather funds from the faithful and the town of Belleville was selected as the most ideal situation for the proposed seminary. When it was first opened in the fall of 1857 the new college, with its staff of four men and two women, welcomed any and all who presented themselves. This open-door enrolment policy unfortunately resulted in discipline problems, personal antagonism, and gossip-mongering on the part of certain board members and the principal. At the end of the first year the principal resigned. His replacement was a young staff member, Albert Carman, who was only twenty-five when he took over as principal. Carman set to work to appease the warring factions and bring some degree of solvency to the new college.

To provide additional financing for the college the offer of government assistance was considered briefly, then rejected. "Let us fling back this hush money," declared the school's governing board, echoing the sentiment of a great many private schools through the years that they would rather be poor but independent than be subsidized by and answerable to political authority. But when it appeared that the college property might have to be sold to Roman Catholic interests this stance underwent a rapid transformation. The possibility was too frightful even to contemplate. Fighting to avert such a calamity, Albert Carman wrote, "The Belleville Seminary turned into a Popish convent! The Belleville Seminary erected by Protestants as an exponent of their principles, a fortress of their literature, and a centre of their light and power, perverted to perpetrate monstrous errors . . . and bind the galling chains of priestly domination and pontifical tyranny about our civil and religious liberties!" It was clearly an unthinkable alternative and government help, the lesser of two evils, was gratefully accepted.

Carman also arranged for those students who were unable to pay the full fee in cash to make up the difference in work, in farm produce, or even in wood—which the more muscular Christians could saw up for a credit of fifty cents a cord. If the students were not wealthy, neither were the schools' benefactors. The College had no monied patrons and received only minimal assistance from the government. It relief heavily on the generosity of people who could ill-afford to give but who did so out of strong personal commitment. Neither was this support confined solely to Methodist Church membership.

Finances, however, were only one of Carman's worries. His major concern appears to have been over a faculty that was predominantly American, a not-uncommon situation in Canadian institutions of learning. "I cannot understand," he groaned, "why the Board threw so strong an ingredient of Americanism into the faculty. Would it not be gigantic mismanagement to take the government of the institution from the hands of men born and educated here and vest the authority in men whose predilections are unmistakably American? Yet such is the plot." He was not the last to make the charge of cultural imperialism, but the number of Americans on his staff was most likely due to the very real shortage of teachers in the province, almost all of whom had to be imported either from Britain or from the United States.

Within ten years of its establishment Albert College received its university charter with the power to grant degrees in arts in connection with Victoria University in Cobourg. It maintained its university status for a number of years, until after the union of the various branches of Methodism in 1884, when the arts and senior theological departments transferred to Victoria University, leaving Albert and Alexandra (the women's division of the College) to fulfill their original destinies at the secondary school level.

Academic training at both Albert and Alexandra placed great emphasis on English composition and public speaking. Attendance at the Saturday morning tutorials for instruction in "Elocution and Composition" was mandatory. The College's calendar took pains to point out, as well, the many advantages of the school's location on the shores of Lake Ontario. Belleville, it seems, was a virtual paradise, and a paragon of sanitation. No mention was ever made of the farm animals which were allowed to run free in the city's streets and gardens, and which from time to time paid their respects to the College. Sheep were known to appear in the halls without warning and once a cow made a well-timed entrance on the assembly platform to greet staff and students as they arrived for morning prayers.

The well-defined separation of Albert and Alexandra Colleges limited the opportunities for socializing, although daily meetings at the communal water pump (called "pump socials") and in the dining hall presented openings for those with romantic inclinations. At table each boy served the "lady" placed opposite him before serving himself, but he would have to receive special permission if he wanted to call on her later—and then he could do so only if a teacher were also present, watchful and vigilant for the duration of the visit. For seniors the rules were relaxed slightly, perhaps in order to better prepare them for the temptations of the wicked world awaiting them beyond the College gates. Senior swains with a dollar and a half to spare could

hire a horse and buggy for a Saturday afternoon jaunt, provided, of course, that the young ladies were returned safely in
time for dinner.

After church union the College entered into an era of extraordinary missionary zeal. Filled with youthful idealism, its
graduates responded in droves to the call. Their letters from the
field and their visits to the school during home leave inspired still
more to follow as missionaries and teachers to the Orient, to
Africa, to South America, or to outposts in the Canadian north.
It is difficult to say whether the female presence had anything to
do with the active part played by Albert College in extending the
work of the church to the four corners of the earth, but the fact
remains that its contributions to the mission field outstripped
those of any single-sex school of its kind.

By the turn of the century enrolment had reached an all-time
high of nearly 350 students, yet the College was still in debt and
the church was reluctant to turn over any substantial funds for
expansion. After World War I, a fund-raising campaign earned
enough to erect a new school. But it opened in the autumn of
1926 minus two departments, with only fifty students in a building created to house 250. Then the early thirties brought salary
cuts of up to fifty per cent, yet none of the staff chose to resign.
Fees were lowered, and entrance standards along with them.
Taxes were left in arrears and there was talk of selling the
building. The principal resigned in despair but by the late thirties hope had been rekindled. The commercial department re-
opened and it was announced that girls would be re-admitted. In
cooperation with Queen's University, first and second year arts
courses were offered, an arrangement which continued well into
the forties.

But money remained, as ever, the primary concern. Dr.
Bishop, the new principal, became the resident plumber and
carpenter in his efforts to help defray rising costs. During the
summer several students stayed on to work under his direction,
repairing roofs, cutting lawns, and weeding the school gardens
that provided the hundreds of quarts of pickles and preserves
that were put down by Mrs. Bishop. The maintenance of the
school became a community effort, and staff and students
worked together to keep the school afloat.

This spirit of making do carried the school through the war

and into the fifties. By now the church, once a source of revenue and support, had all but abandoned its paternalistic role. Education by denomination, once a rallying cry, was now an anachronistic concept. More from necessity than choice the five remaining United Church schools—Albert, Alma, Ontario Ladies' College, Stanstead, and Balmoral Hall—were left to find their own way, to succeed—or to fail—on their own merits and their ability to fulfill current needs. The church withdrew all but nominal support, acknowledging education as a secular matter in which it had little business and as a financial burden it could no longer afford to underwrite.

Today, nonetheless, the religious component of Albert College is still strong. In an age when living the Good Life conjures up a very different picture than it did fifty or a hundred years ago, however, the challenge to foster the Christian Way has never been greater.

Woodstock College
Woodstock, Ontario
1857-1926

Moulton Ladies' College
Toronto, Ontario
1888-1954

Woodstock College and Moulton Ladies' College survive only in the memories of the people who knew them well. Forty years have elapsed since the governors of McMaster University decided to temporarily close Woodstock in 1926, and it is over twenty years ago that Moulton was summarily shut down. But the bitterness that resulted from McMaster's action rings down through the years. The story of Woodstock and of Moulton is instructive, for it demonstrates how schools that were administered by a university finally fell victim to a set of priorities imposed from without, and how they themselves failed to establish the means to rescue themselves.

Like Albert College, Woodstock was co-educational and began as an essentially denominational school, even though its founder, Robert Alexander Fyfe, was a diehard opponent of the principle of education by denomination. "One cries I am a Baptist, or I am a Presbyterian, or a Methodist, and can see no good in any measure which does not directly benefit his particular sect—so wretchedly little are the views of men," he protested. In an age of bigotry and religious factionalism, the young Baptist minister's attitude was startlingly liberal. Advocating the establishment of a provincial rather than a denominational university, he called upon people to put aside their national differences, "be they English, Irish, or Scottish. We ought to look upon ourselves as Canadians and earnestly inquire by what means we can advance the interests of the country." It is not surprising, then, that when Reverend Fyfe founded the Canadian Literary Institute, as Woodstock was known for its first twenty-five years, he chose to call it "Canadian", as opposed to "Baptist".

Fyfe's Institute had barely been established when a fire levelled the main buildings and he found himself not only without premises but deeply in debt. The citizens of Woodstock, however, warmed by the young clergyman's idealism, offered him the use of the Woodstock Hotel rent-free for two years and raised a considerable sum for the reconstruction of the school. To further encourage Fyfe, whose spirits must have been at a very low ebb, an offer of assistance came from Senator William MacMaster of Toronto. It was the first of many McMaster philanthropies, and it was perhaps ironic that the best-known of these — McMaster University — would later bring about the school's demise.

The Baptist community, disunited at the best of times, had every reason to be well pleased with the school. Within a few years of its founding, Woodstock had graduated Canada's first Baptist missionary to India. However, by the early 1870s a movement was afoot to establish a Baptist university in Toronto and to relocate the school's Theological Department there. This did not sit well with the school's local supporters, who believed that the proposed university ought to be located in Woodstock, and Newton Wolverton, the principal of the College, resigned in protest against the "disintegration of the school".

Wolverton's resignation must have created a considerable stir, for he was no ordinary man. Born in Canada, he later moved with his family to the United States. At the outbreak of the American Civil War, while still in his early teens, he had enlisted in the Union Army with his two older brothers and became a wagonmaster in charge of twenty-five ammunition wagons. At sixteen he was appointed spokesman for a special delegation to President Lincoln that was seeking to counteract the pressure of Northern agitators who wanted war declared on Britain because of its aid to the Southern cause. Wolverton is said to have made it respectfully but abundantly clear that while Canadians fighting for the North believed in the Union cause, they were "Canadians, born and bred, who did not enlist to fight against the Mother country". The delegation left with Lincoln's assurance that their fears were unfounded, and shortly thereafter Wolverton was assigned to General Grant as a sharpshooter.

When Wolverton returned to Canada to complete his education he was twenty-four years old, and the girls and boys of the

Institute's preparatory section in Woodstock must have been more than a little perplexed at the sight of their new classmate, who could barely read and write but who was an excellent marksman and chewed tobacco with a vengeance. Within seven years, however, Wolverton had graduated from the University of Toronto with distinction, and when he returned as a Baptist minister to teach at the College he brought with him a worldliness which few of his contemporaries could claim.

During his years on the staff and later as principal of Woodstock, Wolverton became a close friend of Alexander Graham Bell, and had a hand in some of the earliest telephone experiments. When the first long-distance telephone line was installed between Brantford and Paris, Ontario, Bell and Wolverton conversed over the eight-mile wire. Wolverton's own scientific interest centred on the study of meteorology, and for many years the observatory he built on the school grounds was maintained and subsidized by both provincial and federal governments.

Despite Wolverton's resignation in protest over the removal of the Theological Department, the Toronto Baptists had their way, and before long that city also became the home of the new Baptist university, McMaster. A few years later, in 1888, another round was won when Toronto acquired Woodstock's Ladies' Department and renamed it Moulton Ladies' College. After the death of Senator McMaster, his widow Susan Moulton McMaster became interested in the idea of transferring her Bloor Street house to McMaster University for use as a school for girls, and thus the Woodstock Ladies' Department became Moulton. Moulton was administered by McMaster University on the understanding that the university would maintain the school "in perpetuity" exclusively for girls, and that it would underwrite the salaries of four resident teachers. As it turned out, the university lived up to neither of these commitments and in the end it realized a considerable financial gain through the sale of the Moulton College property in 1954. With the loss of the Theological Department and the girls' school, Woodstock College was reduced to "an academic department of the University", and in company with its sister school in Toronto it was to prove a distinct encumbrance to the university administration.

Before the university at last closed Woodstock in 1926, however, it had become a well-respected institution with some notable alumni. In their youth several famous Canadians came to know "the grim wind-sculptured buildings of Woodstock College" (the words of the Canadian poet Wilson MacDonald, who attended the school from 1893 to 1899). Others included Cyrus Eaton (1899-1901) and before him Joseph Whiteside Boyle (1883), millionaire "King of the Klondike" and "uncrowned King of Rumania", whose incredible story is recounted in Kim Beattie's book *Brother—There's a Man*.

Unlike most boys' boarding schools, Woodstock never established an Old Boys' association, an institution that has bailed out several such schools in hard times. And neither it nor its sister school, Moulton, had an independent governing body. With no independent administration and no organized source of loyal support, it is understandable that the affairs of Woodstock and Moulton were relegated to a subordinate position in the concerns of the university. It was only a matter of time before administration by remote control began to create thorny problems. Its Baptist denominational approach to education also worked to Woodstock's disadvantage. After World War I, as public secondary education expanded and became increasingly popular, the demand for the kind of education offered by Woodstock declined.

Woodstock College closed for the last time in 1926 with a marked absence of ceremony. The lights were turned off, the doors closed. For the next two years the school remained empty and unused. Then in 1928 it provided a convenient temporary home for the senior students of Trinity College School, Port Hope, who had been burned out of their buildings. When the temporary students left, the need to sell the Woodstock property became pressing. The Depression had begun and McMaster, in the throes of its move from Toronto to Hamilton, was prepared to accept revenues from any source. When the university sold the property to the Redemptorist Fathers for use as a Roman Catholic seminary, people who had maintained silence over the closing of Woodstock College became suddenly vociferous over the sale of the property. It was almost as if the religion of the new owners was cause for greater concern than the closing of the school had been.

Shortly after World War II, and twenty years after the College had closed, a group of former students organized a reunion in Toronto. They belatedly formed an alumni association and a series of annual reunions followed. The Woodstock College

Laboratory was presented to Moulton College, a memorial plaque was installed at McMaster University, and a Woodstock Memorial chronicle was published, all in an attempt to keep the school's name alive. Over a seventy-year period, 4,600 students had passed through the doors of Woodstock College, yet its name today rarely evokes more than a quizzical look.

The demise of Moulton in 1954 caused even more acrimony. Established in 1888 with an endowment from the McMaster estate, the girls' school was initially so popular that pianos had to be moved to the bathrooms to make enough room for the overflowing classes. The school bore not only the name of its benefactress, Susan Moulton McMaster, but the mark of her influence as well. Even in advanced age she maintained a personal concern for the affairs of the school, where a room was always kept in readiness for her special use. She was a sprightly ninety-four on the occasion of her last visit, and she must have been pleased with what she saw. The standard of scholarship was high, and the curriculum was liberally sprinkled with "refinements" of the type that still marked a superior school for young ladies in the 1920s. The sewing course was described by a prospectus as "one that conducts the student from the first principles of sewing to initiation into the mysteries of various stitches, embroideries, uses of patterns, etc. . . . Much of the work thus executed is devoted to the needs of the poor, and the exquisite needlework that finds its way into some homes must make the recipients feel that a Fairy Godmother has paid them a visit."

Like Woodstock, the school did not fare well with the changing times. Through the Depression and the war, the old McMaster mansion grew shabbier and shabbier, and along with it Moulton's image. In the late 1940s the possibility of moving was raised but the idea was discarded in favour of a program of renovation and expansion at the original site. The expansion program was hailed by the McMaster University Board of Governors as "much the greatest achievement in Moulton's history" and perhaps it was, but within five years the Board had a radical change of heart. The expansion program, according to the Board, was now a "mistake in judgment". The location adjacent to a subway station, once touted as a distinct advantage, had become a "deteriorated site" and a great handicap, and the school of "excellent condition" had become a "declining school" beyond redemption.

In the spring of 1954, without having consulted the school's supporters, McMaster University suddenly announced the closing of Moulton College, a move that resulted in charges, countercharges, and lawsuits. Ironically, it was a defective light fixture that brought about the end. The fire department, which had been summoned when the fixture began to smoke, discovered that the whole building probably needed rewiring. For certain board members of the university it was the last straw. Anxious to be relieved of the responsibility for keeping Moulton afloat, they quickly marshalled the other evidence: the operating deficits, the need for extensive repairs, the unkempt state of the ground, increased traffic, the altered character of the site, and so on. The principal of the school, Miss Marjorie Trotter, was not even present at the board meeting that decided the fate of the school: it was held at the National Club in Toronto, where women were not admitted.

The reaction among parents, alumnae, and friends of the school was immediate, but a request by the Parent-Teachers Association that the Board defer their decision for a reasonable length of time was rejected. A report on the closing of Moulton issued by the Woodstock College Alumni Association, whose members were outraged that history had been allowed to repeat itself, stated that "the McMaster Board followed a calculated procedure in disclosing no information regarding Moulton's problems while there was time for interested groups to seek solutions, and in keeping secret its decision to bring the School to a sudden end". Their indignation was further aroused by the fact that friends of the school had recently donated several thousand dollars to Moulton for the construction of a Woodstock Memorial Laboratory. The donors dispatched a strong letter demanding financial restitution for their contributions and damning the action of the Board as "undemocratic and arbitrary". A special Moulton College committee then engaged a lawyer, and enjoined the McMaster Board to submit its Moulton property sale to the Supreme Court of Ontario. The judgment went in favour of McMaster and the donors' claim for compensation for gifts intended expressly for Moulton College was denied.

In the view of at least one member of the Moulton committee,

such tactics might suit a meat packing firm, bent on obtaining monetary gain to the exclusion of all other considerations. . . . By closing Woodstock College in 1926 and Moulton in 1954 the McMaster board of governors eliminated two fine schools entrusted to its care. To the university and its authorities Woodstock and Moulton are names that will long remain a reproach.

Trinity College School

Port Hope, Ontario
1865

Trinity College School opened in a parsonage in the tiny village of Weston, Ontario, in 1862, as the result of an Anglican clergyman's dissatisfaction with the local school system. Its founder was William Arthur Johnston, a man of great sensitivity and a devout Christian, who had arrived in Upper Canada from England just in time to take part in the Rebellion of 1837. After a brief and inglorious attempt at farming he turned his hand to the work of the church and was ordained in 1852 by the revered and reviled Bishop Strachan. Johnston's devotion to High Church rituals soon involved him in a storm of controversy in his Coburg parish, and it was only with the greatest of difficulty that Bishop Strachan managed to extricate him and arrange for his relocation in Weston.

The school's first three pupils were Johnston's own sons. Within a year several boarders were added to the roster, and between them "Father" Johnston and an uncertified female teacher did their best to improve upon the inadequacies of public education. The success of his endeavour encouraged Johnston to approach Trinity College in Toronto and to ask that his school in Weston be designated as a preparatory school attached to the University. Trinity College, finding merit in the proposal, agreed to assume responsibility for the appointment of staff, provision of prizes, and conduct of external examinations—none of which involved any great expenditure. The burden of financial responsibility still rested squarely on the shoulders of Father Johnston, who was appointed warden and bursar of the new Trinity College School in 1865. Now, however, he had the advantage of ties with the university to help him attract students.

Without Father Johnston the school would probably never have come into being, yet Trinity University chose another man as headmaster, Reverend Charles Badgley, a tall, austere young man "with long black whiskers, a questioning gaze, and a very decided mouth". His qualifications for the post could scarcely have been improved upon, for he was a classical scholar out of Upper Canada College and a graduate of Trinity College into the bargain. His Bachelor's degree from Oxford and a year spent as assistant master in a British public school were further evidence of his eminent suitability. The results of Reverend Badgley's British teaching experience were soon manifested at the school in Weston. According to one former pupil, "he wielded a cane with skill and effect . . . yet he relied more on the honor of the boys than their fear of punishment, and on his moral influence rather than on his compulsory powers. His influence was very great." Another wrote, "The tone of the school was largely due to his ideas of discipline and schoolboy honor. . . . The idea of a master being companionable to a boy, being of assistance to him, being anxious for, or even desirous of, his welfare, or believing that there was anything good in a boy, had never entered into my notion of the realm of possibilities. The effect of this policy on the boys was marvelous. Bad language and untruthfulness were almost unknown."

Reverend Badgley was deeply committed to the humanizing approach to education of Britain's Thomas Arnold of Rugby. His efforts appear to have borne fruit. By the end of the first year twenty-five boys had been crammed into the parsonage, which had to be enlarged to accommodate them. Conditions became so cramped that classes had to be moved to rented space in the village, where the boys received instruction in "all the usual branches of a sound education in Classics, Mathematics, English, French, Drawing, Vocal Music, Fencing, and Drill". The founder of the school, Father Johnston, had been given the post of warden, with responsibility for the religious education of the students. At the crack of dawn each morning, under his watchful eye, the entire school trooped through the parsonage to the little chapel which Johnston and his sons had built in the village.

However, it was the cultural aspect of the school that first attracted the attention of William Osler's parents. Enticed by lessons in music, dancing, and painting, and by cultivated soirees, his parents packed him off to become the school's twenty-seventh pupil and later its first head prefect. During his two years at Trinity College School a lifelong friendship developed between the boy and the school's founder, Father Johnston, who on Saturdays or half-holidays often took the boys on field excursions to collect plant and insect specimens for microscopic study. Osler, who was later to become Regius Professor of Medicine at Oxford University, first learned to use a microscope in the warden's study while recovering from a football injury.

Sports and games were, of course, encouraged at the new school, although the facilities left something to be desired. The outdoor "gymnasium" was studded with outcroppings of stone, the cricket pitch was rock-hard and canted like the deck of a rolling ship, while the football field was strewn with stumps, adding considerably to the hazards of the game. Cadet corps drills also helped to burn up a good deal of the boys' excess energy, though the drills could never wholly succeed in subverting natural tendencies towards truancy and mischief making.

During its first year, the school found itself embroiled in an unsavory lawsuit brought by a former matron-housekeeper after her dismissal and subsequent eviction from the premises. In his history *TCS: The School on the Hill* (1966), A. H. Humble vividly records the saga of the volatile Widow Denham vs. TCS. It appears that the widow, unpopular from the start, had been requested to vacate her room during the summer at her own convenience.

> Six months later, although she had paid no rent, she was still firmly ensconced in her living room which lay directly above the boy's study. Taking offense at a late March snowball fight that ended in the hall, the ex-matron threw slops over several boys on the stairway. The next day, at Osler's instigation the boys barricaded her in her sitting room by tying up the door. Then they made a paste of mustard and pepper which they brewed on the stove in the study. The fumes rose through a stovepipe hole in the ceiling. As fast as the resourceful widow stuffed it with clothes the boys poked them away. They continued to do so even after she sat down on the aperture herself, screaming for help.
>
> She was finally rescued by the Headmaster and the usual punishments were meted out. But the litigious widow, who had already made legal claim against the school for a debt,

had no intention of letting the matter rest there. When she was unable to get a warrant issued in Weston, she went to Toronto and secured a warrant for trespass and assault against twelve of the boys, the youngest of whom was eleven. Their numbers included the warden's youngest son, James Bovell Johnston, a "tiny boy". The hearing lasted two days and was heard by four magistrates. Mrs. Denham stated under oath that her injured arm resulted from large blocks of wood being thrown into the room from below. William Osler testified that the stovepipe hole alluded to by the witness was not sufficiently large to permit sticks of wood being thrown through it. The verdict: a reprimand and a one dollar fine with costs. When it was all over the boys enjoyed "a glorious tea at the English Chop House" and returned triumphantly to school by cab.

Following the episode, Osler's mother was moved to write him a gentle reprimand: "It was an unfortunate affair . . . all you boys being brought into public notice in such a disreputable manner, and although I do not think it was meant to be more than a mere school boy prank, such things often tell against a person long after."

The fledgling school suffered from the publicity given the whole affair. In addition, there were any number of people, even among the Anglicans themselves, who were opposed to the concept of an elitist classical college, particularly one espousing High Church doctrines. To further complicate matters, the Anglican Church opened a church school at Picton in the same year. Fearing competition from the school in Weston, the church proposed an amalgamation of the two schools in Picton. Only the vigorous protests of Father Johnston and two Trinity University professors saved the school at Weston. But while its identity was preserved, it was still in serious financial difficulty, and antagonism between the founder and the headmaster was growing by the day. A special committee of the Trinity Corporation moved that the school be relocated in the town of Port Hope east of Toronto, and several committee members pledged three years' rent and taxes on the Ward Homestead, a spacious two-story frame house with a magnificent view of Lake Ontario and the surrounding countryside. From this vantage point the boys could watch the boats in the harbour—a safe distance from the town where they might encounter scenes of "distress and vice".

With the move to Port Hope in 1868, TCS retained its headmaster, Reverend Badgley, but lost its founder. Disheartened by the decision to remove the school from its birthplace, Father Johnston chose to remain in Weston, though his efforts to carry on his own school met with little success. The school on the hill at Port Hope, however, thrived and grew, although according to reports the food was next to inedible and the canings far more frequent. Headmaster Badgley's own nephew—who twice refused a caning and ran away—was eventually "removed" from the school for his sins. But reports of Badgley's pedagogical methods must have been generally favourable, for two years later he resigned to accept the, then, more prestigious headship of Bishop's College School in Lennoxville, Quebec.

His successor was Reverend C.J.S. Bethune, a former head boy of Upper Canada College and another Trinity College graduate. Bethune came rather reluctantly to the post despite the urgings of his brother, who was already on the staff, and of his father, the Lord Bishop of Toronto, who finally convinced him that it was a duty he could ill afford to disregard. His sense of duty was evidently of the highest order, for Bethune remained as headmaster for nearly thirty years.

Shortly after Bethune's arrival in Port Hope there was talk of renovating the original Ward Homestead, but the young headmaster, then only thirty-two, adamantly refused to settle for anything less than a brand-new building. Before two years were out his wish had been fulfilled and the school had become incorporated as an independent body. Through careful administration, Bethune whittled down the school debt until the fire of 1895—the fourth of a series of lesser blazes—totally demolished the work of a lifetime. The school, the chapel, and the dining hall were all reduced to smouldering rubble. The bucket brigade of masters and boys which had saved the day on earlier occasions was ill-equipped to deal with a raging inferno in the middle of a winter's night. The shivering evacuees, most of them still in their nightshirts, were whisked off to various homes around town, but before the week was out the undaunted Bethune had arranged for classes to be resumed in the Town Hall. Of the 115 boys enrolled, only one was removed as a result of the disaster. A new building designed by an Old Boy, Frank Darling (architect for Toronto General Hospital, the Royal Ontario Museum and the present Parliament Buildings in Ottawa), was erected within the year. In appreciation of his "wise financial management and untiring attention to all the details of a very onerous and responsible position" Dr. Bethune, or the Goat, as he was known by virtue of his ample white beard, was awarded a life membership on the school's Board of Governors when he retired.

Reverend Graham Orchard, the former owner and headmaster of St. Alban's School in Brockville, became headmaster of TCS in 1913. Dr. Orchard was a man of self-control and inflexibility, the ultimate disciplinarian, and he also possessed a driving ambition to mould Trinity College School into one of the finest boys' schools in Canada. Perfection was his goal. "Work must be perfectly accurate, exercises must be perfectly neat, Sunday collars perfectly clean, the dining hall perfectly silent for grace." During the Orchard years TCS also underwent a musical renaissance, owing largely to the efforts of the school's highly talented musical director, Davidson Ketchum. During the 1920s he was joined on the staff by his three brothers, Hugh, Kenneth, and Philip. And in time each one of them left his mark––Davidson at the University of Toronto, Hugh at Lakefield College, Kenneth as headmaster of St. Andrew's College in Aurora, and Philip as Dr. Orchard's eventual successor. As a family their contribution to education probably stands without equal among Canada's independent schools.

Under Dr. Orchard's watchful eye the school indeed appears to have attained near-perfection, but it was once again levelled by fire in the spring of 1928. The Senior School emigrated to the recently vacated Woodstock College until the money—more than a third of a million dollars—to rebuild the school was raised almost entirely by Old Boys. But by 1932, the Depression had become a desperate reality. Enrolment fell off sharply and letters such as the following began arriving with a regularity that became almost predictable. "I am sorry to say that this will be about the last account I will have to pay my Old School. I find that this Depression . . . has so reduced my income that I am unable to send_____ back to TCS next September. . . . however, I am pleased to think that I sent all my sons to my Old School." The staff had to be pared, and those who remained accepted a substantial cut in salary. To make matters worse, as a result of persistent rumors among Toronto's "better families", the academic standards of the school had come into question, and in the end Dr. Orchard submitted his resignation.

In order to appoint Philip Ketchum as Orchard's successor,

the Governing Body had to amend the original constitution, which stipulated that the headmaster had to be "a clergyman of the Church of England in Priest's Orders". At a time when the separation of religion and education was becoming more and more pronounced, it was an unrealistic condition. Clergyman or not, the situation confronting the school's new headmaster was staggering. Incredibly, when the school was rebuilt no provision had been made for married staff quarters, for Ketchum's predecessors had held firm to the conviction that a master could best devote himself to the interests of boys only if he were free of the encumbrances of a wife and family. Philip Ketchum with his family of six went on to confound Dr. Orchard's theory by becoming perhaps the most devoted and enlightened headmaster the school had ever seen. His own three sons attended the school and even his oldest daughter, not to be outdone, once charmed the squadron leader into letting her join the cadet corps for drill.

Ketchum's first decision as headmaster was to close the junior school. Its architects had not even been paid in full and were threatening a lawsuit for the balance. Prospects for raising the money in Canada appeared next to hopeless, and in desperation the headmaster set out on an unsuccessful "begging mission" to the Carnegie and Rockefeller Foundations. Bankruptcy was averted only through the good offices of seven Old Boys who came forward to make an initial payment on the architect's outstanding fees. The Junior School was re-opened the following year and by the late thirties enrolment was on the rise again. Ketchum also engineered the TCS cadet corps' affiliation with the RCAF, making it the first school corps in Canada to become attached to the Air Force. The corps has since been disbanded, but not before 200 citations for gallantry were awarded to Old Boys during World War II.

Ketchum's efforts at educational reform extended well beyond the bounds of Port Hope, bringing unprecedented recognition and respect to both himself and his school. At his instigation a conference on Canadian education was held at the school in 1954, bringing together university presidents, deans, registrars, and other headmasters from across Canada, as well as observors from the United States and Great Britain. The gathering helped set the stage for the reformation in educational thinking of the sixties.

Under his successor Angus Scott, a Ridley Old Boy and a dedicated member of Ketchum's own staff, Trinity College School has today become a first-rank Canadian boys' boarding school. In the traditional mould, its aim is "to expect much of its boys, to give them a right sense of values, to provide an environment which will assist them in developing their individual talents, and to guide and encourage them all along the way. If the school does these things, it will make men of boys, worthy men who will be happy, successful and useful members of the communities of tomorrow."

Trinity College School,

PORT HOPE ONTARIO.

Head Master:

REV. C. J. S. BETHUNE, M.A.

WITH A STAFF OF

SIX ASSISTANT MASTERS.

THE SCHOOL IS NOW IN ITS FOURTEENTH YEAR.

THE

LARGE AND HANDSOME BUILDINGS

Are unsurpassed in the Dominion.

Pupils are prepared for the Matriculation Examinations
of the Universities, the Entrance Examinations
of the Law and Medical Schools, the
Military College, the Army,
Navy, &c.
In the Modern Department special attention is directed
to preparation for Commercial pursuits.

The School premises now include upwards of 20 acres of land, which afford

SPACIOUS GROUNDS FOR PLAY AND EXERCISE.

A GYMNASIUM HAS BEEN RECENTLY ERECTED.

FEES, (inclusive)   -   -   -   - $225 per annum.

Twenty Bursaries, ($100 per annum, each) for the sons of the
Canadian Clergy.

For a Copy of the School Calendar, apply to the Head Master.

T. Hill & Son, Caxton Press, Toronto.

Prospectus for Trinity College School, 1879.

The

Bishop Strachan School

FOR YOUNG LADIES

WYKEHAM HALL

COLLEGE AVENUE, YONGE STREET,

TORONTO, ONTARIO.

INCORPORATED 1868

COUNCIL:

President.—The Right Reverend the Lord Bishop of Toronto.

Right Rev. the Lord Bp. of Niagara.	Messrs. R. H. Bethune.
Rev. Provost Body, D.C.L.	" C. J. Campbell.
" C. J. S. Bethune, D.C.L.	" J. Henderson.
" A J. Broughall, M.A.	" A. M. Howard.
" H. W. Davies, D.D.	" W. Ince.
" J. Langtry, M.A.	" J. C. Kemp.
" J. H. McCollum, M.A.	" G. M. Rae.
" A. Williams, M.A.	

LADY PRINCIPAL - MISS GRIER

This establishment was founded in 1867. Its object is the practical training and instruction of young ladies in the various branches of a liberal education, including Christian doctrine, as contained in the Bible and the Book of Common Prayer.

Prospectus for The Bishop Strachan School, 1870s.

Bishop Charles Inglis, founder of King's College School,
the oldest private school in Canada.

Rose Grier, headmistress of The Bishop Strachan School, 1880s.

Miss Dalton (*centre front*) and staff of Havergal-Winnipeg
(later Balmoral Hall), *ca.*1903.

Three Upper Canada College masters,
1893-95. *Left to right*: J.H. Collinson
(who later founded Hillfield), Robert
Holmes, and Stephen Leacock.

Early photograph of Havergal's
Miss Ellen Knox.

Netherwood's Miss Ganong.

Miss Barton of St. Margaret's.

Miss Maude C. Edgar of Miss Edgar's
and Miss Cramp's.

"Alick" Mackenzie of Lakefield.

The Rev. Heaven of Highfield
(later Hillfield). His counterpart
at Strathallan, the neighbouring
girls' school, was Miss Virtue.

Lord Strathcona (*centre*) with founders and staff of University School, *ca.* 1909.

Miss Jessie Gordon of Crofton House
awaiting their Majesties King George VI
and Queen Elizabeth during their visit
to Vancouver in 1939.

"Min" Gildea of Strathcona
Lodge School.

C.W. Lonsdale, the ex-milkman who
founded Shawnigan Lake School.

Miss Denny and Miss Geoghegan,
founders and co-heads of
Queen Margaret's School.

Ivy Cheetham of
Norfolk House School.

Edith M. Read of Branksome Hall. In the background, the girls' kilts are being
measured to make sure they are regulation length.

E. Gordon Waugh, owner and principal of St. Clement's
for nearly fifty years.

Miss Lowe, headmistress of
Bishop Strachan School (*centre*),
and Miss Rosseter, head of the
Junior School, with the members
of the Board. Late 1920s.

The school nurse with Miss Lonsdale,
the founder's sister, at Shawnigan
Lake School, *ca.* 1920.

Games mistress, 1920s.

Hockey coach, 1930s.

Bishop Strachan school staff room, 1940s.

Bishop Strachan senior girls practise the art of pouring tea.

The Junior Boys of King's College School in their school caps, 1890s.

The girls' art class at Alma College, 1880s.
Drawing by H. Bell-Smith, RCA, Alma's art instructor.

A BSS graduating class of the 1890s.

The Bishop Strachan School

Toronto, Ontario

1867

Among the Anglican Church of Canada's first ventures into the realm of female education, The Bishop Strachan School for Young Ladies has since become the most prestigious and prominent of Canadian independent schools for girls. Its preeminence, its critics hasten to add, has tended to be more social than scholarly; but social pretentions certainly played no part in its beginnings. It was founded because of a deepening conviction that the church should be responsible for the education of girls as well as boys.

Before the school opened, several well-intentioned Toronto ladies were already conducting their own little private enterprises and charging astronomical fees for their services. This had forced a number of Protestant parents to choose the less costly Roman Catholic convents as an alternative, in spite of what they surely regarded as the manifest perils of such a course. From the Anglican point of view it was a deplorable situation, though only a few stalwarts felt sufficiently moved to seek a remedy. Among these were the school's founders, Reverend "Father John" Langtry and other Anglican clergy and laymen. They were appalled that "from one end of the Dominion to the other" there was not a single institution "for the proper training of those who exercise the deepest and widest influence over the character and happiness of the rising generation".

With the founding of Bishop Strachan in Toronto and Bishop Bethune College in Oshawa, Ontario, a noble beginning was made. For many years close ties existed between these schools, named after Toronto's first and second Anglican bishops; although Bishop Bethune College, intended primarily as a school for the daughters of Anglican clergy, never attained the success of its wealthier sister and closed in the early 1930s. A third undertaking was launched two years later in London, Ontario, by Bishop Isaac Hellmuth, a German Jew converted to the Church of England and a man of culture and intellect. Neither of the two schools which bore his name lasted beyond the turn of the century.

Of these three ambitious ventures into female education only Bishop Strachan has withstood the onslaught of change. Considered a calculated risk when it was first opened in the heart of downtown Toronto, on land now occupied by the Art Gallery of Ontario, it quickly blossomed into a promising school of thirty-three boarders and forty day girls. The second year, encouraged by its initial success, the Governing Council decided to move the school into the residence of its recently deceased namesake at the foot of Yonge Street. But even the Bishop's Palace, or See House, and another house known as Captain Strachan's Cottage could barely contain the influx of new pupils, and a search was begun for still larger quarters. By the beginning of its third year the school had found a more permanent home in Wykeham Hall, the former home of Sir Joseph McCaulay, on College Avenue. At that time the site was well to the north of the city centre and still offered some of the charms of rural life. There was an old wooden toll gate at the entrance to what is now College Street, and groups of BSS girls could often be seen making their way through the tall grass along the slopes of the nearby creek in search of violets and strawberries.

Here, under the watchful eye of Miss Frances Dupont of Quebec, a disciplinarian and task-mistress of the highest order, BSS girls were not only afforded "the pleasures of a woodland setting", but also received a first-class education. Although she was only thirty when she took over the school on College Street, Miss Dupont had already run a private concern of her own in Belleville, Ontario. She was a woman of extraordinary independence with a strong appetite for challenge, and no sooner had she put BSS on a firm footing than she left to open a competitive school of her own. For a good many years Miss Dupont's School, along with Miss Veal's school and later Miss Neville's, Westminster, St. Margaret's, and Havergal College, vied openly with BSS for the privilege of educating the daughters of Toronto's first families.

The administration of the school was subsequently taken over by a Mrs. Thompson, the widow of an officer in the Indian army who was "a frail little lady in widow's weeds with a gentle voice and quiet step". Her words of advice to one Leaving Class indicate that she was also a woman of sense and sensibility: "Remember, girls, you are not going home to be social butterflies of fashion. The Bishop Strachan School has been endeavouring to fit you to become useful and courageous women." Her stay at the school was also confined to a few brief years, but her successor, Rose Grier, not only was to assure the school's permanent survival, but was to determine its tone and philosophy for many years to come.

Described as a "warm, devout and courageous Christian", Rose Grier was also a thoroughly competent administrator. Her business sense was sorely needed, for there had already been some discussion about the wisdom of keeping the school open in its semi-rural location. Enrolment had begun to fall off and the school's financial condition was shaky. To ward off financial disaster she immediately recommended the sale of a portion of the school property (many years later the site of Eaton's College Street store).

For the next twenty years Miss Rose Grier, the personification of refinement and culture, made it her business to shape the destiny of her school and inspire her girls to new academic heights. To at least one of these, the daily round and common task had its dreary moments. An autograph book, returned to the school long afterwards, contains this timeless schoolgirl lament, penned in a fine copper-plate hand:

> What cannot be cured
> Must be endured
> And such is Life
> At the B.S.S.!!!!

While the Grier Years were years of stability and scholarship, they were also years of subtle change in curriculum and in educational style. Finishing courses, needlework, art, music, and dancing were offered along with stenography and bookkeeping, although preparation for university was stressed for the studiously inclined. When Trinity University began admitting female students in 1883 it gladly welcomed graduates of the school, and for many years BSS graduates went on to Trinity almost as a matter of course.

When Rose Grier retired in 1899, she left confident that BSS would be in the best of all possible hands—the hands of a woman she herself had trained and nurtured. Before her appointment as Miss Grier's successor, Helen Acres had spent two years in England studying developments in women's education in that country. On her return she put her observations into practice both on the games field and in the classrooms. As muscular Christianity at long last became acceptable for girls, basketball, cricket, and later lacrosse, the "national" game, joined the curriculum. The cricket matches have long since been dropped, but lacrosse at BSS has remained a tradition.

The creation of the Old Girls' Association, the BSSA, was another of Miss Acres' innovations. She recognized the worth of maintaining "old school ties", and, in turn, its members can be credited for the preservation of the school name. When the College Street site was abandoned for a new location further north, certain members of the Governing Council (then all-male) favoured changing the school's name, but the BSSA would hear none of it. They protested vociferously and the idea was permanently laid to rest.

Creeping commercialism was encroaching on the once-peaceful College Street oasis, and it was clear that a decision would soon have to be made on a new location. Before the move from Wykham Hall, BSS had attempted a smaller branch school in the then-fashionable Parkdale district of the city's west end, but local support was not as great as the Council had hoped and the small satellite soon closed down. The first BSS Junior School, which for a time included several small boys, proved a much more successful experiment. Set up in rented premises near the school's present Lonsdale Road site, it helped to accelerate plans to acquire the "College Heights" property nearby.

The College Heights location was rendered more attractive than it might otherwise have been by the rumour that Upper Canada College, the boys' school two blocks to the east, was preparing to move further into the country, having acquired property in York Mills. As it turned out, the planned exodus never occurred and since 1915, when BSS moved into its new Collegiate Gothic quarters, the proximity of the two schools has remained a mixed blessing, to the staff if not to the students. Much neighbourly nonsense has been attributed to the tempting nearness of the two schools, such as the appearance of a skull and crossbones on the BSS flagpole (in the days when it could be reached only by climbing the school's central tower) and the tolling of the chapel bell at midnight (ingeniously operated from across the street on a pulley system).

Many of the first residents of the "new" BSS found its outward appearance less than inviting. "It looked for all the world like a penitentiary . . . a penal colony . . . just sitting in a field with its grey stone walls and scarcely a tree to be seen," one recalled. The inside was formidable in a different manner. "It was so beautiful that we weren't allowed to put our hands on the banisters, in case someone marred the lovely shiny finish. . . . Those were Miss Walsh's instructions, and believe me, we towed the line." To question the school policy of Miss Harriet Walsh, Miss Acres' successor, was to court disaster. Miss Walsh's direct and withering gaze and well-honed mind intimidated parents and girls alike, and the headmistress was not easily persuaded that her way was not, in fact, the only way.

During Miss Walsh's tenure as headmistress the school's handsome Gothic chapel was added to the main building. Although a chapel in Rose Grier's memory had been part of the original plans for the new school, the drive fell short of funds during World War I and it was another ten years or more before enough money was raised by the BSSA and other friends of the school to begin work on this long-awaited tribute to the beloved and respected former headmistress. Since then, chapel service has always been part of the school routine. Thirty years ago "order marks" were liberally dispensed by the school prefects to anyone unable to stifle whispers, sighs, and girlish giggles during chapel. The one escape was to faint, a malady that from time to time reached epidemic proportions. Under its vaulted ceiling successive generations of brides and bridesmaids have proceeded up the central aisle—cautiously—for the grating underfoot was made for oxfords, not for slender heels. And under the same vaulted ceiling the babies of these brides have been dutifully christened.

Miss Walsh's successor and former pupil, Margaret Lowe, together with her friend and advocate Victoria Rosseter, the

Junior School's principal, carried Bishop Strachan through two more decades to the end of World War II. Since, 1948, however, the great oak front doors have opened and closed on a series of principals. None has stayed more than six or seven years and one or two have taken their leave under some duress.

The Council's decision, in 1969, to appoint E.S. "Ted" Jarvis as the school's first male principal precipitated shock waves of disbelief that reverberated far and wide, but this startling departure from tradition was only one of several. Since 1970 small boys have been admitted once again, from pre-kindergarten to grade four. The addition of the Early Education Centre at BSS is indicative of a more innovative and outgoing approach to education at all levels.

Unlike many city schools for girls, Bishop Strachan still accepts boarders from grades seven to thirteen. Although the "escape tunnel" that led to the "outside" through the heating plant has been sealed off for years, the problems inherent in any boarding school situation have tended to increase rather than diminish in recent years. On the other hand, a century of traditions has not prevented BSS from meeting the future on its own terms. To quote Mr. Jarvis, who retired in June, 1976, "We're no longer trying to protect the kids from life—we get them out into it!" For better or for worse, sighed a recent graduate, "BSS just isn't what BSS used to be!" The declared purpose of BSS today is "to foster in each individual the pursuit of excellence in all aspects of school life". Though the world has changed vastly since 1867, it is essentially the same purpose envisaged by the founders of BSS more than one hundred years ago.

King's Hall

Compton, Quebec

1874-1973

The founders of Bishop Strachan School in Toronto were not alone in their concern over the number of Anglicans who had chosen to send their daughters to Roman Catholic convents. Reverend J. Dinzey, the Anglican rector of the village of Compton, in Quebec's Eastern Townships, expressed similar misgivings in his proposal to the Bishop of Quebec for the establishment of a church school "where girls, and daughters of the clergy, in particular, might receive a sound education at a minimum charge".

The first board of trustees of Compton Ladies' College (later King's Hall) included the bishop himself and four male appointees of the synod, although the practicalities of building and running the new school were left to Reverend Dinzey and his wife, Compton's first "Lady Principal". As lessees, they managed the school together, and within a year had attracted nearly fifty boarders. Despite its initial success, within ten years the school found itself deeply in debt. The "minimum charge" had been too low to meet expenses, and for two years the school had to close altogether. When Compton Ladies' College re-opened the Corporation had assumed full control of its management, but the next fifteen years would see no less than seven successive lady principals in one door and out the other—hardly a formula to ensure stability and continuity.

The turning point came in 1902 when Compton Ladies' College was reincorporated as King's Hall, to commemorate the coronation of Edward VII. In a mood of confidence, the new trustees turned back the annual $200 grant from the provincial government; it would be another sixty years before they would

109

have to reconsider the question of accepting government assistance. The school's new principal was Gena Smith, described as "a lady of exceptional culture and charm". The prospectus of that year announced that the girls would be in the charge of "Real English Ladies", who were referred to forever after as RELs. The RELs took a dim view of Canadian schoolgirls, as one Old Girl recalled. "We were lazy and incompetent. We walked on our heels and talked through our noses. We were rude, and altogether poor material! Life became one long series of rules. You must not use the front door, or go up the front stairs nor go below the road. You must not run or talk in the corridors or leave a class under any consideration, or raise your voice at any time." The list of "must nots" was interminable in the days of the RELs, who apparently never felt the cold even though the water froze in the wash pans and the ink in the inkwells. Still, there were the compensations of rural life. "The country was beautiful in the fall and spring. We went for walks every day and picked flowers in the woods. In winter we always went to a 'sugaring off'. In the swamp behind the school we caught polliwogs, every spring, and kept them in glass jars until they got cute little legs and turned into frogs."

After a few years at King's Hall, Gena Smith was persuaded to take on the headship of another Anglican girls' school, Edgehill, in Windsor, Nova Scotia. The board was again faced with the perplexing problem of finding a headmistress who would extend her stay at the school for more than a token period, and who would give it the leadership it deserved. In Miss Laura Joll they found such a woman. Almost immediately the enrolment climbed, and a program of remodelling and expansion was undertaken that included the building of the "glass passage" which joined a new wing to the original school. The idea of moving King's Hall to a more central location was also considered, but was abandoned for lack of financial support.

Miss Joll stayed on as headmistress for twenty-three years. Although she too was a "real English Lady", she was both loved and respected by everyone. "She was strict, but not unapproachable. Never a martinet, and never unfair!" recalled one of her Old Girls. By the time she retired in 1928, King's Hall was considered to be one of the finest girls' boarding schools in the country.

Two years later, the Board appointed Adelaide Gillard as headmistress and the school acquired the ultimate in continuity. With only six years of teaching experience at St. Clement's School, Toronto, she managed to keep King's Hall in the front ranks for the next thirty-eight years. No two King's Hall girls have quite the same memories of her, but all remember her profound moral impact: the sting of her vituperation, her Saturday morning "talks", her admonitions, and her warm and forgiving heart. "She was unabashedly sentimental, romantic, old-fashioned, but never puritanical or prudish. The strength of her convictions, the consistency and passion of her idealism, somehow made important the tritest old moralities." And, like her mentor E. Gordon Waugh, headmistress of St. Clement's, she was determined not to produce snobs.

But by 1968 many things in the world had changed. In her last year at King's Hall, Adelaide Gillard wrote a particularly difficult message:

> For the first time in my years here, some girls have given me the feeling that they have accepted and preferred the highly publicized but basically invalid standards of modern youth. As a group you are not really interested in principles and standards of integrity, kindness, consideration and service to others . . . courage in facing difficulties and disappointments, appreciation of what is done for you . . . all the things I have tried to instill over the years. Some have classed them as outmoded. . . . Far too many young people do not show the slightest interest in anything that is not of immediate benefit to them and the idea of sacrificing their own personal pleasures for the general good is unthinkable.

It was a sign of the times. If Adelaide Gillard's girls were no longer living up to her ideals, the world had perhaps grown less interested in those ideals that she had spent her life striving to impart. By 1970, amalgamation with Bishop's College School in Lennoxville was being seriously if not openly discussed. Gillard Hall, King's Hall's new residence for 150 girls that had been completed just two years before, was only half-full, and at Bishop's College School the "empty bed" problem had become too acute to ignore. The following year the headmaster of Bishop's College School became the headmaster of King's Hall.

On paper, the plan to combine the schools held great promise. The Boards would operate jointly, the King's Hall property would be sold and a new Gillard Hall would be raised on the Bishop's campus. Yet although the new residence was ready by the fall of 1973, it was finally decided that there would be no amalgamation. Bishop's College School, instead, would become a co-educational boarding school and King's Hall would close for good. It remains so today, although the buildings are leased during the summer by the Ontario Ministry of Education for French immersion training for teachers, and during the school year by nearby Champlain College as an overflow residence.

Ontario Ladies' College

Whitby, Ontario

1874

Despite the existence of the Wesleyan Ladies' College in Hamilton, established in 1861, there was a strong feeling among certain Ontario churchmen that another school operated for the education and edification of young ladies would be an undertaking of merit. The apparent success of no less than three such ventures fostered by the Anglican church—Bishop Strachan School in Toronto, Bishop Hellmuth College in London, Ontario, and Bishop Bethune College in Oshawa—may well have provided added encouragement to the group of shareholders involved in raising the capital to start the Ontario Ladies' College.

The imposing baronial hall which became the home of the school had been christened Trafalgar Castle by its original owner, Nelson (hence Trafalgar) Gilbert Reynolds, a county sheriff and an Upper Canada College Old Boy, with visions of grandeur. At the time of its construction in 1859 the white brick and cut-stone mansion, complete with seventy-five rooms, fifteen stately octagonal towers, a magnificent grand staircase, stained glass windows, and even a secret chamber, was said to be the largest private residence in the Dominion. But it was not public spirit or religious charity that moved Reynolds to make his monument available to the new school at a fraction of its original cost. It was debt. His single-minded determination to achieve the pinnacle of social status was for a time gloriously rewarded, but it turned out to be his ruin.

The high point of Reynolds' career came when he somehow managed to entice the Royal party—including Prince Arthur, Queen Victoria's third son and later Governor-General of

Canada—to attend a luncheon at his castle in company with a throng of dignitaries who included the then Governor-General, Baron Lisgar, the Prime Minister, Sir John A. Macdonald, and the Ontario Premier and Lieutenant Governor as well. But the creditors were not far behind, and as they clamoured for their money Reynolds is said to have sought refuge in the castle's secret chamber between the first and second floors of the flagstaff tower. (Fifty years later the chamber was re-discovered when a group of girls on an exploratory foray stumbled upon the hidden entrance and crept inside. They emerged, festooned with cobwebs, to be greeted by the principal, who then pad-locked the door and eventually arranged for the chamber's removal.) In desperation, Sheriff Reynolds sold the castle for $15,000 to the Ladies' College and in return was rewarded with a charter membership on the new school's Board of Directors.

With his love of ceremony, Reynolds was undoubtedly one of the keenest participants in the formal opening of the College by the Governor-General of Canada, the Earl of Dufferin. Despite an unrelenting downpour, as His Excellency's carriage swept through the arch at the entrance to the College grounds twelve little girls (nearly half the total enrolment) decked out in red, white and blue, and bearing Union Jacks, greeted the official party with flowing curtseys. In his address to those assembled for the momentous occasion Lord Dufferin expressed the fond hope that the Ontario Ladies' College would always uphold "a standard of refined taste in its teaching", and predicted for the College "an honoured and durable fame".

Uniquely, the College, since its inception, has appointed only male principals (all of them Canadians), presumably on the premise that a man is better equipped to contend with the financial and organizational aspects of running a school and raising funds, with an associate Dean of Women to assist him in attending to the day-to-day needs of the girls on a more personal level. When the College was first established it had not only a male principal, Reverend Dr. J. J. Hare of London, Ontario, but a "moral governor" as well. But within a few years Dr. Hare had assumed both responsibilities and the school had prospered sufficiently to warrant the addition of a new wing to the castle. Together, Dr. and Mrs. Hare devoted nearly forty years to

Ontario Ladies' College. In his 1910 report on the ladies' colleges and preparatory schools of Ontario, J. George Hodgins expressed high hopes for a school so well begun. "So great are the present possibilities of the College with its superior buildings, appointments and surroundings . . . that what has been accomplished is but the beginning of what will be realized."

But a facade does not a school make. The "standards of refinement" so hopefully prophesied for the school in 1874 became the target for criticism by the Massey Foundation Report of 1921 dealing with the secondary schools of the Methodist Church of Canada (which, after church union, included all Wesleyan schools as well). There was, the report contended, entirely too much "refinement" and too little genuine scholarship to be found both there and at Alma College in southwestern Ontario. "Skill of hand," the report commented, "will seldom go far with an ill-furnished head." It was felt, furthermore, that the College's general organizational structure was "somewhat pretentious". The various departments, such as fine arts, music and domestic science, had each become separate "colleges", each granting its own "degrees" and sending forth accomplished "graduates" from its various "faculties". (For a time, like Albert College, the collegiate course at Ontario Ladies' College offered post-secondary education to the second-year level.)

The commission's recommendations were duly noted and in time concessions were made in several areas. "Degrees" later became diplomas, though the term "faculty" was retained and the school motto, "*Veritas, Virtus, Venustas*" continues to advocate Truth, Virtue, and Loveliness. There continued, as well, an emphasis on the study of music, speech arts, and drama. The school's annual "May Day" celebrations, a demonstration of gymnastics and dancing, along with the crowning of the May Queen, have been, as one Old Girl puts it, "an OLC tradition since time immemorial".

Despite its criticisms of the girls' schools, however, the Massey Report noted with distress that the Wesleyans and Methodists had never managed to establish a boys' residential school. By tradition the schools of both the Methodist and Wesleyan churches were co-educational, and at the time of the Massey Report there were no fewer than ten such schools. However, it was clearly the opinion of the commission that while co-education had its own virtues, the merits of single-sex education should not be overlooked. Perhaps the male commissioners were somewhat nettled by the fact that for once, boys were denied an opportunity already available to girls.

Through the years there have been extensive additions to the school, but it continues to make good use of its original building, whose "Old World dignity and charm" are still commended to parents in the school prospectus, along with its swimming pool, chapel, and "Christian atmosphere". The College's affiliation with the United Church of Canada is still one of its strong selling points in spite of the Church's drastically altered policy with regard to educational institutions operating under its auspices. Most of the original and essentially Canadian traditions of the Ontario Ladies' College (even to the honey and buns on Sundays) have been assiduously maintained, and, in fact, cherished by those associated with the College during its first hundred years.

St. Helen's School

Dunham, Quebec

1875–1972

A second Eastern Townships school for girls with Anglican sponsorship opened just a year after Compton Ladies' College (King's Hall). Ironically, with nearly a century behind them, they would both close in the same year. St. Helen's was a diocesan effort, incorporated as The Dunham Ladies' College under the chairmanship of the Bishop of Montreal. Several other local parishes had competed for the privilege of having the new ladies' college, but Dunham, with its offer of free land and a $5,000 retainer, was the highest bidder. An early school prospectus describes its "elevated and beautiful surroundings... with well-wooded hills and mountains in the distance". The village's seclusion was another advantage. "The numerous and beautiful country walks are beneficial for the health of the students and for the retirement necessary for study," it promised. The school's relationship with the village of Dunham was close and harmonious. Many of the local clergy and laity helped to build the school out of rose-tone bricks manufactured in the village. The facade of the rambling old building, with its mansard roof and enormous 200-foot verandah, remains virtually unchanged after a hundred years.

As at Compton Ladies' College, the first quarter-century at the Dunham School was plagued by lack of continuity, and it opened and closed several times under a variety of principals. Stability came at last when Miss Winifred Wade, a young staff member from England, offered to lease the school from the church as a private concern in 1911. Determining that the school should have a new identity, she re-named it St. Helen's. Until her retirement in 1947, this remarkable woman, who jounced and rattled at breakneck speed along the country roads at the wheel of her "motor car" (one of the first in the district), became widely known and respected. Her emphasis on the necessity of "graciousness" and the "ethics of the dining table" left its imprint on many young ladies or would-be young ladies. Every evening, with formidable dignity, she would appear at the head of the main staircase, and each girl in turn would mount the stairs, curtsey, shake her hand and say good-night.

Winifred Wade's capable management immediately enhanced the fortunes of St. Helen's. Though devoutly religious, she was a hard-headed businesswoman. Mary Grant, who later became headmistress of the school, has vivid recollections of the invincible Miss Wade during the years of World War II.

> I can see her now, with her big boots on, wearing a ski cap and an old fur coat, out there with a gang of the girls digging potatoes. She had a lot of fields plowed and planted and ran a farm as well, with a few horses that the girls could ride. Life was very simple in those days. There wasn't much contact with other schools for games and so forth. Transport was a major difficulty, of course.

The post-war years brought many changes. Miss Wade retired to England, selling the farm and the house in the village called the Gate House, which had been used as a Junior School. The fate of St. Helen's was once more dropped into the lap of the Bishop of Montreal. Although by this time his connection with the school was rather tenuous, it was decided that St. Helen's should be maintained at all costs, and it again became incorporated. The Board appointed as headmistress Miss Helen Hague, an outstanding athlete and a teacher of great talent and versatility. A trained librarian, she reorganized and expanded the school library, and there was a renewed emphasis on physical fitness. Groups of girls were often seen puffing along the road behind Miss Hague's car to "improve their wind", and those who accompanied her on long rambles in the country gained an appreciation and detailed knowledge of wildflowers.

Miss Grant, a long-time staff member who succeeded Helen Hague in 1956, knew that modernization was imperative, but she also wished to retain all the important traditions associated with St. Helen's. Among these was the school's encouragement of bilingualism, which dated from its earliest days. In its latter years, the family of a former student, Grace Elliot Trudeau, donated an annual gift to the school in appreciation of their mother's happy girlhood there.

With Miss Grant's retirement in 1970 and the appointment of Warren Reid as principal a new "ten year plan" for St. Helen's was eagerly discussed in anticipation of future expansion. It dwindled to a two-year course in survival. When a school closes, there are inevitable doubts and recriminations. Could it not have been saved somehow? Was every effort made? Every possibility explored? Whatever the answers, the closing of a school produces a common feeling of deep regret. St. Helen's was never a big school, nor did it aspire to be one. In the end, its size, always one of its greatest charms, was also its most serious drawback.

After St. Helen's closed in June 1972, the town of Dunham took over the school library, and the building is now used for special classes by the local school board. To those who fondly remember St. Helen's as it was, it is of some comfort that the building is still performing a useful educational function and being preserved as a historic landmark.

Rothesay Collegiate School

Rothesay, New Brunswick

1877

It was not until nearly 100 years after the founding of King's Collegiate School in Nova Scotia that the Maritimes acquired a second collegiate school for boys, in the town of Rothesay, near St. John, New Brunswick. Like Father Johnston's Trinity College School at Weston, Ontario, which had opened twelve years earlier, it too was born out of one man's dissatisfaction with the quality of local education. The founder of Rothesay, William Thompson, MCP, was not a clergyman but a Master of the College of Preceptors, a degree granted to educators in England. As a man who could speak with authority on the subject of education, William Thompson was almost bound to find fault with local standards. His first classroom is said to have been located in a house that happened to be on the way to the local railway station and occasionally on blustery winter days commuters would stop in to warm their fingers and toes. Mr. Thompson's eleven pupils must have found these impromptu visits an amusing and welcome diversion from their stern regimen.

Thompson's methods were evidently of a superior calibre, for within the next few years he had attracted a great many more pupils to his little school, including a few girls, who came in the afternoons "to share the advantages of this excellent school". It expanded into the rectory of the Anglican church in the village, and it is possible that the close ties that developed later between the church and Rothesay began in those days.

Another of Thompson's objectives was the preparation of boys for admission into the Royal Military College at Kingston. It was the start of a military tradition that Rothesay has maintained to the present day. After the school's reorganization in 1908 as a church-based boarding school, the Rothesay cadet corps, drilled to perfection by their Sergeant Richmond "Dickey" Dooe, became one of the finest anywhere in the Maritimes. Until recently the corps had a long-standing affiliation with the Black Watch Regiment and today is affiliated with the Royal Canadian Regiment. Rothesay is the only remaining independent school that requires the boys to wear the cadet corps uniform as regulation dress.

The school in the rectory had been operating successfully for several years when, in 1891, James F. Robertson, son of a country clergyman, purchased for the school its present site, College Hill. The new property overlooked the rooftops of Rothesay and the broad Kennebecasis River and extended back into a hilly, wooded area. There were also two houses, a barn or two, a coach house and some good farm land. As a "Canadian Church School for Boys" under headmaster Reverend George Exton Lloyd, later Anglican Bishop of Saskatchewan and a founder of the city that bears his name, it was a boon for country parsons, whose sons could receive a first-rate education at little or no charge.

The school stressed the virtue of discipline not only through its military affiliation but through its rigorous daily routine. The Rothesay calendar of 1892 included not only an extensive clothing list but also a request that each boy bring along "a six foot rug or carpet for the bedroom", probably to ward off the winter cold. Punctuality was, of course, essential and the boys were warned that "the great bell will ring 100 strokes, after which late marks will be given".

But if the school was strict with its charges it was no less so with their parents, as a headmaster's message from the 1890s proves:

> If it is true that a poor beginning is one half-done, then it is a poor sort of boy who always has to stay just one more day after the holidays are over. Neither does it say much for the wisdom of those Parents who tolerate such loose methods of work. . . .
> At what age [it continues] should a boy be sent to a residential school? Two important factors are to be considered, the boy and the School. If the boy is wilful and petulant, having been brought up in a spoiled indulgent way, then for the good of the School, keep him home altogether. Such boys are never welcome, and are only tolerated in the

hope that firm discipline will improve their tone. If, on the other hand, a boy has been well-trained by his Mother, then, by all means let him go into residence as soon after 12 years of age as possible. After that, five years without break or change.

Parents were further advised to look carefully into the selection of a school for their sons.

Your boy's character is of more value than anything else. . . . Enquire closely into the workings of the school. The Masters should be total abstainers and non-smokers and the boys' habits should be scrutinized. Do they smoke? Do they chew? Do they use bad language?

In final warning, the headmaster exhorted:

Be kind, but firm, considerate but not coddling. . . . One of the greatest needs of this age is discipline. What a shame it is to see a boy, with all the materials for making a fine, striking man, bright intellect and a good heart at bottom, gradually being spoiled by an indulgent Father or a weak, foolish Mother. . . . The Mothers are the worst!

A survivor of the rigors of the Rothesay regimen in those early days, H.G.D. Ellis, recalled that there was one tin bathtub in each house, and a list posted in the hall informed each seeker after cleanliness on which night he was to take his bath. Even in the nineties the boys were expected to wear a uniform. "Short pants were worn by one and all with long black stockings, and in the winter overstockings and 'larrigans', like moccasins, but of a much heavier cut of deerskin, which had been soaked in seal oil, until it was waterproof. They had a terrible odor, but we wore them all through the winter."

The Christian ethic and its educational implementation continued to apply at RCS long after its purchase by the Anglican Diocese of Fredericton in 1908. In the business of making men of boys, knowledge of the Christian faith and its principles was essential, and the practice of those principles was to be gained through participation in team sports. A Rothesay headmaster of the 1950s voiced a conviction shared by many educators when he asserted, "It is on the athletic filed where many of the most important lessons of life are learned."

Since 1930 Rothesay has operated as a corporation under a

Board of Governors, and there have been a series of new buildings and improvements. In one sense, RCS has come almost full circle, for once again girls are "sharing the advantages of this excellent school". With the near-unanimous support of the Old Boys, the academic affiliation of Rothesay and Netherwood, a nearby girls' school, was made official in 1972.

Aside from its program of organized sports, a continuing emphasis on the outdoor life is encouraged by Rothesay's location, with its nearby woods and trout streams. At one stage in the school's history boys were paid to cut hardwood, which had to be piled by a roadway and measured exactly—an effective way of learning both the dimensions of a cord of wood and the value of a hard-earned dollar. And although the pedagogical methods may have changed, the goal of building character both in and out of the classroom has not.

Alma College

St. Thomas, Ontario

1877

Bishop Albert Carman, the dynamic and visionary general superintendent of the Methodist-Episcopal Church, was instrumental in founding two church schools in southern Ontario—Albert College in Belleville, and Alma College in St. Thomas. During the 1870s Carman had travelled extensively throughout the province and was struck by the need for a church school in southwestern Ontario. The central position and accessibility of St. Thomas (nearly a dozen railway lines passed through the town), along with its distance from "the vices and snares incident in overgrown cities", made it an ideal location.

Carman was wise, too, in seeking broad local support for the new venture. He secured the endorsement of St. Thomas' leading citizens of all denominations, who supported him in a resolution to establish "an educational institution designed to afford young Ladies a liberal course of instruction in all attempts to make their lives useful, happy, and their tastes elevated and refined". The citizens of St. Thomas were among the first to contribute towards the new school. Eventually nearly 10,000 individual subscribers donated funds, often at considerable personal sacrifice. Several ministers of the church subscribed out of their own meager salaries, relying on Faith and Hope to cast away doubts about the practicality of this charity. Bishop Carman confidently proclaimed that his protégé would rise above "all the clouds of financial distress to where potential sunshine shall settle upon it".

Although the charter for Alma College was secured in 1877 the building process was drawn out over four financially embarrassing years. The money situation was hardly to improve in the first decades of the school's existence. The church union of

1883, just two years after Alma College had actually opened, only increased the number of schools which had call on an ever-dimishing communal purse, and later, local crop failures led to a sharp decline in enrolment.

Still, when it was finally completed, the towered and turreted school building was as handsome a monument to high ideals and great ambitions as any in the country—despite the fact that its construction very nearly involved a lawsuit. At least twenty architects had submitted plans for the building, attracted by the Board's offer of a premium to its first and second choices. But when funds ran low the premium was cancelled, and one of the more irate competitors declared that he intended to sue the Board until a benefactor of the school finally intervened. The competition was eventually won by James Balfour of Hamilton, perhaps because of the philisophic originality of his plans. His ambitious design was intended to represent the union of Home, Church and School—with the church in the centre, flanked by the school on the right wing and the residence on the left. The honour of naming the new institution was given to one of its most enthusiastic local supporters, Sheriff Colin Munroe, whose wife Alma had died shortly before the laying of the College cornerstone in 1878. As a tribute to her, and to her daughter and namesake, Sheriff Munroe decided upon the name Alma, and the council of the school agreed that it was indeed a suitable name, in harmony with the names Albert and Alexandra, the church colleges in Belleville.

Like many girls' schools of the era, Alma was much given to rampant symbolism. The school colours each represented one branch of the College's original three departments: blue for Literature, gold for Art, and crimson for Music. (One of the professed aims of Bishop Carman had been "to fill our Homes, our Churches, and our Sunday Schools with wholesome song".) The downstairs corridors were dedicated to Literature (Tennyson, Burns and later Lampman), the second floor to Music (Beethoven, Mendelssohn, Chopin and Wagner), and the top floor to Fine Art (Turner, Rembrandt and Millet).

The fact that the community as well as the church was involved with the beginnings of the school has probably had a great deal to do with its continuing success. Its original twenty-one-member board of management included several prominent

Anglicans and Presbyterians as well as a quorum of thirteen Methodists. It was their desire that the College should be "virtually a public institution, open to sons and daughters of all citizens, without distinction of race or creed", and that "the teachings and curriculum should be free from sectarian tenet and dogma". While the school never did become co-educational, as originally intended, it did try to honour freedom of worship. Each girl was encouraged to attend the church of her own denomination, a practice that finally got out of hand during the 1890s as close to a dozen separate groups sallied forth each Sunday—each properly chaperoned—to their separate places of worship. As the girls proceeded home from church a police escort had to be requested to ward off the amourous advances of certain local youths. It was thereupon decided that, for evening services at least, everyone would attend the Methodist Church.

The College's Fine Art department, under the distinguished F. M. Bell-Smith, RCA, professor of painting, drawing, and elocution, quickly gained for the school a reputation as one of Canada's leading art schools. Its exhibits at the Indian and Colonial Exhibition in London, England in 1886, and at the Chicago World's Fair won an impressive array of medals and diplomas. The school's general literature course soon came to include shorthand and bookkeeping, and Alma became a pioneer among Ladies' Colleges in Canada in the teaching of domestic science.

Handsome though it may have been, and dedicated as it was to "noble work", like the Ontario Ladies' College, Alma too became the object of criticism in the Massey Foundation's 1921 report on Methodist schools. Its narrow Gothic windows let in far too little light. Its servants' quarters were located impractically. Its dining room was in the basement. Its kitchens and bathrooms were antiquated. In fact, there was practically nothing to commend the College from the point of view of physical facilities. The commissioners, however, could not fail to be impressed with the general tone of the school and noted that from the first the College had flourished and was "still doing good service to the community". As with the Ontario Ladies' College, however, the Commission expressed concern over the "narrowly technical courses" offered by the College and noted with horror that the girls could "take what subjects they pleased". There were, in their view, too many frills and not enough substance in the curriculum.

Until 1953, when Dr. Flora Sifton, formerly a Dean of Women at the College, was appointed principal, the destiny of Alma rested primarily with three distinguished and devoted church-men. The first, Reverend B. F. Austin (1891-1897), was a graduate of Albert College and Victoria College, Cobourg, and was also a prolific if not altogether successful writer. His private publishing enterprises put him deep into debt and eventually brought about his resignation. Austin's successor, Reverend Dr. R. I. Warner (1897-1919), was another Albert and Victoria College graduate. An original Alma College staff member, he had experienced at first hand its growing pains. Dr. Warner had a charismatic personality, and it was mainly owing to his efforts that Alma's enormous debt was gradually liquidated. He established scholarship funds as well, and when Dr. Warner retired just prior to publication of the Massey Report the school was debt-free at last, though badly in need of renovation.

The contribution of Reverend Dr. Perry Silas Dobson (1919-1947 and 1951-1953), an Albert College graduate and former Stanstead staff member, was monumental. During the Dobson years Alma acquired a gym, a swimming pool, a music building, and its picturesque and unique garden amphitheatre. However, Perry Dobson will more likely be remembered best as a man with a sense of humour "who thought of us as kids growing up—not as some kind of material to be moulded into a church pillar".

Under Dr. Sifton and her successor Elizabeth Bone, as a school Alma has become less community-centred, and its student body is increasingly multinational. It is still, in essence, a "Christian school"; roughly one quarter of its present board members are clergymen. Its curriculum is geared to practical courses, and it offers a two-year intensive secretarial course as well as a special course for church secretaries. A part of the school has recently been made available to local senior citizens, who live on the premises and share its facilities. A girl can still work off part of her tuition by working in the laundry or washing dishes; Alma is virtually the only school left where such arrangements still exist. The traditions of the College, and pride in its heritage, are readily apparent.

Lakefield College School

Lakefield, Ontario

1879

Like William Thompson of Rothesay in New Brunswick, Sparham Sheldrake, the founder of Lakefield (or The Grove, as it has become known to several generations of Old Boys and friends) was his own man — a schoolmaster constrained by neither a governing body nor the demands of a clerical collar. Mr. Sheldrake was motivated by the need to earn a living as well as by an earnest desire "to give his whole and undivided attention to the instruction of a limited number of young gentlemen in all elementary branches of an English Education". Many of the fathers of his students were retired British army officers who had settled in the Kawartha Lakes district, and to them he gave his assurance that he would pay "every possible attention to their [the students] domestic comfort and happiness", and that greatest care would be taken "to inculcate moral and gentlemanly behaviour".

When Sparham Sheldrake settled in the village of Lakefield, most of the surrounding property was already owned by Colonel Sam Strickland, whose two married sisters, Catherine Parr Traill and Susanna Moody, publicized through their literary accomplishments the joys of pioneering in the Upper Canadian wilderness of the 1830s. The trail which led to the Moody's log house among the cedars crossed property which would later become the ground of the Grove School. The association between the school and these pioneer families has been of long standing; recently a historic house on the edge of the school property, once occupied by a daughter of Catherine Parr Traill, was acquired by the College as additional accommodation for its boarders – and renovated to preserve its unique charm and individuality.

Mr. Sheldrake's school, like so many other small private ventures flung out across the Dominion, enjoyed modest success in its early years, and its future was virtually guaranteed with the arrival in 1893 of the young Anglican clergyman, A.W. Mackenzie. Within a year, Mr. Sheldrake stepped aside and Mackenzie became headmaster of the small, haphazard cluster of buildings set in magnificent natural surroundings.

In a tribute to his former headmaster, who dedicated forty-three years to the making of this remarkable school, John Morgan Gray writes: "Young Alick Mackenzie, who loved the out of doors, at once gave the boys of his small School almost all possible freedom. He delighted in swimming and canoeing, and they learned both. He knew the woods and relished campfire meals; so, in time, did they." These happy expeditions gradually became institutions. There were sleigh rides and skating parties on the lake and snowshoeing, and sometimes a few boys went off to fish for the school's breakfast. "The woods to the north were filled with cunningly concealed huts (the boys' own architectural wonders, built from every imaginable material that could be begged, borrowed or scrounged) and of a Saturday afternoon or Sunday, Grove canoes were to be seen anywhere on Lake Katchewanooka." Boating is another of Lakefield's long-established traditions. The school's first boathouse was built by the boys and masters who cut down the trees, hauled the logs, made the crib and filled it with stones. "Yet," Gray remembers, "only someone coming on his tall figure, standing on the top of the hill, as he looked out across the lake for some overdue canoe could have guessed at the price he paid in worry for the freedom he gave us."

The school motto, "Mens Sane In Corpore Sano", expressed Mackenzie's belief in the values of athleticism, self-restraint, self-denial, and endurance of hardship. "A spirit of lean living and right-doing" was to become the Lakefield way of life, as was good sportsmanship, and no boy left Lakefield without having learned to swim. "The man who is a good sport will always earn respect and liking wherever he is," he believed. Yet Mackenzie was nevertheless outspoken in his criticism of schools where sports were "overemphasized to the students' detriment", and early in his career he had already begun to question the undue stress placed on external examinations.

Alick Mackenzie understood boys—their high spirits, their pranks, and their next-to-insatiable appetites. In his account of a harvest festival held at Lakefield Church he observed, "The Festival's chief attraction is the generous tea provided in the town hall, where a boy can have a reasonable allowance of four helpings of turkey or a dozen pieces of cake without being subjected to any ill-bred, officious remarks." His formula for developing all-around boys was simple and straightforward: hard work, thoroughness, moderation, patience, honesty, and a firm religious faith.

Mackenzie's death just a year before the outbreak of World War II was keenly felt. A newspaper reported his funeral as follows:

> With the masters of the School acting as pallbearers, the beautiful open casket was carried out to where there awaited a bob-sleigh drawn by workhorses and driven by the village expressman, and Dr. Mackenzie's good friend. The coffin was placed on the sleigh, draped with a large Union Jack and heaped with flowers. Immediately in front of this sleigh was another, filled, garlanded and spilling over with rosy blooms of all descriptions, and drawn—not by horses—but by six Schoolboys. . . . The Schoolboys stood at attention, their red and green toques in their hands as the procession got under way, and passed slowly from the shadowed School grounds into the early spring sunshine of the village street. There were no cars, everybody walked, and the only sound was the tinkle of the sleighbells as the single team of horses moved along.

Shortly after Mackenzie's death, Lakefield Preparatory School became an incorporated non-profit institution, and Dr. Mackenzie's son, Kenneth, served as headmaster until his enlistment at the outbreak of World War II. During the war years and well beyond, the headship of The Grove was taken on by Gordon Winder (Windy) Smith (1939-1964). As a student at Lakefield and later at Upper Canada College "Boody" Smith had been an athlete of some note. When he returned to Lakefield he had already taught at both St. Andrew's College and Upper Canada. At Lakefield he re-introduced the naval cadets in 1940, and following the war he undertook an ambitious building and renovation program. Yet he remained a man of simple tastes, "careless or casual in his dress, and with no great interest in conventional comforts—with a wholeness about him that mystified and then usually captivated high-powered parents and distinguished visitors. Integrity and love governed his life." Unassuming, uncomplicated, and deeply loyal to his school and to his boys, Winder Smith became to new generations what Alick Mackenzie had been to the old.

At his own request he retired in favour of J. (Jack) E. Matthews, whom he had persuaded to enter the career of teaching and soon recognized as his potential successor. Because of his desire to continue to serve the school, the Board appointed Winder Smith as Dean with special responsibilities, and he maintained his close association with the school until his death in 1970. He was a man greatly admired and fondly remembered.

Jack Matthews, a keen outdoorsman with dynamic energy, maintained Lakefield's family atmosphere while bolstering its academic standards and improving the facilities. Sailing, canoe tripping, kayaking, and cross-country skiing flourished under his headship. He left the school in 1971, to establish the Lester B. Pearson College on Vancouver Island.

J.T.M. "Terry" Guest, Matthews' successor, was quick to perceive Lakefield's unique qualities and potential, and he stresses the advantages of a close, familial relationship in a rural setting. "Being small and almost completely residential, we have a strong sense of community. Our closeness to natural beauty around us tends to release the tensions and diminish the complexities of modern living." It remains one of the school objectives to make the boys aware of the great, still-unspoiled country which is their heritage. The original stucco and beamed Grove house has been lovingly maintained as part of the Lakefield complex. It is a symbol of that tradition—without pretension—that has given the school a place unique among Canada's older boarding schools.

Halifax Ladies' College

Halifax, Nova Scotia

1887

The oldest independent school for girls in Atlantic Canada can trace its beginnings to a meeting room in the Halifax YMCA. The professors, lawyers, doctors and Presbyterian churchmen had assembled there to organize an association which would operate "a College for Ladies in Halifax, in connection with the Presbyterian Church of Canada". Two Presbyterian girls' schools were already flourishing in Ontario, one in Ottawa and another in Brantford, and they were sure that a Nova Scotian effort would be equally successful. Money to open the Ladies' College in Halifax was raised in the usual way, by issuing shares, at twenty-five dollars apiece, but it soon became more practical to dissolve the original joint stock company and operate the school as a non-profit trust.

For more than thirty years after its founding, the most influential force behind the school was the first chairman of its Board of Governors, Reverend Robert Laing of St. Matthew's Presbyterian Church. Credit for the success of the College was also shared by its first principal, Miss Anna Leach, who came to the School from Wellesley College in Massachusetts. She was, according to one recollection,

> very good to look at, with dignity and character that compelled the respect and admiration of the girls. It was whispered that she had lost her lover and that the black dress which she always wore, as well as her slightly remote air, were due to a broken heart. It is far more likely that any remoteness in her manner was due to the worry of coping with eighty troublesome girls, but it pleased us to think that she had loved and lost. Every morning she wrote a sentiment or quotation of moral worth on the blackboard which we had to copy in our commonplace books provided for

that special purpose — a collection of virtuous platitudes.

Like a number of other private schools, Halifax Ladies' College has moved from one location to another, to another. Its first home, originally built by a member of the prominent Uniacke family, was a large, rambling wooden house surrounded by an iron fence with a huge gate, with at least two duels and a flight of "ghost stairs" in its background. Every Monday Miss Florence Blackwood, a successor of Anna Leach, would allow the girls to use the main entrance of the historic old house so that they could admire its elegant winding staircase, marble fireplaces, and crystal chandeliers.

·Before many years had passed the College had gained a reputation for high academic and cultural standards. It became an affiliate of Dalhousie University and developed an outstanding art studio. Later the Halifax Conservatory of Music opened a branch in conjunction with the school, and became the centre of music studies in Atlantic Canada.

Among the students of the Conservatory during the 1890s were two children whose grandmother had once served as governess to the children of the King of Siam. Anna Leonnowens' daughter and her family in Halifax received fairly frequent visits from "Grandmama" and a schoolmate of her grandchildren recalls one memorable day when Grandmother Anna came to look the school over. Ever the schoolmistress, she cast a critical eye over the children's lessons and found them wanting. It is not widely known that the famous Anna retired to Montreal when extensive travel and lecture tours became too much for her, to live out her life in genteel poverty.

If Grandmama Leonnowens found that her grandchildren's education lacked substance, it was probably because the school at that time, like most girls' schools, encouraged refinement first and scholarship second. Certainly the original motto of the College, "That our daughters may be as cornerstones polished after the similitude of the Palace", conveys the impression that its graduates should be "finished" in every respect. It is not surprising that Halifax Ladies' College was one of the first schools to open a domestic science department, which attracted a great many students and included every imaginable facet of home-making.

But while it may have been academically insubstantial, as a church school it was conducted on the principle that "the Christian Faith is the true basis of the highest culture". Any girl with a burning desire to teach in connection with mission work was admitted free of charge. The twin emphasis on the domestic virtues and on the religious was designed to promote an atmosphere of a Christian home, "in which the students may have the daily advantage of association with scholarly and cultivated ladies". The physical health and well-being of the girls were another important consideration, though this did not include competitive sports until decades later. Entire afternoons were often given over to games and "calisthenics", with compulsory exercises with dumbbells and Indian clubs. Boarders also participated in "the Morning Walk" and midnight fire drills, which involved sliding down a firepole or lowering oneself from a window with a rope.

The disastrous explosion in Halifax Harbour in December 1917 made a vivid impression on the girls then attending HLC. Two ships, one laden with munitions, collided at the Narrows and created the largest man-made explosion prior to Hiroshima. More than 2,000 people were killed outright and another 8,000 injured or maimed. The entire north end of Halifax was levelled and windows were shattered over sixty miles away. "We were at prayers in the gymnasium when we heard a strange rumbling sound, followed by a crash," one former student recalled. "The windows rattled and broke and even the floor began shaking, but there was no real panic. We were too stunned and helpless to be really afraid." Repairs to the building were hastily made and within a week of the disaster the school was converted into a 250-bed hospital, with a number of teachers and senior girls acting as volunteer relief workers.

Just after the outbreak of World War II, the old house was taken over as a hostel for the armed forces and, at the same time, the school's long association with the Conservatory of Music came to an end. Halifax Ladies' College moved to its new home, "Armbrae", on Oxford Street in the autumn of 1940 and the school continued there until Dr. Marion Dauphinee, the school's principal for over thirty years, persuaded the Board that a new building was imperative. The curricular emphasis, by this time, had swung from cultural and domestic accomplishments to university preparation and new facilities were desperately needed. The new plans made no provision for the accommodation of boarding students, and HLC became a day school only for the first time in its history.

Over the years Halifax Ladies' College has developed into a school geared to students with high academic potential. Recently, however, two co-educational day schools with similar objectives have opened, the Halifax Grammar School, which began as a boys-only effort in 1958, and Dartmouth Academy, which opened in the 1960s. They are highly competitive alternatives that offer a challenge to the Ladies' College to maintain its high academic reputation.

Trafalgar

Montreal, Quebec

1887 (incorporated 1871)

Trafalgar is English-speaking Montreal's oldest independent school for girls. Thanks to the explicit and exacting terms of its Scots Presbyterian founder's will, it was also, until recently, a school with perhaps the most incredibly complex system of management in Canada.

Trafalgar's founder, Donald Ross, arrived in Montreal at the age of fifteen, a penniless Scots immigrant. Through an advantageous marriage and a keen business sense, he accumulated a substantial fortune. In 1871, obsessed with the idea of using his money to perpetuate his mother's memory, he set down his plans for the creation of a "seminary" for the educational training of "the middle and higher ranks of female society". Never has a legacy been trammeled with such stipulations. Ross was a man with very firm and fixed ideas of how the school was to be administered, and his bequest embraced every consideration from the marital status of the teachers to precise specifications for the glass panes in the school greenhouse, an edifice he considered absolutely essential and "of much value to the scholars, especially in the winter".

But at his death, six years after the incorporation of the Trafalgar Institute, there was not enough money in the estate to cover the expense of building a school, let alone the chapel he had also envisioned. Without a substantial donation of $30,000 from his old friend Donald Smith (Lord Strathcona), the school never would have been built. Lord Strathcona's generosity, however, also had its own provisions, thereby violating Ross' wishes with respect to his school for the first, but hardly the last, time. Lord Strathcona stipulated that the Trafalgar Institute must be located within the city limits, which precluded the property on Côte des Neiges Road that had been designated by Ross as the future site of the school. Instead, Chalderton Lodge, "a fine residential property on Simpson Avenue", was acquired for the school in 1887. The Lodge, built originally as a replica of a gracious old English home, was located on a historic tract of land. A portion of it had once belonged to the explorer Sir Alexander Mackenzie and later to Sir George Simpson of the Hudson's Bay Company. It had taken sixteen years from the date of Trafalgar's incorporation for the school to become a physical reality.

Not only had Ross specified a "suitable" site, but he had also hand-picked the men who would serve as Trafalgar's Governors, men he felt certain could be relied on "to erect, establish, and even maintain" the school entrusted to them. But the good intentions of his last will and testament, full of Hallelujahs and Praise ye the Lord's, would cause a collective headache in years to come. Until very recently the school's charter required it to be administered by a Board of Governors which had to include the principal of McGill University, the principal of Queen's University, the Anglican Archdeacon of Montreal, and the minister of the Presbyterian Church of St. Andrew and St. Paul, as well as several members of the Presbyterian Kirk Session and trustees of Queen's University. It is not hard to believe that most of these men had more pressing commitments than the administration of a girls' school.

Originally, the school was to be open only to girls over the age of fourteen. They were under no circumstances to be lower-class girls but must belong rather to "families of the respectable and middle ranks . . . mechanics' children, as well as the children of merchants in reduced circumstances or any other . . . being Protestants . . . to whom the privilege of the Institute might be an object". It was also stipulated that they must possess the means to suitably maintain and clothe themselves during the whole term of four years. Trafalgar's first pupil later recalled that she spent her first month at the school living in solitary splendour, waiting impatiently for more boarders to arrive. By the end of the year there were six, including two sisters from the West Indies who came with only one overcoat between them and had to take their winter walks by turns. The Governors of the school evidently did not take Ross' wishes about proper clothing too much to heart.

Ross wanted scholarships, too, the bulk of them to be awarded to daughters of Protestant ministers, with preference given to Presbyterians. The principal of the school, "the prudent, loving, anxious Mother of the Girls", was to be a married lady but a childless one, "free from the encumbrance of a young family". Trafalgar's first headmistress was, in fact, a spinster but Ross would probably have been mollified to know that she was at least Scottish. The teachers, on the other hand, were to be unmarried or widows, ready and willing to live in the residence, "punctual and faithful . . . endeavouring to improve themselves as much as their pupils". Fortunately, they were also to be well paid, "in order to secure the highest talent".

The first principal, Miss Grace A. Fairley of Edinburgh, presided over the new Trafalgar Institute for the next quarter-century and helped it grow from a tiny school of eight pupils to a sizable one with more than eighty, and then 180. The standards of the school were high and by 1911 it was an affiliate of McGill University. After a few unsettled years during World War I, a second Scotswoman, Miss Janet L. Cumming, was appointed headmistress. She would remain at Trafalgar and serve it with ability for twenty more years. In fact, periods of extended service have been the rule rather than the exception for Trafalgar's headmistresses. Jean Harvie, its recently retired headmistress, has had a personal connection with the school that dates back to 1926, when she herself was a pupil of Miss Cumming.

Today Trafalgar is one of three girl's schools that serve English-speaking Montreal. In the course of its development it has adhered very closely—some might think too closely—to the spirit of Donald Ross' will. It is proudly conservative by virtue of its constitution, and devoted to its traditions.

Ridley College

St. Catharines, Ontario

1889

Aside from Rothesay Collegiate School and Lakefield (The Grove)— both private rather than denominational ventures— Ridley College was the first church-sponsored independent school for boys established since Trinity College School, founded twenty-five years earlier. To its supporters the success of Bishop Ridley College, and later of Havergal Ladies' College in Toronto, meant that a long-overdue Low Church alternative at last existed to counter the High Anglican presence in education.

Since mid-century, Anglicans in Ontario had been taking up sides in the battle of ritualism versus evangelicalism. Huron College, the precursor of Western University in London, Ontario, was Bishop Benjamin Cronyn's answer to John Strachan's Trinity University in Toronto. Cronyn, an Irishman who had had the temerity to question Strachan's divine right to rule the Anglican roost, had been labelled "a political agitator" by Strachan. Then, in 1879, Wycliffe College opened its Divinity School in Toronto to accommodate those who had chosen to take the Low Road, and it appeared that the two factions were beyond reconciliation. What had begun as a theological rift had blossomed into knock-down, drag-out ecumenical warfare.

To the evangelicals the idea of educating a son or daughter at a High Church establishment such as Bishop Strachan or Trinity College School was not merely unacceptable, it was totally unthinkable. Education and religious principles, the Evangelicals believed, must never be set apart, and therefore they considered it imperative to establish their own schools as quickly as possible.

By the 1880s there were, of course, numerous public schools in Ontario, but the British boarding school tradition still ran deep among the "Principal People". The association between Trinity College School and Trinity University already served as a fine example of the merits of a "feeder school" located in a small community where the distractions and temptations of city life would be absent. Thus a Low Church search party was recruited to seek out a suitable location for the establishment of a preparatory school for boys.

The College promoters included men who had been deeply involved in the formation of Wycliffe College, such as Sir Daniel Wilson, later President of the University of Toronto, Sir Casimir Gzowski, Sir Edward Blake, and Archibald Campbell. They finally settled upon the stately and spacious Springbank Sanitorium in St. Catharines. The town's ready accessibility, both by rail and by lake steamer, plus its reasonable proximity to Toronto, Hamilton, and several American border cities, rendered it ideal from all points of view. The school Governors were unanimous in their choice of the name Bishop Ridley College, after Nicholas Ridley, immortal martyr of the sixteenth-century Protestant Reformation, who was tortured and finally burned at the stake for failure to renounce his faith. To the Anglican evangelicals, Bishop Ridley's name personified the struggle to uphold the Protestant faith "simple and purified", free of the taint of Roman mystic ritualism. The school coat of arms, three pelicans and three bishop's mitres, represented Bishop Ridley and his fellow martyrs, Cranmer and Latimer. The original College motto, chosen by the first principal J. O. Miller, was the family motto of Thomas Carlyle; though it was changed later to "Terar Dum Prosim": May I be consumed in service. Probably few of the school Governors knew that Miller's choice of orange and black as the school colours was prompted by romantic sentiment. Earlier that year, at a party in Toronto, a particularly attractive young lady wearing an elegant orange gown covered in black tulle had caught Miller's eye. She subsequently became his wife.

Ridley's youthful principal, a Wycliffe graduate and one of the founding members of the College, was only twenty-seven when he undertook responsibility for the new school. For the next thirty years Ridley College took on its own particular shape and form under this extraordinary, inspiring, and dynamic personality. J. O. "JoJo" Miller chose his staff with utmost care, finding men of brilliance and scholarship. (In the competition for the post of classics master, Stephen Leacock lost out to H. J., later Canon, Cody.) In the beginning canings and strappings were employed only as a last resort and were considered a sign of failure on the part of the masters, not the boys. Dr. Miller's attitude was that "it is far better to come a cropper by taking a firm stand than to sit on the fence like a petrified wren", and he violently disapproved of hazing, initiation rites, and fagging. His book, *Studies in Ethics*, a scholarly work published in 1895, brought new academic acclaim to the school.

Two years later Ridley opened its own Lower School—the first preparatory school for younger boys from about seven to thirteen attached to any Canadian independent school. Its first head was a man of great warmth and rare understanding, H. G. "Rep" Williams.

Both Upper and Lower Schools placed such emphasis on games that most boys spent the major portion of their hours out of class "consumed in service" either on the playing fields or in the gymnasium. Every boy was required to spend at least two hours out of doors every day, regardless of wind or weather. "J. O." himself was an ardent cricketer, but he also promoted football over lacrosse, and with the Welland Canal virtually on the school's doorstep it was only natural that swimming, canoeing, and rowing would soon become popular as well. Over the years Ridley's rowing teams have won many honours both in North America and abroad, and the school now boasts its own indoor rowing tank.

Fishing was also a popular pastime—at least until the day a group of boys lugged back a six-foot, seventy-eight pound sturgeon that had become trapped in the canal. The headmaster ordered its instant burial and the ungodly stench emanating from its shallow grave served to discourage future anglers from hauling home anything that would not fit into a frying pan. While the canal's proximity was useful from the recreational standpoint, it also had its drawbacks—a virtual plague of rats, attracted, no doubt, by the endless variety of edibles stashed in the school dormitories. Only an edict banning food in the dormitories averted a major pestilence. Meanwhile, on the hills near the banks of the canal someone discovered that the school's dining room trays were particularly well suited for tobogganning. The sport gave vast amusement to the school's Chinese laundryman, who is said to have remarked, "Zippee half-a-milee—then walkee back? Phoo!"

More enterprising were the organizers of a scheme to convert the call of the wild into a profitable fur-trapping business venture. Several companies of gentlemen adventurers sprang up before a scarcity of muskrats and the inevitable calamity (one of the adventurers fell through the ice in the canal) combined to put them all into bankruptcy. The boys then had to content themselves with less profitable pastimes such as "corridor curling" with the granite chamber pots that made ideal "stones". Until the introduction of plumbing fixtures, bonspiels of this sort were fairly common in many Canadian boarding schools.

The days of gaslight and chamber pots at Springbank came to an abrupt end one cold October night in 1903. By the following morning only the smouldering ruins of the old sanitorium remained. But as at Trinity and Bishop's when they were devastated, virtually no boys were withdrawn from the school. Most of them were put up in a local hotel until the new Ridley—with its electrically-lit corridors—arose on the other side of the canal. At its new location the partnership between Dr. Miller and Ridley College continued for nearly twenty more years until 1921. For another ten years, H. C. "Harry Griffiths," an Old Boy, athlete, and a noted football coach (his Varsity team won the first Grey Cup), ran the school jointly with "Rep" Williams of the Lower School. In 1924 Ridley's shareholders relinquished or redeemed their stock certificates and the school became a non-profit corporation and hence relieved of its tax burden. It proved to be a well-timed change in status, for the Depression claimed Ridley's closest neighbour and competitor, Lake Lodge School, a small private venture in Grimsby, Ontario.

Following the retirement of "Rep" Williams as co-head, "The Griff", as he was known to several generations of Ridley boys, remained in command until 1949. J. R. Hamilton, a master since 1922, then took over as headmaster, but his collapse and sudden death in the school chapel led to the appointment in the mid-sixties of E.V.B. Pilgrim, a former master at Bishop's College School.

For Ridley, the post-war years have proved among the most difficult in its history. The reputation of a school rarely rests on its bricks and mortar. Richard Bradley, the present headmaster and only Ridley's fifth, arrived from England in 1971 to promote and project Ridley's new image as an "emancipated" Canadian boarding and day school. Girls—a very limited number of them—are now admitted to the senior classes as day students. Though Ridley maintains its status as one of Canada's foremost "Establishment" boys' schools, the school administration is keenly aware that very often a school must accommodate itself to changing times in order to survive.

Ashbury College

Ottawa, Ontario

1891

Like Lakefield and Rothesay Collegiate School, Ashbury was started through the efforts of a single individual. Its founder was George Penrose Woollcombe, a graduate of Oxford University and later an Anglican clergyman. He had taught at both Trinity College School and Bishop's College School before deciding to embark upon his own enterprise a venture which would incorporate the best of both the Canadian and British systems of education.

Since Confederation, Ottawa had been expanding at a rapid rate and there was a clear need for the sort of school George Woollcombe had in mind, a school that would prepare boys for university and "provide a superior education" for the sons of the many families that had moved to the capital to help shape the destiny of the young country. Essentially Ashbury has remained an Ottawa school and, almost inevitably, it has become a school for the sons of foreign diplomats as well.

"Mr. Woollcombe's School", which opened the same year he was ordained into the Church of England, began with nine boys, one of them the son of Sir Charles Tupper. It was first located in the Victoria Chambers, then a part of the old Victoria Hotel facing the Parliament Buildings. Before long it was moved down the street into three grey stone houses on Wellington and was re-christened Ashbury House School, with its playing fields at the corner of Sparks and Bank. Later it was moved again, this time into an old centre-town mansion on Argyle Avenue. In 1900 Dr. Woollcombe, who had adopted the name Ashbury from his ancestral home in Devonshire, incorporated his school as an educational trust and changed its name to Ashbury College.

Ashbury continued to attract more and more boys each year and soon even the large Argyle Street property grew cramped. In 1910 Ashbury moved for the last time to the village of Rockcliffe. Although Rockcliffe has grown considerably since then, it remains a haven of quiet respectability, its expanses of houses, lawns and trees unmarred by commercial development. With the ready accessibility of the Gatineau Hills, as well as the many attractions of the capital, Ashbury has enjoyed the combined advantages of the city and the country. Even today Ashbury and the outside world are almost as well separated as they were when Dr. Woollcombe moved his school to Rockcliffe Park over sixty years ago.

For more than forty years the school bore the mark of its quiet, unassuming, and scholarly founder, who had a handshake like steel and determination to spare. At his instigation a Junior School was opened and has continued to maintain its own identity as a separate unit of the school. Ashbury's house system, prefects, compulsory sports, daily chapel services, and cadet corps, which is affiliated with the Governor-General's Foot Guards, are all elements of the school's British heritage. The years following Dr. Woollcombe's retirement in 1933 have brought relatively few changes in its basic orientation, although the relationship between Ashbury and Elmwood, a neighbouring school for girls, has recently undergone a transformation that many Old Boys and Old Girls would find almost incredible. Interchange of classes at the senior level, joint ventures in drama and music, and more intermingling in all facets of daily school life are signs of a willingness to move with the times.

Edgehill School

Windsor, Nova Scotia

1891

In Nova Scotia, the Edgehill Church School for Girls was established just four years after the Halifax Ladies' College. Perhaps its Anglican promoters were reluctant to be outdone by the Presbyterians, but while the Anglican Church may have played an important part in the beginnings of Edgehill, another factor was equally, if not more, significant. Windsor was a university town, the home of King's College, and the sons of its faculty were almost predestined to attend its well-established preparatory school of the same name. But the education of the professors' daughters was another matter. Among young gentlewomen everywhere a mood of exasperation and restlessness was growing. If boys had no monopoly on brains, they certainly did have the benefit of educational advantages that had been largely denied their sisters. The main objective of Edgehill's founding fathers was to provide an exemplary education for their daughters, as well as their sons, and perhaps to show the Presbyterians in Halifax a thing or two while they were at it.

From start to finish the creation of Edgehill took under six months. That their school opened in the dead of winter gives some indication of the promoters' impatience to begin. Their first problem was that there were far more applicants than the building could comfortably hold, and work on a new residence was begun at once. Edgehill's first principal, Miss Hannah Machin, was imported from a girls' school in Quebec, and with a handful of pupils in tow from her former school she assumed her position full of hope and enthusiasm.

Life at Edgehill was a strictly regimented existence, but those who endured it remember their school with uncommon affection. Miss Machin was a woman of great dignity, who warned everyone of her impending arrival with the musical tinkle of a tiny golden bell attached to her watch chain. She also attracted to the school a staff whose lessons were liberally spiced with "a God-given sense of humour".

Her successor, Miss Blanche Lefroy, from the Ladies' College at Cheltenham, England, also chose her staff well. They must be qualified, yes, but more important, they must be adaptable, understanding, and able to approach their work "with vigour". Miss Lefroy encouraged vigour in all aspects of life. She believed heartily in outings, sports, and open windows, and she ordered several sleds to be built, so that winter walks could be varied by coasting and skating. During these years nearly all the mistresses, like Miss Lefroy, were English and unaccustomed to Canada's great outdoors. Their efforts to learn the rudiments of skating and snowshoeing were the source of constant amusement to their Canadian pupils.

But their tenacity won them both respect and affection. One new mistress from England arrived in Halifax in the winter of 1905, to be greeted by the news that a blizzard had blocked all the railway lines and that the drifts had reached thirty feet in some spots. After several days as a guest of the Halifax Ladies' College she determined to wait no longer and set out from Windsor, only to be stranded in an empty hotel along the rail line. At last she arrived at Edgehill by sleigh, but not before she had spent some time in a snowdrift when the sleigh overturned. Because her luggage was delayed for several weeks, she had to face her new charges in borrowed shoes, many sizes too large. But with characteristic heartiness she declared that it had all been "great fun, really".

Although visitors to Edgehill were as carefully screened as the staff, all the vigilance in the world could not prevent occasional clandestine contact between the boys at King's and the Edgehill girls. In the early days, the girls' fencing classes were held at King's, and the services at the parish church afforded at least a glimpse at the opposite sex. Thus, friendships invariably sprang up between "the dwellers on the two hills". In later years, when ground hockey for girls became fashionable, the sport gained instant popularity at Edgehill. The heavy grass roller on the King's College School field where the girls played hockey served as an undercover post office, where notes could be deposited and retrieved. Riding also became very popular, and the King's-Edgehill version of the Pony Express is said to have done a thriving business.

After the World War I, Edgehill lost many of its English staff members and acquired a new headmistress, Miss Mildred Roechling. The former housemistress of Havergal in Toronto spent the next twenty-seven years at The Hill and saw it through some of its happiest and most difficult times: the flapper years, with dances and sleigh rides and tobogganing parties, the "thrifty thirties", as she described them, "when everything toppled like a house of cards", and the forties, "when all hell broke loose!" Fifty English schoolgirls from Rodean, Edgehill's sister school in England, arrived on the doorstep in June of 1940, where they remained for the duration of the war. Almost the entire town turned out to greet them. Before the night was out every scrap of food in the school had been devoured, and Miss Roechling had to make a midnight ride to awaken the town baker so that there would be something for Sunday breakfast.

The next morning a small refugee appeared at Miss Roechling's door and thrust a very crumpled and grimy handkerchief into her hand. The grubby handful contained an impressive collection of family jewels, entrusted to the child by her grandmother in the event of a German invasion. Before long Miss Roechling had accumulated a sizable mound of similar treasures for safekeeping.

During the first summer the war guests were farmed out to private homes, but when school reopened in the fall they became part of Edgehill, sharing candy, bicycles, and friendships. After the war, the Rodean account was paid in full and formed the basis of a scholarship fund at Edgehill.

Having weathered the war years, Miss Roechling turned the running of the school over to Miss Barbara Briggs, one of two Rodean mistresses who had come to know Edgehill well. She returned to the school as an old friend but she found the times more difficult to contend with than any during the war. At one stage the teaching staff even took turns getting up early to cook breakfast for the school. A stint as a short-order cook was scarcely what they had bargained for when they had signed on. But a feeling of community and of pulling together has always been part of Edgehill's history. It is an intangible bonding process that has helped the school survive even when it seemed that all the cards in the deck were stacked against it.

As of the fall of 1976, Edgehill amalgamated with King's College School.

St. Mildred's-Lightbourn School

Oakville, Ontario

1891

A third endeavour with Church of England ties began in the same year as Ashbury and Edgehill. This school, however, was not underwritten by prosperous Anglican professional men, but was financed from the proceeds of a second-hand store run by seven impoverished women.

St. Mildred's promoters were seven Sisters of the Church, a religious order established in Chester, England in 1870, whose members have devoted themselves primarily to work with children. Since its founding the order has established nearly a dozen schools in Britain, Australia, and Canada. St. Mildred's, the order's first school outside England, began quietly in downtown Toronto. Before the Canadian enterprise could get under way, however, the seven Sisters had to raise enough capital to pay the rent on a school building. For a time they all lived above a store on York Street, selling used clothing until their accumulated assets reached the point where they were able to afford the rent on a house on D'Arcy Street. Had their venture into the world of commerce been less successful, St. Mildred's might never have been born.

But the school prospered, and they were soon able to move to larger quarters on Beverley Street, into what later became Georgina House, an Anglican girls' school residence. In the early years, both St. Mildred's and the Sisters who ran it were viewed with a certain antipathy, if not outright hostility, by many Toronto Anglicans. To begin with, they were English, a fact that did nothing to enhance their stature in a community that was growing more and more conscious of its distinctive Canadian character and resentful of things British. Bishop Strachan, the officially blessed High Anglican church school for girls, was by now well established, and the Low Church promoters of Havergal College, which opened three years after St. Mildred's, were scarcely delighted by competition from yet another High Church school—and a convent school at that. The Sisters of the Church, however, persevered, with the support of a few devoted families. Apart from their Toronto school they also set up branches in Hamilton and Ottawa, although only the Toronto school managed to survive the exigencies of two wars and a Depression.

By 1908 "fashionable" Toronto had begun expanding northward and when a large home at the corner of Walmer Road and Lowther Avenue was offered for sale it was decided to move uptown. The mother house in England granted its permission to make the purchase, just as today it still ratifies all major decisions by its overseas branches. Here St. Mildred's settled for the next sixty years, and in time it gained the acceptance and grudging respect of its High and Low Church "sisters". At least three future Canadian headmistresses passed through its doors: E. Gordon Waugh, of St. Clement's School, Toronto, Maisie Mac-Sporran of Miss Edgar's and Miss Cramp's School, Montreal, and Gwen Murrell-Wright of Balmoral Hall, Winnipeg.

For quite some time, St. Mildred's was regarded as a school for younger children, and one with a restrictive religious atmosphere. But with the acquisition of a totally separate convent in 1923 and the addition of more lay teachers, several of whom were Canadian, the school took on a slightly different and more Canadian character.

Despite its controlled way of life, a good many children were quite happy there. One former Walmer Road pupil says, "I remember the Greek myths and the small classes. A happy place for a small child—with the exception of the long horrifying hymn we had to memorize, *The Story of the Cross*—with itemized suffering." Another Old Girl of St. Mildred's remembers the Sisters, "in their coarse black serge habits and heavy stockings", as "models of infinite simplicity and self-sacrifice". Even gloves were considered an unnecessary luxury. Instead, on wintery days, their hands remained under their voluminous black cloaks or were thrust into the broad sleeves of their habits.

With the separation of the convent and the school, St. Mildred's acquired its first secular head, and in the late thirties its first Canadian-born headmistress, Sister Anna. The decision of the Sisters to move their convent to Oakville, Ontario, just west of Toronto, in the 1960s had a profound effect on the fate of St. Mildred's. Here they found a new challenge for their mission, taking over a private elementary school in Oakville, Miss Lightbourn's.

While 1923 is the official founding year of the Lightbourn School, it actually began a year or two earlier when Miss Ruth Lightbourn agreed to teach the two daughters of John Guest, the headmaster of nearby Appleby College. The arrangement proved to be such a success that before long she found herself with a burgeoning school set up in one room in her parents' home. As more and more little girls kept appearing, space became a critical problem and a series of moves began, first to a larger house, then, in the Depression years, back to a smaller one, and later to larger quarters once more. Until Ruth Lightbourn's retirement in 1960, when the school became incorporated, the entire undertaking was self-financed—one of the last of its kind.

Not long after the formation of the Lightbourn School's Board of Governors, a permanent site was purchased, and in 1964 the Sisters of the Church were approached with a request to take over the administration of the Oakville school. Somehow, for the next five years they managed to run both the school in Oakville and the school in Toronto. Finally, in 1969, the two schools became one in Oakville. There, the new St. Mildred's-Lightbourn School has been fulfilling the area's need for an independent day school at both the elementary and secondary levels.

Havergal College

Toronto, Ontario

1894

The creation of Havergal Ladies' College was the final feather in the cap of the Ontario Evangelical Anglicans. First had come Wycliffe, a divinity college; then Ridley, a university preparatory school for boys. Havergal, a sister school to Ridley, helped to complete the separation between the High and Low Anglicans in the heart of cultural and cultivated Toronto. Bishop Strachan, the High Church's foremost girls' school, was situated in Toronto, and it is possible that Havergal's founders felt honour-bound to choose that city as the location for their school—just as Ridley's founders had chosen to follow the lead of Trinity College School by establishing a boys' boarding school in the country. Many of Ridley's original investors were also involved in the Havergal enterprise, and it can be safely assumed that those "evangelicals" who were not actually shareholders gave the new ladies' college their full moral support.

Time has helped to smooth the ecumenical divisions within the Anglican Church, and Ridley and Havergal are no longer the evangelical strongholds they once were. But in the beginning even the names of the two schools were interrelated. Havergal was named after Frances Ridley Havergal (1836-1879), a prolific Church of England writer and hymnist, and a Christian gentlewoman to her Victorian fingertips. By happy coincidence she also bore the name Ridley, after her godfather (a descendant of the martyr), which only helped to make the choice more obvious.

If there were any Canadian applicants for the position of first headmistress, the Board must have rejected them out of hand. In the late 1800s there were many English women with more impressive qualifications, willing to emigrate, whose training and experience could only prove invaluable in a new venture such as Havergal. A staff member of the famed Cheltenham Ladies' College, Miss Ellen Knox, was put forward as a woman eminently well suited to Havergal's needs, and in spite of personal doubts and reservations she agreed to accept the post in the spring of 1894. Without the encouragement of her brother, the Anglican Bishop of Coventry, she might never have come. Only his assurance that Canada was a land of golden opportunity on the threshold of unparalleled prosperity and development convinced her to take up the challenge. And Ellen Knox did prove to be an empire builder of sorts. Believing that it was her duty to make Havergal "a vigorous stronghold of learning in our land", she established outposts all over the city: the Rosedale Junior School, Havergal-on-the-Hill on St. Clair Avenue West, and the St. George Street School. To meet local demand, both the Rosedale and the St. George Street schools admitted small boys as well as girls.

Havergal's first home, however, must have presented a sorry aspect to its new headmistress. Morvyn House, at 350 Jarvis Street, had seen better days. The building had already passed through several hands as a school when it was purchased by Havergal's Board of governors from a Miss Lay, who had decided to close up shop. Within four years, however, Ellen Knox had taken a firm hold on the future. Adjacent houses were acquired and connected by "Bridges of Sighs" to the original house, and in these "three peninsulas connected by two isthmuses and an island across the way" there was a perpetual shifting and shunting of classrooms to bedrooms and bedrooms to classrooms. Miss Knox once referred sympathetically to the plight of "poor Wylie Grier", the school's art teacher, who moved his studio in one of these annexes back and forth from basement to attic "until he was justly weary".

The Board soon agreed that a "proper" school must be built as soon as it could be arranged. Land just north of Morvyn House was acquired and a new Havergal arose, a sprawling red brick structure which later became the Toronto headquarters of the Canadian Broadcasting Corporation. Before the school had even moved in, a fire severely damaged the building's roof and top stories, but by Thanksgiving of 1898, in the midst of an unseasonably early blizzard, the new school was officially opened.

A large number of Havergal's earliest boarders came from the United States and there was, as well, a large contingent from the west, mainly Winnipeg. But Miss Knox's teaching staff were preponderantly British, "in order," she said, "to best combine the best features of English and Canadian education". All of the resident staff were either maiden ladies or widows. There was, in addition, a large staff of visiting teachers and specialists of various kinds. Nothing but the finest of everything would do—the best available equipment, an indoor "swimming bath", a gymnasium, and thirteen pianos (often all being played at once), lectures, recitals, debates, botanical expeditions. There was even a Havergal Académie Française complete with pen pals in France.

Havergal's one-time reputation as Canada's answer to the Cheltenham Ladies' College is not altogether unjustified. In Ellen Knox's time alone, no fewer than twelve future Canadian headmistresses came to their posts with Havergal experience behind them: they included Miss Dalton of Havergal College in Winnipeg; Miss Edgar and Miss Cramp of Montreal, Miss Hardy of Trafalgar in Montreal; Miss Virtue of St. Alban's, Prince Albert, Saskatchewan, and founder of Strathallan in Hamilton; Miss Elgood and Mlle. Shopoff, founders of Ovenden at Barrie, Ontario; Miss Cumming of Trafalgar; and Miss Roechling of Edgehill in Windsor, Nova Scotia. These future headmistresses were usually hand-picked and carefully groomed by Miss Knox herself, even to their choice of headgear. For this one's hat a flower—for that one's a feather, or a ribbon, or a rosette. Miss Knox saw to it that her staff maintained an image of good taste and respectability at all times.

During her thirty years as principal Ellen Knox's admonitions and advice to her girls were liberally sprinkled with Cheltenham ideology, and they echoed the duty of public service stressed in so many boys' schools. The girls were "to see the world as a place in which you can use your influence towards bettering the conditions of women workers and neglected children". For a time there was an active working girls' club at Havergal, whose purpose was to provide the girls with an opportunity of meeting young women of the working class, presumably so that they might develop a greater awareness of social problems and societal inequities. Havergal was also the first private school in Canada to set up its own YWCA branch. Ellen Knox's girls were to be prepared "to take a stand for the right" all through their lives. "Turn away from Laura Secord's and creaking shoes," she urged them, coming down hard on chocolates and patent leather as symbols of idle self-indulgence.

It would be an exaggeration to suggest that the silver-haired, ample-bosomed but often fearsome Ellen Knox, who clumped in dignity along the halls of the Jarvis Street building in her men's boots, was universally loved and admired by all who knew her. On the other hand, neither her motives nor her basic kindness could be called into question. The school was her life, her love, and her child. Her death in 1924 came just three years before the completion of still another Havergal, the Lawrence Park School erected on twenty-seven acres of land on north Avenue Road. Though it is now the only Havergal, it pleased her to think that her Havergal empire was still expanding, for as she had claimed many years earlier, "A school which never threw out new life or new buildings would be as dull as ditchwater." Tall (over six feet), dignified Marion Wood, at her right hand almost since the first day, became Ellen Knox's successor. She is said to have been a scholar and a woman of great faith and courage, qualities she would need in full measure during the dark days of the Depression.

The Board had planned to finance the new suburban Havergal by the sale of the Jarvis Street property. But the deal fell through, and the school was left with two substantial properties on its hands all during the Depression years. Both were operated as schools (in order to avoid paying city taxes), but, it was a difficult time at best. Eventually, the Jarvis Street building was rented to the Women's Division of the RCAF, who remained there until the end of World War II, when the property was purchased by the CBC. The story goes that during the renovations undertaken at that time a large cache of chamberpots was unearthed, each bearing the Havergal crest on its lid. One of the architects involved in the renovation, a Ridley Old Boy married to an early Havergalian, took it upon himself to forward several of these "treasures", splendidly wrapped, to his wife's former schoolmates. One gracious acknowledgment came back to him written in elegant script—on a roll of toilet tissue.

When Miss Wood returned to England in 1937, Miss Gladys Millard was appointed to replace her. She saw Havergal through the war years, although it was her helpmate and vice principal, Miss Constance Ellis, who actually held the school together during Miss Millard's latter years when she was in ill health and confined to a wheelchair. In 1952 Havergal acquired its first Canadian-born headmistress, Catherine Steele. An Old Girl and former staff member, "Stainless"—as she was inevitably christened—was well imbued with a sense of Havergal's history and traditions. She was succeeded in 1972 by Mrs. Audrey Southam, and, in 1975, by Miss Mary Dennys, who was also an Old Girl and a staff member of long standing.

Havergal has not, like some other schools, sought outsiders to lead it, nor has it pursued the new educational trends with unqualified zeal. It appears unlikely that its commitment to stability, structure, and disciplined learning will change very radically.

Netherwood

Rothesay, New Brunswick

1894

Within three years of the founding of Edgehill in Nova Scotia, Miss Mary L. Gregory of Fredericton acquired an old gabled house and three-and-a-quarter acres of land, in the picturesque little New Brunswick village of Rothesay, for the site of Netherwood School. Unlike both of the other Nova Scotian Schools, Edgehill and Halifax Ladies' College, Netherwood began as a private venture and continued as such for more than fifty years, even though its idealistic young founder's career as headmistress proved to be very short-lived. A romance with one of the masters at nearby Rothesay Collegiate School saw to that. Within a year of opening Netherwood, Mary Gregory had married and was off to Japan as a missionary. It would not be the last time that the proximity of the girls' and the boys' schools encouraged romance—to the frequent despair of Netherwood's headmistresses.

As luck would have it, Mary Gregory had an aunt, Mrs. Jane Armstrong, who was also trained as a teacher and who agreed to carry on her niece's work. Just two years after Netherwood opened, the village of Rothesay was blessed with yet another school for girls, Kinghurst, whose Board was, by coincidence, almost identical to that of the Rothesay Collegiate School for boys. The presence of another girls' school created unforseen problems for Netherwood, whose financial position was precarious at the best of times. But another romance saved the day. The headmistress of the rival school, Kinghurst, left her post to marry J.F.F. Robertson, benefactor of Rothesay Collegiate School, and Kinghurst promptly folded.

There remained the problem of proximity to the boys' school, although it later became a moral, not a financial, issue. When

Mrs. Armstrong passed Netherwood over in 1905 to its next proprietors, Susan B. Ganong (of the Ganong chocolate family) and Miss Pitcher, she advised them to make every effort "to widen the distance between the two schools as far as possible". This they did, and many years later were able to announce proudly that "for a period of over forty years no girl lived under a cloud while at the school nor left it with any disfavour as she went out of it".

With Netherwood's new management came an increased emphasis on academic excellence in order to prepare more girls for university entrance, usually to Dalhousie or Mount Allison. It was not an easy transition. The headmistress wrote: "We were not very successful with our first Graduating Class [in 1906]. The social whirl and Coming-Out parties seemed to be the great objective and a natural confusion to the restricted years of school life."

During Miss Ganong's and Miss Pitcher's first years at Netherwood they purchased a horse and carriage so that they might refresh themselves each afternoon after classes by taking in the beauties of the countryside. Their first ride was very nearly their last, for the horse they were sold—on the recommendation of the local vicar—was a highly neurotic beast who lept from one side of the road to the other, shook his head violently, and pawed the air. Deciding to eschew all clergymen's advice on the matter of horse-trading, they found another horse of "a more stolid disposition" and could often be seen hauling a whole sleighload of Netherwood girls on winter outings.

One parent, on entrusting her daughter to Miss Ganong's care, was unprepared for the headmistress's youthful appearance. "You look far too young to be managing a school," she announced. "I am leaving my daughter but if she is not happy and I don't approve of your administration I shall remove her at once." Mamma's fears were unwarranted, for Susan B. Ganong knew very well what she was about. To this day grown women, whose formative years were spent in her charge, swear that they can see her face before them if ever they are tempted to tamper with the truth.

The problem of permanent ownership was resolved in 1912 when Miss Ganong bought the Netherwood property from the Armstrong family. Miss Pitcher retired and for the next thirty years Netherwood became Miss Ganong's school. An outdoor camp was acquired, "a place where the stirring multitude would have freedom to wander under conditions of rare charm and beauty". Miss Ganong's eye for beauty was not limited to nature, for every summer she would return from visits to the Continent with new objets d'art for the school—chandeliers, paintings, carvings, and even stained glass windows. . . .

Susan Ganong was without question one of Canada's most remarkable headmistresses. In her patient understanding of individual needs and differences she was decades ahead of her time. She encouraged individual accomplishment rather than competitiveness. "It is surely a mistake to hold up any member of a school as a golden example to others," she believed. "The same standard of excellence cannot be reached by all." She felt that there were two approaches one could take towards the management of young people—one based on discipline, fear and punishment, the other based on confidence and trust. She ran her school on the second of these principles. The school prefects were chosen by both teachers and girls. "The vote of the latter was always considered important," she commented, "since girls know each other in their intimate life far better than the staff, who often feel they know them and sometimes are mistaken."

Miss Ganong's views on bilingualism and biculturalism were, again, enlightened for her time. "If the two races in Canada —each with different backgrounds of training and education —are to have intimate and sympathetic touch with each other, a mutual understanding must be created by an interchange of language and literature." It was her belief that the teaching of French should stress enjoyment and appreciation of the language rather than the memorization of long lists of vocabularies and grammar rules. "When the English of Canada have a knowledge of the French language and literature, such as many French people have of English, many of the natural misconceptions and prejudices will be lost sight of."

When Miss Ganong retired in 1944 the school continued under the auspices of the Netherwood Foundation, a group that included several interested citizens of Rothesay and three local Old Girls. But the day of the small country boarding school was on the wane, and many closed in the years that followed World

War II. By the early 1970s the growing trend towards co-
education in the United States preparatory schools provided an
answer to those seeking ways to survive. An academic amalgamation of the two neighbouring schools, Rothesay and Netherwood, was effected in 1972. Today Netherwood is little more
than a female adjunct of Rothesay. It is a compromise solution,
but it is, perhaps, all that is possible in a world of changing
priorities and financial constraints.

Crofton House School

Vancouver, B.C.

1898

The West's oldest independent school for girls, like any number of other Canadian private schools which sprang up in the next century, began modestly as a private venture undertaking. Most eastern girls' schools had opened as joint stockholding companies with well-established denominational ties; but Crofton House—then "Miss Gordon's School"—opened the year of the Klondike gold rush in the basement room of the Gordon family's home on Georgia Street, with only four pupils. Of the several private venture schools established around the turn of the century in Vancouver and Victoria, Crofton House alone would survive.

As a young girl Miss Jessie Gordon had emigrated with her family from Scotland, making the cross-country journey to Vancouver via the newly constructed CPR line. Once in Vancouver, her father entered into partnership in a pioneer newspaper, the *News Advertiser*. Two years later, when his health began to fail, the family packed up again and returned home. For several years they remained in Britain, but by 1892 with the father's health restored the Gordon family headed west once more, leaving Miss Jessie to continue her studies at Newnham College, Cambridge. Her stay at the Crofton Cottages there was cut short when she received word that the family's fortunes had dwindled to a pittance. She hurried dutifully to their aid. After attending Vancouver High School, which then provided the only teacher-training course in the province, she became a qualified teacher.

At the beginning Miss Gordon's motive in opening her school was simply economic necessity. In time, however, her school acquired its own chaplain and the support of the Anglican

Church, which had previously sponsored a girls' boarding and day school at Yale, B.C., called All Hallow's. All Hallow's had opened in 1885 as an Indian mission school to provide the native girls with an "industrial education". The evident success of the mission school soon resulted in the addition of a "Canadian" school, designed for the daughters of clergymen and well-to-do families. Although the two schools shared the same property, a marked separation was maintained between the "young ladies" and the Indian pupils, who lived totally segregated lives with the exception of their participation in the school chapel choir. "The services were beautiful and inspiring," recalled one graduate, without a hint of irony. "We always had a choir of twelve — Indian girls on the one side with red pinafores and red skull-caps, and the Canadian girls on the other side wearing white veils." After war was declared in 1914, however, the government transferred the mission school to Lytton, B.C., where there was already an Indian boys' school, and All Hallow's closed.

By this time Jessie Gordon's school, now Crofton House, was ready to take up the slack. Emily Carr taught art there for a brief period, taking her pupils sketching in North Vancouver or along the CPR tracks. Sports and games were encouraged as part of the educational process, although cheering was unladylike and was not tolerated. Riding also became popular, and the annual musical rides and displays of horsemanship at the old Horse Show building were a highlight of the year. Gradually Miss Gordon's little school became a city landmark at its new location on the corner of Jervis and Nelson streets in Vancouver's west end.

Miss Jessie managed her school's financial affairs with extra-ordinary acumen; even today Crofton House is one of the few Canadian independent schools that operates without a substantial deficit. But though she may have been frugal, she knew when to be generous. A pupil at the original Miss Gordon's School remembers trundling her lunch to school in a basket and receiving each day, without fail, a cup of cocoa "never equalled in flavour or importance," served to her personally by Miss Gordon or one of her two sisters. Their teaching methods, too, have yet to be improved upon, for it is a rare child who fails to respond to individual attention. Punctuality and good attendance were en-couraged by awarding an alarm clock to the girl whose record was untarnished at the end of each term. Integrity, consideration, and simple good manners were taught as well, both by word and by example. In the Misses Gordons' ambitious new quarters at Jervis and Nelson, with Miss Jessie as headmistress and Miss Mary and Miss Edith as housekeeper and kindergarten mistress, their pupils were still expected to be Ladies, or at least to try to behave as such. The two-by-two boarders' crocodile rarely left the premises without the reminder, "Remember, girls . . . the eyes of all Vancouver are upon you!" At prayers they were often informed, in tones of abject horror, that someone had been seen on the streetcar . . . without gloves!, or that "one of our girls did not stand up for an older person".

Thanks to the Misses Gordon, the school's character was essentially British for many years. "We were trained to think and be as British as possible," recalls one Old Girl, "and I had to keep it a deep dark secret that my father was an American." The day Queen Victoria died Miss Jessie arrived dressed in black from tip to toe and closed the school for the day.

Miss Gordon cherished certain Victorian attitudes towards discipline and morality long after the death of that queen. During the 1920s and thirties, wrongdoers were condemned to "sit on the box", an ominous camphor trunk covered with a faded rose chintz that was strategically located just outside the staff room. Each passing teacher in turn would pause to ask the sinner exactly why she was there, and she in turn would have to hop to her feet and go through the agonies of explanation again and again. At Crofton House, as in most reputable girls' schools, any mail that arrived was opened for inspection before being passed on—especially after a group of Shawnigan Lake School boys sent one of the girls a nude valentine. Miss Gordon's reaction was no doubt as amused as Queen Victoria's would have been, and the incident probably served to strengthen her conviction that censorship was in the girls' best interests.

By the late 1930s, having weathered the worst of the Depression (at one point they were down to eleven boarders), the Gordon sisters came to the painful but inevitable decision that the time had come for them to retire. Crofton House, their labour of love for nearly forty years, would have to be either sold or closed down permanently. If it had not been for the school's twenty-seven-year association with Canon Harold King of St.

Paul's Anglican Church, the school would probably have suffered the fate of most private ventures; but Canon King assembled a Board of Governors who continued the school as a non-profit educational trust. In 1938 Miss Sarah MacDonald, formerly principal at St. Hilda's, Calgary, and a teacher at Edgehill and Branksome Hall, was appointed head of the newly incorporated Crofton House. She was followed five years later by Miss Ellen K. Bryan, a Havergal protégé and a former principal at Trafalgar in Montreal. Miss Bryan's appointment coincided with a move to Crofton House's present site at Forty-first and Blenheim, a spacious ten-acre property. Then in April, 1958, after nearly sixteen years as headmistress, Miss Bryan was taken ill and Muriel Bedford-Jones, a long-time staff member who had also been at Trafalgar, became principal. For the next twelve years she brought to the school her "gentle wisdom, and a warm affection for each and every girl".

Under her vice-principal and successor Rosalind Addison, Crofton House jubilantly celebrated its seventy-fifth birthday in 1973. Crofton House has seen Vancouver grow from a shanty town where some of the sidewalks had to be built on stilts because of the swampy ground, into a sprawling metropolis. Crofton House in turn has grown from a basement schoolroom into what it is today, an institution still dedicated to preserving high educational standards and Christian principles of living.

St. Andrew's College

Aurora, Ontario

1899

The last school to be founded during the era of Christian gentility and joint stock companies was the fourth and final member of Ontario's famed "Little Big Four" schools. Along with Upper Canada College, Trinity College School, and Ridley, St. Andrew's was to become a strong contender in the education of the sons of Canada's Establishment families.

St. Andrew's College made its first home in Rosedale, one of Toronto's most fashionable suburbs. Both Trinity College School and Ridley had elected to become country boarding schools, leaving Upper Canada College as the only real competition in the vicinity. When St. Andrew's opened in Chestnut Park, Rosedale, it could hardly have been considered an inner city school, but it was more centrally and strategically located for prospective day boys than Upper Canada, whose new (1891) Deer Park location was still in open country to the north.

In contrast to Ridley, a most carefully planned creation, St. Andrew's began as an almost haphazard adventure on the part of several prominent men who agreed to become joint stockholders, among them Robert C. Kilgore, Hamilton Cassels, and George Dixon (a former principal of Upper Canada College and an active member of the Board of St. Margaret's, a local girls' school).

At first glance, Chestnut Park seemed an ideal place to launch the school. The former estate of Sir David Macpherson, a very Scottish gentleman, it was surrounded by lawns, gardens, conservatories, fountains, hedges, and ten acres of orchard with winding walks. There were even tennis courts and a ballroom built specially in the 1860s to entertain the Prince of Wales. Sir David's profitable partnership with Sir Casimir Gzowski (an original Ridley backer) had made him enough money in railway construction not only to buy Chestnut Park but to extend and embellish it liberally with the mark of Scotland. In every nook and cranny were carved Gaelic inscriptions and crests, and portraits of Scottish chiefs peered down from the library walls.

No school of Scottish descent could have asked for a finer legacy, yet by the time the SAC stockholders acquired it, Sir David's once-magnificent home had become a semi-mouldering manor. The state of disrepair went almost unnoticed by the day boys. They could return home each night to their comfortable beds, their nannies, and their running water. But for the first SAC boarders, who often had to break through a layer of ice in their washbasins on winter mornings and who climbed into bed armed with hockey sticks to ward off scavenging rats, daily life presented more of a challenge.

Although St. Andrew's College's first home was less than ideal, the calibre of the men who formed its staff assured its instant success. To the delight of the college Governors, most of them Presbyterian, Reverend Dr. George Bruce, an outstanding personality in Canadian Presbyterian circles, was persuaded to leave St. David's, his church in Saint John, New Brunswick, to help organize the school in Toronto and become its first principal. One of the "originals" on the staff was the late Dr. Percy J. Robinson, who remained as classics master at St. Andrew's for nearly fifty years and was a foremost authority on the French period in Canadian history; a truly wonderful gentleman and scholar.

According to Dr. Robinson, the school was not as ready as it might have been to receive its first students. The day before the school opened the staff was confronted with what Dr. Robinson described as "an amazing situation. Beds and bedding had been provided and adequate arrangements for feeding the boys had been made but there had been no provision made for teaching—no desks, blackboards, chalk, schoolbooks, paper, or maps. There were not even any chairs to sit on." With the greatest diplomacy, Dr. Robinson and another master managed to convey their agitation to Dr. Bruce and obtain permission to make the necessary purchases. A whirlwind buying spree ensued which included three dozen kitchen chairs, yards of blackboard cloth, and a farm bell. "In that Scotch-Canadian soil of

Chestnut Park, Scotch Presbyterian St. Andrew's flourished and took root like a thistle in a plowed field—and with lots of prickles," Robinson remembered, "In a surprisingly short time it meant something to be a St. Andrew's boy."

Much of the credit for St. Andrew's early reputation belongs to the school's second headmaster, Reverend Donald Bruce Macdonald, one of Ridley's original prefects. Dr. Bruce's unexpected resignation owing to impaired health before the first year was out placed the Governors of the school in a predicament. The board chairman's son, young Bruce Macdonald—then only twenty-seven—was a graduate of the University of Toronto's Knox College and had just returned from post-graduate theological studies in Edinburgh. In this desperate moment, his father's position as chairman of the board seemed of little consequence. In any case he happened to be away on business at the time, and although on his return he offered his resignation to avoid a possible conflict of interest, it was too late to protest. His son was already installed as the youngest headmaster of any Canadian boys' private school at the time.

"Mac", as he was known both affectionately and respectfully, was an "all-around" man, keenly interested in physical training as well as in scholarship (the Macdonald Medal is still awarded annually by the Old Boys to the SAC boy who distinguishes himself in both fields). For the next thirty-five years, hundreds of boys would bear the distinctive stamp of St. Andrew's College under the influence of this outstanding personality. The autumn following his appointment as headmaster a junior preparatory division was added to SAC with a female teacher for the youngest class (an innovation quickly adopted by several other boys' schools). By September, 1902, the school had expanded into two houses on Roxborough Street and one on Macpherson Avenue, and enrolment had doubled. Dr. Macdonald's selection for the Scripture lesson the first morning of that term was the Third Psalm, "Lord—how are they increased that trouble me! Many are they that rise up against me!" That same year, W. L. "Choppy" Grant joined the SAC staff from Upper Canada College, where he later returned to distinguish himself as its headmaster.

By the fall of 1905 a masterfully designed and "thoroughly modern" new St. Andrew's College with chapel, gymnasium, lockers and dressing rooms was opened in north Rosedale. The year of the move the now familiar kilted cadet corps of the school was formed in affiliation with the 48th Highlanders Regiment. One of the original officers of the corps was Vincent Massey, later the first Canadian-born Governor-General of Canada.

In 1911 St. Andrew's, like many other private schools, was dissolved as a joint stock company and incorporated as a non-profit educational trust. Its later benefactors included such famous names as Sir Joseph Flavelle, Lady Eaton, and Colonel Sam McLaughlin. After World War I, as at Pickering College, the school buildings were offered to the government to provide much-needed hospital accommodations for convalescing servicemen. The school moved for a time to Knox Theological College, but by 1920 it had returned to its north Rosedale location. There it remained until its move in 1926 to the town of Aurora, twenty miles to the north. In Aurora St. Andrew's became an exclusively residential school, and its new rural setting became a selling point in the school prospectus. Certainly its vast playing fields and handsome Georgian brick buildings, valued at over three million dollars, created an imposing effect. Dr. Macdonald, however, insisted on maintaining the same close contact with his boys that he had encouraged in the city. His own house adjoined the senior boys' residence so that the boys could come and go as they pleased, making use of his extensive personal library.

K.G.B. "The Crow" Ketchum, who had served as acting head since 1933, succeeded Dr. Macdonald in 1935, just two years after his brother Philip Ketchum had been appointed headmaster of Trinity College School in Port Hope. He acquired his nickname by virtue of his high, beaked nose and flapping black gown. For the next twenty-five years, except for a leave of absence during World War II when he served as Director of Studies at the Royal Canadian Naval College, Ken Ketchum remained in command. A master of quippery, he knew his boys often better than they knew themselves.

In 1958 Kenneth Ketchum was replaced as headmaster by J. R. Coulter, a well-known football coach. In 1974, after sixteen years as head, Dr. Coulter was succeeded by Thomas A. Hockin. One strength of the school is undoubtedly the extraordinary continuity provided by these men, for the current headmaster is only the fifth in the school's seventy-five year history.

The Rise of
The Private Venture School
1900-1950

Overleaf: Selwyn House School, Montreal, P.Q.

I N the new century the provision of a Christian education and the building of character continued to be the central theme of private education in Canada. But as the years advanced, the churches assumed less and less of that responsibility and their direct influence declined. The nineteenth century had seen a proliferation of church-based schools, but only a token few of the schools established after 1900 had well-advertised ties with any specific denomination. Organized denominationalism was giving way to personalized ideologies. At the same time, schools promoted by joint stockholding companies began to become the exception rather than the rule. Most of the newer and younger private schools were funded almost entirely by the men and women who ran them—usually with the help of friends, relations, and bank managers. These extraordinarily dedicated people often had tenures that ran into decades. Not uncommonly, they did not relinquish their control to a Board of Governors until faced with retirement, when they began to feel the need of ensuring the continuation of the school after their deaths. When such provisions were not made, the school was apt to expire along with its founder, although in a few cases dying schools were rescued by dedicated alumni. As the creation and life work of one or two individuals, the private venture schools were impressed with the stamp of their founders.

One reason for the growing reluctance of the churches to extend themselves directly into education was, of course, because education had come to be regarded as the duty of the state. Yet while the public school elementary system was well established by the turn of the century, the early growth of the public high school was slow, and in means, ends, and student population it differed little, at first, from its private counterpart. The principle of the free high school was a product of the Victorian age, an extension of the nineteenth-century belief in society's duty to promote the natural aristocracy of talent. The high school was intended to train gifted youngsters for the professions or for leading roles in the business world. In fact, however, social background still determined the level of education attained by most children, and secondary education was available only to a tiny minority. In 1873 only one-half of one per cent of the entire popularion of Ontario were attending high school. It was not until after World War II that most Canadian children could look forward to a high school education.

In the interim, the nature of public education changed dramatically. As Canadian society became increasingly urbanized and industrialized, the public schools were called upon to prepare children for their future roles as skilled or white-collar workers. The formalistic, academic Victorian curriculum was gradually abandoned for more practical studies designed to prepare the work force of the next generation. Manual and vocational training were introduced in the town and city high schools; agriculture was taught in the rural schools; and, for girls, "domestic science" became ubiquitous in private as well as public schools. Public secondary education had become mass-oriented.

The private schools on the whole were far slower in curriculum innovation. Well into the twentieth century many continued to offer the formalistic, classical studies far more appropriate to nineteenth- or even eighteenth-century ideas about the education and training of the bourgeois Christian gentleman. Yet as the public high schools gradually became egalitarian and job-oriented, the private schools found new support from those seeking the values and the intimacy of a traditional, liberal education. As public schools developed into huge, state-run bureaucracies, many well-to-do, well-educated parents began to view them with mistrust and dismay, and looked to the private school not only for an ostensibly better education, but for a more personal approach to the education of the child.

Between the years 1900 and 1950 the newly founded girls' schools continued to outnumber those established for boys by almost two to one. However, they were quite different from the church-sponsored Ladies' Colleges of the nineteenth century. Almost without exception they were brought into existence through the efforts of strong-minded and determined women who were not at all enthralled with the prospect of being at the beck and call of a male Board of Governors. On the other hand, only a few of these women undertook the creation of their schools single-handedly. Women founders and headmistresses tended to come in pairs or triplets, and in one instance a multitude of six. Conversely, only one or two boys' schools were under joint administration. Most headmaster-founders apparently preferred to shoulder the burden of responsibility alone.

Male or female, many of these people established their schools because they were dissatisfied with the quality of available public education. They were convinced that unfulfilled needs—moral as well as scholastic—could best be met independently and individually. That many of them, and the teachers they hired, were uncertified by provincial authorities was perhaps incidental. Official certification did not necessarily ensure either competence or dedication, and furthermore, uncertified teachers were cheaper. The salary structure of most private schools was notoriously low. Job security and opportunities for advancement were almost non-existent. Whether they liked it or not, headmasters and headmistresses often had to take on staff who had come to them out of sheer desperation. Dedication and devotion to the school might—and often did—follow, but a significant number of teachers accepted their positions not as a lifetime vocation but quite simply as a stopgap measure. Because teachers in private schools received lower wages, it might be assumed that the quality of their work was bound to be inferior. Perhaps it was, yet it would be impossible to make any accurate assessment in retrospect. In all probability it ran the gamut from exceptional brilliance to glaring incompetence. There were tyrants and milquetoasts, spell-binders and drones, just as there are today in any school, any province, any country.

There is no question, however, that because of the lower salaries and because there was no necessity to be certified, the private schools did attract more than their share of teachers from the British Isles. Those who arrived expecting to find colonial replicas of British public schools were often in for a rather rude awakening. While it is true that most private schools established in Canada before 1900 were patterned and cut from British cloth, in the new century these same schools, and the new private venture schools, grew increasingly Canadian in character, retaining only a few tattered remnants of nineteenth-century British tradition to remind them of their origins and heritage. Although well over half of all the Canadian private schools were both started and staffed by British-born and trained teachers, they found that the new land demanded new ways. Those who were flexible and open-minded soon adapted, but more than a few beat a hasty retreat—often before their contracts had expired. As an added inducement to prospective teachers from Britain, several girls' boarding schools offered free return passage. Before long, however, they began to stipulate that the teacher remain for at least two years to be eligible for the return portion of the fare. Many of those who chose to stay on became permanent fixtures in their schools, and for some the School became the centre of the universe.

In the Canadian landscape many of these expatriate Britons found both a challenge and an inspiration. The new Boy Scout troops and Girl Guide companies were actively promoted in many private schools, not so much because of their British origin or basic Christian tenets, but because they were geared to out-of-doors activities. Stalking, tracking, hiking with maps and compass, fire-building and camping out were all ideally suited to the Canadian environment. It was not long before a number of people recognized the potential of the great outdoors beyond the realm of scouting and guiding. Several schools founded summer camps, particularly in Ontario and Quebec, and there were, in addition, a substantial number of private camps owned, operated and staffed almost entirely by private school personnel. For certain children the growing-up years soon became one long and predictable cycle of packing and unpacking from boarding school to camp and from camp back to school again, with a few weeks at home sandwiched somewhere in between. Is it any wonder that some of these privileged children felt happier and more secure at school or at camp than they did at home?

As Canadian cities mushroomed and expanded from suburb to suburb, the country boarding school concept began to lose some of its earlier appeal. Slowly but surely, urban schools began dominating the scene. After 1900, for every school established in a small town or country setting, two or three opened in a city. Several of the new city schools were non-residential, but many of them welcomed boarders; and in the years prior to and including World War I it was not uncommon for six- and seven-year-olds to be sent into boarding, often in the child's own home city. Thus the inconvenience of transporting the child was avoided, leaving the parents unencumbered but secure in the knowledge that their "darling" was being well cared for, well disciplined

—perhaps even well educated. The child's own feelings about this arrangement were generally considered immaterial. It was not a child-centred age. If the child was happy—so much the better; if not, the experience would help build character.

By the late 1940s the boarding schools began to go into a rapid and irreversible decline. Not the least of the reasons for their disappearance was the considerable change that had come about in people's notions of child-rearing. The end of World War II, not unnaturally, brought a renewed emphasis on the importance of family life. Father was home from the war, Mother's services were no longer required at the canteen or the Red Cross every day, and the proponents of familial togetherness were heard throughout the land. And children were now distinctive members of the family unit, each an individual with his own unique set of abilities, needs, and wants. Not only had the boarding school outlived its usefulness, the very notion of the boarding school had taken on a hint of moral repellence.

At the same time, the public schools preparing for the onslaught of the post-war baby boom, managed to lure away substantial numbers of private school staff with offers of higher salaries, superannuation benefits, and pension plans. In a system which was expanding at an unprecedented rate, there was the additional "carrot" of promotion and increased earning power, to say nothing of job security. It is surprising only that the private schools did not lose more teachers than they did to the state system. Staff benefits of any sort were still completely out of the question at most private schools; the money was simply not available. To say that the financial rewards of a teaching career in an independent school were insubstantial would be an understatement. They were, simply, nothing short of a disgrace. The boarding schools in particular, with their after-school programs and evening and weekend supervisory chores, were demanding far more of their teachers and paying far less than local boards of education. Teachers prepared to devote their lives to a school for the mere satisfaction of shaping young minds were no longer in abundance.

The smaller schools especially had enormous difficulty attracting well-qualified new staff to replace those who had retired or defected—a difficulty which, in some cases, was ultimately insurmountable. The staffing problem was only compounded by outdated and ill-equipped premises, dilapidated buildings, worn furniture, faded drapes, threadbare carpets—the kind of creeping shabbiness that goes unnoticed by the people who see it every day, but that is all too apparent to the rest of the world. In wartime "making do" had been a first cousin to patriotism. In peacetime it quickly lost its charm.

By 1950 the situation had become grave enough to inspire the Headmasters' Association, then consisting of eighteen schools, and then as now wary of self-promotion, to put out a small directory which it hoped would serve as a guide and an induce-ment to parents with school-age sons. In most instances the text for each school was provided by its headmaster, and reflected the widely divergent personalities and philosophies of several memorable characters: Pickering College's Joe McCulley; the Ketchum brothers, Philip of Trinity College School and Ken ("The Crow") of St. Andrew's; Vancouver's Johnny Harker, the only headmaster without a degree; Shawnigan Lake's ex-milkman C. W. Lonsdale, and Lakefield's "Windy" Smith. Only two of the eighteen headmasters were ordained clergymen, a fact that further reflected the church's waning influence. The concerns that prompted the Canadian headmasters to issue their directory were shared by their female counterparts. But the girls' schools were less concerted in addressing themselves to the problems at hand, and on the whole have been less amenable to rapid change. They are more inclined to hold fast to the old ways, whose worth has been well proven, than to try new methods or approaches toward the kinds of problems that never seem to change. In all but a few instances Canadian headmistres-ses have proven themselves more conservative, more set in their ways, and more tradition-bound than their male counterparts. That conservatism, added to the girls' schools' less generous or nonexistent endowments, led to a high post-war mortality rate.

And what of the post-war generation of students, growing up in the shadow of A-bombs and H-bombs and bomb shelters at the bottom of the garden? When the War Guests departed, they found life to have changed very little. A private school graduate of around 1950 sums up the attitudes of the era:

> Sure, we were concerned about what was happening in the world—the possibility of being blown to smithereens in a nuclear attack seemed very real and pretty frightening if

you stopped long enough to think about it. And I suppose most of us did, at some point or another, but—let's face it—we were a lot more concerned about little ordinary everyday problems like what to wear to the Battalion Ball or how you were going to talk your parents into letting you have a breakfast party afterwards ... and whether you really wanted to go steady after only three dates with Bob ... even if your secret passion was already pinned to somebody else and had never given you so much as a sideways glance. For us that was the "real" world. In fact, the part of our lives spent in school was just a neccessary evil, something we just had to make the best of because-—God knows—we couldn't change it.

If the notion of changing the system had not yet dawned on the students of 1950, neither was any fundamental change in the private school philosophy envisioned by the people who led and taught in them. True, they had lost ground dramatically. Some, like St. John's-Ravenscourt, and later Balmoral Hall had to amalgamate to stay afloat. Those that had survived two wars and a depression faced an even grimmer future, especially those with small enrolments, the country boarding schools, and the private venture schools whose founders were reluctant to relinquish control. But despite their financial straits and declining enrolments, the private schools had not yet begun to re-evaluate their role in Canadian education. Co-education, "child-centred" learning, unstructured classes, and broadened curriculums were hardly gleams on the horizon. Those debates still lay many years into the future.

Hillfield-Strathallan College

Hamilton, Ontario

1901

In 1962 Hamilton's Hillfield College for boys and Strathallan, a neighbouring girls' school amalgamated to become Canada's first "coordinate" independent school. It was a new concept, in which each school would share a common campus but retain its own identity. Today the schools are a single co-educational entity, a response perhaps to financial and administrative stresses as well as to the increasing demand of students everywhere for integration of the sexes.

Hillfield College dates back through two previous schools, several generations, and many moves to the early years of the century. The original Hillfield was an outgrowth of a school called Highfield that opened under the sponsorship of several prominent Ontario citizens, including the Lieutenant-Governor Sir John Hendrie. Highfield's first headmaster, John H. Collinson, had already taught at other Canadian boys' schools, and had gained a reputation as an outstanding teacher of higher mathematics at Upper Canada College.

There he had also begun a lifelong friendship with his fellow master Stephen Leacock. It must be assumed that Mr. Collinson was blessed with that essential headmaster's prerequisite, a sense of humour. The story goes that once when the two friends were journeying by train to Montreal Leacock decided to break the tedium of the trip by ringing the porter's bell beside Collinson's berth. Protesting total innocence each time the porter appeared, Leacock persisted with his prank until poor Collinson was put off the train, while the real culprit rolled merrily along.

When the new school opened it was known for a short time as Ontario School, but its name was soon changed to Highfield. By

1910 it had already become a school of some stature. Its vast Gothic mansion, with several acres of lawns, gardens, and woods was the perfect home for the small boarding and day school "in the best British tradition". Each year the school magazine chronicled the events of the cricket, hockey, and football seasons, and there were also several patrols of "Baden-Powell Boy Scouts" at Hillfield who received their orders, by mail, directly from the Chief Scout himself. The school cadet corps became an affiliate of the Royal Hamilton Light Infantry and for a time close to half of Highfield's graduates continued on to the Royal Military College in Kingston.

In 1918 fire swept through the school's upper story. The building was sold and Mr. Collinson returned to England, placing the management of the school in the hands of its assistant head, Reverend Cecil A. Heaven. In 1920 Highfield was converted to Hillcrest, a day school for boys in a new location. As Hillcrest, it enjoyed modest success until 1928, when a group of Highfield Old Boys and Hillcrest backers formed a joint board to incorporate the new Hillfield College. No sooner were plans for their new country day school under way, however, when the stock market crashed, leaving the new Board with a substantial property donated by one of its members and very little else. Fortunately, the man chosen as Hillfield's first headmaster was equal to the challenge. Like his predecessor John Collinson, Arthur Killip had also come out from England to teach at Upper Canada College, and had spent a good many years on its staff before accepting the Hillfield post. When the position was first offered to him, he had been reluctant to accept, partly because his ideas and the architect's plans for the new school building were incompatible. Eventually he was persuaded to draw up his own master plan which was approved by the Hillfield Governors. For the next twenty-one years he directed Hillfield's course with wisdom and wit. His successor, Colonel John Page, another Upper Canada Old Boy, took over the reins in 1950 and became, in turn, the first headmaster of Hillfield in its new cooperative venture with Strathallan School in 1962.

Established privately in 1923 by Miss Janet Virtue and Miss Eileen Fitzgerald as an elementary school for girls, Strathallan soon expanded to include the upper grades. For the better part of the twenties, Hamilton parents were placed in the enviable position of entrusting their daughters to Strathallan's Miss Virtue while their sons were being guided along the paths of righteousness by Reverend Heaven, the headmaster at Hillcrest. Between Heaven and Virtue it is hard to imagine any child falling from grace.

At Strathallan, Miss Virtue and Miss Fitzgerald aspired to instill "self-reliance, independence of thought, consideration of other . . . the appreciation of real values in life and a true conception of the Divine". Their partnership worked well. Although it was very like any number of Canadian girls' schools in its basic orientation, Strathallan reflected clearly the distinctive personalities of its two proprietresses. Miss Fitzgerald is well remembered by Strathallan's Old Girls for her theatrical bent. Play upon play was produced in the Little Theatre, a converted barn at the back of the school. The event of the year, however, was the annual school play, held either at the Conservatory or at McMaster University. Latecomers, left to cool their heels till the first curtain, soon learned that when the meticulous Miss Fitzgerald was in command performances began precisely on time. When asked why she spent so much time embroidering one small ornament for a costume—something which could scarcely be seen from a distance—she replied, "But I shall see it!" Her keen blue eyes missed nothing, whether on the stage or in the classroom. Miss Virtue, her Scottish partner and a former member of Havergal College's staff, was a taskmistress of a different sort. Her job was to set the standards and cope with the administration of the school. Miss Virtue with her stern exterior and tender heart, and Miss Fitzgerald, "always bright, shining, pleasant and smiling", but hard as ice if she had to be, constituted an effective team.

In 1931, Strathallan became a non-profit corporation. Finally, in 1948, the school's silver anniversary, Miss Virtue and Miss Fitzgerald retired to a house just across the street from the two old homes in which their school was located. It would be neither out of sight nor out of mind.

By 1960 the Governors of both Hillfield and Strathallan had begun discussing the idea of a joint operation. Although both schools were prospering, it looked as if the future could be made even more secure with some coordination and cooperation. By 1962 a joint board of thirty-seven Governors had acquired a fifty-acre site on Hamilton Mountain, and a year later both schools had settled into their new site. For several years the original coordinate concept was maintained. Then, little by little, to the chagrin of some board members, staff, and former students of both schools, the schools began to integrate. In 1969 a new headmaster, Barry Wansbrough, son of V.C. Wansbrough (a former headmaster of Lower Canada College), was appointed to administer the two colleges as one "co-educational and up-to-date academic institution" that included a Montessori primary program inherited from Hillfield. Today the future of Hamilton's only "independent alternative" seems more promising than ever before. Socially and economically its students are no longer all cut from the same cloth. It is a welcome diversity. As Hillfield's former headmaster Arthur Killip said recently, "the only criterion of elitism which is not acceptable is one based on class or money rather than brains. The time has come . . . to get away from the idea of privilege." At Hillfield-Strathallan, the reality appears to be approaching that ideal.

St. Clement's School

Toronto, Ontario

1901

Like most people who believe in independent education, the co-founders of St. Clement's School, Canon Thomas Wesley Powell, the rector of St. Clement's Anglican Church, and Mrs. Constance Waugh, were committed to the ideal that a sound education and Christian principles should go hand in hand. The superficiality of the religious instruction doled out in the public schools concerned Canon Powell deeply, as did the marked absence of what he liked to call "joy" in education. In his own school he was determined to supply both needs.

When St. Clement's School first opened its doors in the barn-like parish hall of the little brick church, the village of Eglinton was little more than fruit orchards and farm houses. A rather unpredictable radial tramway connected it to Toronto proper and in the springtime children sailed paper boats in the ditch which ran along the west side of Yonge Street. That first term there were five or six pupils, ranging from a five-year-old to a young fellow of twenty-one who had never learned to read or write. But under the tutelage of Mrs. Waugh and Canon Powell, both inspiring and brilliant teachers, it was not long before several graduates from the little school's three bare classrooms had been awarded university scholarships.

Word of the school spread rapidly, and by 1909 the older boys had moved to a new location on Blythwood Road to form St. Clement's College, under Canon Powell's direction. After Canon Powell's departure to become president of the University of King's College, however, St. Clement's College was reorganized as a boys' boarding school and moved to Brampton, Ontario. Without Canon Powell's dynamic leadership it was less successful and within ten years had closed for good.

Mrs. Waugh, in the meantime, had kept the younger boys and all the girls with her at the parish hall. By 1917, when her daughter Effie Gordon stepped in, the original school had also begun to falter. It would not falter again. E. Gordon Waugh's name and the name of her school were to become respected well beyond the confines of North Toronto. A graduate of the University of Toronto, with an M.A. from King's College in Nova Scotia, she had inherited all her mother's intelligence and determination. Her students soon discovered that behind a rather severe countenance there lurked a magnificent sense of humour. It never failed her, even when in later years crippling arthritis took her from one cane, to two, to a wheelchair.

Within five years of taking over her mother's school, E. Gordon Waugh had St. Clement's firmly back on its feet, having mortgaged her soul and her life insurance to purchase Number 21 St. Clement's Avenue, a white stucco farmhouse just a block from the parish hall, and the site of the present school. By the early thirties, there was no longer enough space for active and energetic young boys, and so Miss Waugh and her ever-present assistant Alma Conway, in a reversal of the usual procedure, decided that the boys would have to go.

As the years passed E. Gordon Waugh remained a remarkably impressive personality. More than one parent was made to squirm uncomfortably during her end-of-year speeches as she took them to task for hypocrisy or double standards. She never hesitated to press home her point, even if it meant treading on a few toes.

To Miss Waugh, smoking was among the cardinal sins. Her disapproval of this "revolting" habit was well known. One memorable morning she announced that three of "her girls" had been seen smoking in their school uniforms *in public*, and she commanded the guilty to present themselves after prayers at her tiny office by the school's front entrance. But she had not specified *which* three culprits had been spotted, with the result that anyone who had ever smoked in uniform felt honour-bound to confess. Instead of three girls waiting outside her office she was confronted with close to thirty, most of whom felt so sorry about letting her down that the entire front hall was soon awash with tears. Even the police were not exempt from her loathing of tobacco. Once her permission was requested to use the school building at night as a police stake-out. She was pleased to lend the police her cooperation until one of the officers inquired where he might find an ashtray, a request that jeopardized the entire operation.

Between Miss Waugh's retirement in 1960 and the formation of a corporation in 1966 the fate of St. Clement's hung in the balance. Through the years she had sloughed off all suggestions that she relinquish ownership and place her school into the hands of a Board of Governors. Rather than see the school close, Miss Margaret Thompson, a former student and staff member even assumed ownership when Miss Waugh's immediate successor left to be married. But costs were rising at an alarming rate and St. Clement's—private and unendowed—was among the first to feel the pinch. In the spring of 1966, notices sent home with the girls announced that St. Clement's would not be re-opening the following September. The announcement produced immediate action by a group of concerned parents, who established the St. Clement's Foundation and began campaigning vigorously for funds. The Old Girls responded, and gradually the future took on a brighter aspect. Perhaps the unusual harmony which has existed between the Board and the school since then can be attributed to the fact that the Board was formed to save the school rather than to create it.

Soon after incorporation the old building was replaced, ending the days of mixed aromas in the cafeteria, where the smell of gym shoes mingled with that of freshly backed oatmeal cookies. Aside from the building itself, however, very little that is important has changed at St. Clement's School. There is still no stigma attached to being very bright, but on the other hand there is no trace of intellectual snobbery, or, for that matter, snobbery of any kind. The warm and friendly spirit of this unpretentious little day school, as well as its reputation for academic excellence, have remained basically unchanged and unchallenged for seventy-five years.

Branksome Hall

Toronto, Ontario

1903

St. Andrew's College for boys was in its infancy when Branksome Hall, a school for girls which was to acquire an equally Scottish tone, opened in an old estate on Bloor Street East. Fear of competition appears to have had no bearing on the choice of location, for Moulton Ladies' College, a Baptist stronghold of long standing, was situated just one block to the west. Miss Margaret Scott and her friend and associate Miss Florence Merrick, Branksome's founders, shared the determination of several other remarkable headmistresses of this era to operate their new school in their own way, without the help or the hindrance of a Board of Governors.

Margaret Scott's many years of experience with a variety of school administrations perhaps contributed to her penchant for autonomy. Her teaching career had begun at the Institute for the Blind in Brantford, Ontario. Next had come the Ottawa Ladies' College, a Presbyterian school of some distinction at the time. Here she served as principal for several years before going to Toronto to take over the administration of the Girls' Model School for teacher training. In her seventeen years as principal of the Model School she acquired a host of loyal supporters and admirers. In the light of such a varied and extensive career, it is hardly surprising that she embarked upon her final educational venture, the creation of Branksome Hall, with very little trepidation. Nor was her confidence misplaced. Former staff, daughters, and even a few granddaughters of former pupils flocked to her school.

Like Canon Thomas Powell and Mrs. Constance Waugh, who had opened their little St. Clement's School just two years earlier,

Miss Scott's foremost objective was to instill Christian principles into education. A thorough study and knowledge of the Scriptures remains a cornerstone of Branksome education to this day, although it has admittedly lost much of its original impact. Some of Branksome's more reluctant Christians remember spending countless hours committing Scripture passages to memory, and heaven help the hapless souls who were unable to recite chapter and verse when called upon. The open Bible at the centre of the Branksome Hall crest could scarcely be improved upon as a symbol of the founder's dedication to the word of God.

Another of Margaret Scott's interests that has endured was the Ramabai Mission in India. Mukti ("The home of salvation"), a school for child-bride widows and orphaned children, was first opened in 1896 at the instigation of a young Indian widow, Pandita Ramabai. Her world-wide appeal for funds eventually brought her to North America, where Margaret Scott was among the first to respond, thereby establishing another Branksome tradition.

The death in 1909 of Florence Merrick, Miss Scott's close associate and confidante, had a devastating effect on the aging headmistress. It soon became painfully obvious that if Branksome was to be kept on the rails its direction would have to be given over to a younger woman, someone with ambition and drive. In 1910, just such a woman purchased Branksome's assets from Margaret Scott, who then retired as Honorary Principal. Until her death in 1921, she maintained a voluminous correspondence with her Old Girls, along with a continuing interest in the school's welfare.

Dr. Edith MacGregor Read, the daughter of a Halifax physician, arrived at Branksome in 1906, fresh from the staff of Netherwood in New Brunswick. She was to lead the school for nearly fifty years and would become something of a legend among Canadian headmistresses. But no sooner had Edith Read taken on her new responsibility than she was faced with a dilemma. The Bloor Street house that had been leased to Miss Scott was sold over her head and she was forced to find new quarters or close the school. As luck had it, a house which is now part of the Selby Hotel on Sherbourne Street was available for rent and conveniently close to the old school. She leased it but immediately set her sights on finding something more permanent. She found a stately Rosedale mansion just north of Bloor Street, and in 1912 Number 10 Elm Avenue became Branksome Hall's permanent address.

For Miss Read it was just the beginning. Havergal's Ellen Knox may have been an empire builder, but Miss Read's talent for finance and real estate was second to none. Before she had finished, Branksome's assets included close to a dozen buildings and nearly thirteen acres of land, including a large ravine lot. It is rumoured that she was once offered a million dollars for this particular property, but turned it down flat, with a crisp "It is not for sale. It is Branksome. It is priceless!"

By that time, however, Miss Read was not technically in a position to sell anything, having long since reorganized her school as an educational trust. But there is no doubt that if she had wanted to sell the land, or anything else, her decision would not have been questioned for a moment. The Board knew that Miss Read knew best. It was a fact that had been made abundantly clear from the day of the first meeting of the Board in 1920, when the newly appointed directors arrived at the school fully prepared to offer counsel, encouragement, and practical suggestions. Instead they were served up a cup of tea and a biscuit, informed of Miss Read's plans for the school and its future in a brusque and businesslike manner, and then politely but promptly shown to the front door.

Many years later when the school property was sliced in half by a downtown expressway route, Miss Read's forceful personality was felt as far as City Hall. Shortly after Branksome's gray-haired but sprightly headmistress stepped into the early morning traffic wearing a bright red coat and brandishing a homemade stop sign, signal lights were installed at the Branksome intersection. Several years later, a petition to construct an overpass at this same intersection passed through City Council with barely a murmur of protest.

For many years the Branksome property also included a farm north of Toronto called Clansdale Heights. Both boarders and day girls spent many happy hours skiing there until, following a series of fires, it was sold in the late 1950s. Rebuilding was not considered worthwhile; money was short and, with the advent of ski-tows, cross-country skiing was temporarily out of fashion.

Although Branksome Hall acquired its Scottish heritage through Margaret Scott, it was Edith Read, a Nova Scotian, who cultivated and nurtured it. In 1931, a system of clans was introduced and three years later she shepherded a group of Branksome girls through England and Scotland to visit and compete in games with several girls' schools. The Stewart tartan, however, was not adopted as part of the official school uniform until 1940, a memorable year for Branksome Hall in other respects as well. Miss Margaret Sime, Branksome's headmistress from 1968 to 1974, vividly recalls the arrival of forty-four schoolgirl evacuees from the Sherborne School in England.

> The girls with the three mistresses who were accompanying them were in mid-Atlantic when Britain cut off the export of sterling. It came as a terrific shock as they had planned to set up their own branch school on arrival. Naturally, we took them in as a temporary measure until some other arrangements could be made for them. As it turned out, there weren't any other arrangements to be made. In the end, Miss Read went to her friendly trust company and said "I will have a house for a dollar a year" and so they gave her 40 Maple Avenue. The three Sherborne staff members joined our staff and the girls came to our classes. Of course, they came in their own uniforms at first, but it wasn't long before they were bursting to get into ours. They remained at the school until after the war and it was a very very happy experience for everyone.

The close bond between Sherborne School and Branksome Hall and the ensuing exchange scholarship scheme have continued since 1945.

In the meantime, Branksome's no-nonsense headmistress was on her way to becoming a living legend. For close to fifty years, Edith Read continued to preach the gospel against educational faddism and frills, while keeping rules and regulations to a reasonable minimum. Although Dr. Read herself was no mean scholar, holding honour degrees in mathematics from Radcliffe, she insisted that scholarship must never be rated above fair play, diligence and honesty. "It is the students and staff who put the heart, the character and the spirit into any school," she declared shortly before her retirement in 1958.

Now under the direction of Allison Roach, an Old Girl,

Branksome's present enrolment of nearly 700 includes a number of boys to the third grade. It is not, however, a radical departure in philosophy, but is merely an extension of Branksome Hall's pioneer co-educational pre-school program which was set up more than twenty-five years ago. While other schools have faltered or failed, Branksome Hall's spirit and character have been carried on from generation to generation. The affection and loyalty of its Old Girls are as real as the half moons ground into the stair treads of Number 10 Elm Avenue.

St. Michael's-University School

Victoria, B.C.

1906

As its hyphenated name suggests, St. Michael's-University School is another product of amalgamation, a merger of Victoria's two oldest existing boys' schools in the spring of 1971. It is not widely known, however, that University School, the older of the two by four years, was itself the product of an earlier union of three privately owned schools, two in Victoria and a third in Vancouver. All three were owned and operated by British gentlemen with a common interest in the education of boys.

The initial merger took place in 1906 between the two Victoria schools, Reverend W. W. Bolton's St. Paul's Junior School in Esquimault, and James C. Barnacle's University School, so named because it was designed to prepare boys for entrance to a provincial university which did not yet exist. Reverend William Washington ("God") Bolton, described as a "hardy Cambridge man", was a champion swimmer, runner and boxer; articulate and benign-looking, "but not quite as benign as he looked". James Clark Barnacle was a vigorous and rugged north country Englishman, a graduate of London University, and "every inch the schoolmaster and disciplinarian". The third member of the founding trio, Captain Robert Valentine Harvey, joined the others a year later. He was a British army man, and like the others was a hearty outdoorsman and hiker who camped out for weeks at a time during school holidays, in addition to being one of the first enthusiasts of the new Scouting for Boys movement in Canada.

Plans for uniting under one roof were not finalized until 1908, when the premier of British Columbia, the Honourable R. Mac-Bride, laid the cornerstone of the new University School on a site near Mount Tolmie overlooking the city of Victoria. By the following winter seventy-four boys were ready to move in, including a few day boys who, for want of more dependable transportation, commuted on horseback. The local press hailed the new school as "a place where a boy can receive instruction that cannot be found in books—that comes from the personal interest of the instructors in each individual boy". Reverend Bolton ("The Warden"), an eloquent speaker on any occasion, predicted that the school would soon become "the supremely great boarding school of the West". A visit from an aging but still impressive Lord Strathcona the following autumn helped to enhance the growing prestige of the new University School yet further. Officially, all three men were joint headmasters, but unofficially it was Mr. Barnacle—the decision maker—who was the commanding presence in the eyes of the boys.

In its splendid new buildings, under its trio of administrators, the new University School grew in stature and size (with the exception of its first gymnasium which, according to Reverend Bolton's meticulous daily record, lasted one week before the roof fell in). With the onset of the World War I, Captain Harvey left with his regiment for overseas duty and died in a German prisoner-of-war hospital. The news of his death was received with a deep sense of personal loss at the University School. Ironically, all three founders died far from their school in Victoria: Mr. Barnacle in the Barbados, where he retired in the early twenties, and Reverend Bolton in the South Seas, where he had chosen to live out his last fifteen years alone.

For one brief year—1921—it was decided that the University School would become a military college. Everything would be done by bugle. The boys would wear uniforms at all times, either khakis or their best "blues", and passes would be issued for those wishing to go into town on "leave". With pacifism sweeping the country, the plan was bound to be a dismal failure. The University School's bugles and uniforms were soon set aside for cadet corps use only. In 1970, during the course of a second anti-militaristic era the school cadet corps, then affiliated with the Canadian Scottish regiment, The Princess Marys, was disbanded altogether.

The years following Mr. Barnacle's departure were difficult ones as a succession of headmasters came and went. In 1925 a

$100,000 bond issue was floated to private shareholders for renovations, a swimming pool, and a separate headmaster's residence (known ever since as "the Palace"). But it was not until after 1935 that the University School was restored to stability with the appointment of Reverend George Herbert Scarret, a British schoolmaster's son and a "Barnacle man" who had joined the staff in 1919. As headmaster he fashioned himself in the same mould as Barnacle. He was a ramrod and unrelenting disciplinarian. To the University School boys who failed to perceive his noble intentions, he was "Judas Iscariot". As a schoolmaster he carried his rigid morality into the classroom, and eventually sought ordination as a Church of England clergyman. From 1919 to 1948, when he died suddenly, G. H. Scarret's impact on University School was equalled only by that of its original founders.

Some time before Scarret's death, in order to reduce the school's debt, it became incorporated as a non-profit organization. This incorporation was revised in 1971 to include another of Victoria's schools, St. Michael's Preparatory School.

St. Michael's was the life-work and labour of love of Kyrle C. Symons, his wife Edith, and subsequently their two sons, Ned and Kyrle. The founder's charmingly personal account of the history of St. Michael's School, *That Amazing Institution*, is recommended reading for anyone who believes that private venture schools were started only for financial gain. Begun on less than a shoestring as a single-room school built onto the family home, within a decade St. Michael's had grown into a sizable school of four classrooms and a gymnasium. Although the following years brought several more additions, by 1958 the inadequacies of both the buildings and the property had made it impossible to continue the school as it was. In the midst of the school's annual Christmas concert seven civic officials, including the police chief, arrived with the tidings that the building had been condemned. St. Michael's had only eight months to rebuild or move.

Early in 1959 a partial solution was found by incorporating the school as a non-profit society, and within months two-thirds of the $120,000 needed for new property and buildings was raised through private donations. By the autumn, St. Michael's was settled in its new Victoria Avenue home. As the preparatory school division (grades three through seven) of the newly incorporated St. Michael's-University School, it has remained at this location. The amalgamated school is today the only boys' independent school offering secondary education in Victoria. A quarter of its students are boarders, many of them from Hong Kong.

Probably the most recent innovation at SMU is its "cooperative" liaison with Norfolk House Girls' School in the higher grades. However, the many traditions of both St. Michael's and University School will not be cast aside without careful deliberation. As the handbook for new boys states: "[School tradition] is a very personal and private thing. Others who don't belong to your school can't have it. . . . A steady gentle pruning of the old traditions is essential, yet it is with the pruning hook that we work, not with the axe. Speak up for your new ideas, by all means, but do not shout and rave. Listen to the old ways. There is good in each."

St. Margaret's School

Victoria, B.C.

1908

The oldest remaining girls' school on Vancouver Island opened
in the four-year interval between the founding of the new University School and Kyrle Symons' St. Michael's. It was not, however, the first attempt at female education in Victoria. Fifty years
earlier a ladies' school had been undertaken by the sisters of
Reverend E. Cridge, colonial chaplain to the Hudson's Bay
Company. Their task was to educate the daughters of company
officials, and, for that matter, the daughters of anyone else who
could afford the $200 fee. Several other ventures flourished and
faded before the turn of the century, notably the Mt. St. Angela
Seminary, another of Victoria's pioneer schools for girls. St.
Margaret's itself began with the arrival in Victoria of two young
English women, Miss Isobel Fenwick and Miss Margaret Barton,
who had struck up a friendship several years earlier while at
finishing school in Germany. Having seen Canada coast to coast,
the friends had to decide whether to move on to the Orient or to
pause on the Island to catch their breath. Miss Barton, the more
restless of the two, was for moving on while her friend, Isobel
Fenwick, seemed more inclined to remain in Victoria. In the end
Victoria's charms were greater than Margaret Barton's persuasive powers. Her journal reads,

> Early in 1908, Isobel went to teach in Mrs. Blaicklock's Little
> School and a few girls came to me for private lessons. . . . A
> few months later I went to Japan hoping Isobel would
> follow, but instead she took on my three little girls. Very
> soon these three were joined by so many others that Isobel
> was very glad when her sister Edith came out to help her.
> Edith had been living in Cheltenham with Lady
> Baden-Powel. . . . From the little house on Fort Street,

Edith and Isobel moved to a small house on Cook and then rented a larger one on the same street. Here St. Margaret's School was born and I joined my friends in November, 1909.

Within a year there were forty pupils and three mistresses were added to the staff, but then tragedy struck. Miss Barton's journal continues:

> At Easter, 1911, we decided to spend the vacation on Salt Spring [Island]. We set off early on April 10th for Sidney and boarded the little steamer "Iroquois" which plied between Sidney and the Gulf Islands. The weather was very stormy and soon after the Iroquois left Sidney the cargo shifted and the boat foundered. In the disastrous wreck of the Iroquois both of our dear Misses Fenwick drowned.... During the wreck Isobel and I were put in a little lifeboat and before it swamped and overturned, Isobel was handing her lifebelt to a poor woman near her.

Miss Barton, one of the only survivors of the tragedy, was washed up on a beach more dead than alive. Alone and bereaved, she must have been sorely tempted to give up everything and return to England. Instead she chose to remain in Victoria and carry on St. Margaret's, so newly begun, as a memorial to her friends and the dream they had shared. By September, 1912, a new school for boarders and day girls (many of them from the state of Washington) was ready for occupancy at the corner of Fern and Fort Streets.

The years following the outbreak of World War I were not easy ones. The number of pupils, 150 at its pre-war peak, decreased rapidly; staff had to be let go and grades combined. But in the off-hours, Girl Guides and Brownies and work in the school vegetable garden kept everyone cheerful. On weekends there were tally-ho's to the Esquimalt Lagoon or to Cordova Beach where whole afternoons were spent "chasing crabs and getting sand in the sandwiches". There were other diversions: "hoofing it" to Gorge Park or Mount Tolmie and, of course, the cricket matches against the boys of St. Michael's School.

Then in 1924, just at the close of the school year, the upper two stories of the main building were demolished by fire while the girls were at a farewell banquet in town. It was a disheartening blow. A few years later Miss Barton sailed back to England, retaining her ownership but leaving St. Margaret's in the care of a new headmistress. That same year, St. Margaret's joined forces with St. George's, a rival girls' school that was also privately owned, on the understanding that the name St. Margaret's would be retained. The 1928 amalgamation of the two schools helped to ensure their survival through the Depression and the war that followed. In the mid-thirties, Miss Barton, who still retained ownership, briefly came out of retirement in England to run the school for two years. Persuaded that the school's future would be more assured if it were to become an educational trust, she incorporated it in 1938.

By the late 1960s the school buildings, erected over fifty years before, were finally past saving. After much deliberation an attractive site was chosen on the outskirts of Victoria, and by 1970 the school had moved into its new home on Lucas Avenue. The low buildings set among the tall fir trees must have seemed a world apart from the St. Margaret's of Fern and Fort. The move was both a necessity and a form of insurance for the future. Any independent school ignores the future only at its peril; for there is no guarantee that what was once an asset will not one day become a liability. That attitude is as true of well-loved traditions as it is of buildings. Survival demands many sorts of adaptability.

The prefects of King's College School, 1904.

The Boy Scouts of University School, *ca.* 1912.

Prize Day at Appleby College, *ca.* 1912. Sir Edmund Walker makes a presentation to a pigeon-toed Raymond Massey.

Three generations at a Prize Day during the early 1920s.

The young ladies of St. Margaret's in their crocodile promenade past the Empress Hotel in Victoria.

Domestic Science in the 1920s.

Chapel—an integral part of life at any independent school.
(This one is at Bishop Strachan.)

The boys in the band. Rothesay Collegiate School, before World War I.

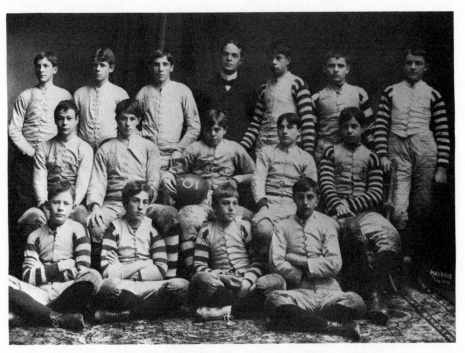

The fourth football team. Upper Canada College, 1901.

The baseball team. Rothesay Collegiate School.

The gymnastics team. King's College School, 1920s.

Swedish drill at Crofton House.

The basketball team. Halifax Ladies' College, 1902.

Havergal girls with snowshoes.

Bishop's College School cadet corps, around World War I.

King's College School cadet corps officers and men, 1920s.

Shawnigan Lake's first cadets.

A grand reunion at an Old Boys' picnic. Bishop's College School during the 1890s (?).

The Old Girls of St. Margaret's hold a children's tea party in the 1920s.

Above and opposite: Independent young school ladies of two centuries.

Red River Academy-St. John's, Winnipeg, 1850.

The castle that became a college. Ontario Ladies' College, Whitby, Ontario, 1870s.

Upper Canada College, Toronto, Ontario. Drawing by H.G. Kettle, the art master, dated 1936.

Appleby College, Oakville, Ontario.

St. Michael's-University School, Victoria, B.C. Drawing by Edward Goodall.

The chapel of King's College School, Windsor, Nova Scotia.

Trafalgar School, Montreal, ca. 1900.

The dining hall at Trinity College School, Port Hope, Ontario.

Selwyn House School

Montreal, Quebec

1908

By the time Selwyn House was founded in Montreal, the city's two solitudes were already well established. Several other Montreal private schools also date to this same period of WASP entrenchment. Miss Edgar's and Miss Cramp's, The Study, and Weston School were all founded between 1900 and 1920. Whether or not their founders shared any unity of purpose, every one of these schools bears the stamp of the determined individualists who created them.

In the case of Selwyn House, however, the influence of its founder was of short duration. Algernon Lucas, a graduate of Selwyn College, Cambridge, devoted only four years to the establishment of his school in Montreal before going into retirement. Had he not been fortunate enough to find someone willing to take over his school, it would have followed the all-too-familiar pattern of closing before it had barely begun. By coincidence, the school's new owner and headmaster, C. C. MacAulay, was also a graduate of Selwyn College. From its original quarters on Mackay Street he moved the school to a neighbouring house on Sherbrooke that would accommodate his increasing numbers of students. When a staff member, Geoffrey H. Wanstall, bought Selwyn House from MacAulay in 1929 the prospects appeared excellent. Strangely, the stock market crash had little or no immediate effect on enrolment, and in 1930 another move was under way to a house on Redpath Street. But as the thirties advanced, like most privately owned schools Selwyn House was put to the test. Although it survived, Geoffrey Wanstall's death in 1945 once again created a situation which seemed likely to end the school. The ownership had fallen to his heirs, all of whom lived in England and none of whom were in a position to take on the management of their unexpected and most likely unwelcome bequest. This time, some of the school's Old Boys and friends committed themselves to saving the school, forming a non-profit corporation to operate it.

In the past thirty years Selwyn House has grown to a school of over 400 day boys. Its few boarders have long since departed. Moving on has become something of a habit, and in 1961 the school moved once again to the large grey stone building which had once been the home of the old Westmount High School. Much of the credit for Selwyn House's expansion and success belongs to R. A. (Bob) Speirs, a long-time master at Lower Canada College, who accepted the invitation to take on the headship of the rival school. More than twenty-five years elapsed before the school's board had to worry about making a new appointment, and they found it difficult to locate a man of Speirs' calibre to replace him. Private schools may encounter little difficulty in filling such a vacancy, for the position carries enough prestige to make it attractive to any number of qualified people. But if the choice is not the right one, as many schools have learned to their sorrow, it can take years to undo the damage. Alexis Troubetzkoy, the present headmaster, came to Selwyn House from the staff of Appleby College in Ontario. Under his guidance there is every indication that Selwyn House will continue to provide some lively competition to Lower Canada College in the Montreal area, while maintaining its hard-won standards of academic excellence.

Lower Canada College

Montreal, Quebec

1909

Unlike Upper Canada College in Toronto, which pre-dates Confederation, Lower Canada College in Quebec did not come into being—at least by that name—until long after the province had ceased to be known as Lower Canada. But although its official date of founding is 1909 its story begins in 1861, when its predecessor, St. John's School, was established. St. John's School was originally a choir school, an adjunct to the Church of St. John the Evangelist in Montreal. England had a long tradition of choir schools, such as the Westminster Abbey Choir School and those attached to colleges at Cambridge and Oxford. A similar arrangement in Montreal would at once provide ready-made recruits for the St. John's Church choir and supply an educational need within the English-speaking community. The one flaw was that the author of the plan, Father Edmund Wood, was first and foremost a churchman, and though his desire to ensure the best possible education for the boys in his charge cannot be questioned, the work of his church always had precedence.

Father Wood had emigrated from England in order to care for his widowed mother and two sisters, who had come over several years earlier. When he arrived in Montreal, however, he found his less than helpless mother conducting a small school for girls and apparently managing very well on her own. It may be that her interest in education influenced her son's decision to start his own school in conjunction with his work as the curate of St. John's. When his school first opened, classes were held in the Wood's house on Aylmer Street. Within a few years "Wood's School", as it was then known, had expanded and changed location several times to accommodate an ever-increasing number of pupils. Father Wood ran the school for eighteen years before Father Arthur French assumed control, leaving Father Wood to devote all his time to his church.

A fatherless boy, Father French had come to the school as its first boarder, or houseboy, as they were called in those days. Like Father Wood, his interest lay first and foremost with his parish. During a smallpox epidemic in the city it is claimed that Father French was the only clergyman willing to take the risk of accompanying caskets to the graveside for burial services. Morally stern about others' principles as well as his own, his persistent admonitions from the pulpit about Montreal's "Ladies of the Evening" and "The Demon Drink" resulted in the enforcement of stricter laws, although they brought reminders from prominent local citizens that such matters were really above and beyond his responsibilities as a clergyman.

In the first decades of the school the teaching was done on an irregular basis by assorted clergy. The academic program was designed to prepare boys for university or for the Royal Military College at Kingston. As a concession to the business world there were extra courses in shorthand and typing. Gradually other activities were introduced. In the summer there was a choir camp at Sorel. The cadet corps, which had enjoyed an ingloriously brief existence during the time of the Fenian raids in the 1860s and then been disbanded, was revived under Father French. But the school's future fell into doubt with the church's appointment of a successor to Father French who, alas, lacked the moral rectitude of his predecessors. Under the headship of this particular curate, the headmaster's rooms became the site of champagne parties after Sunday evening Vespers, and echoed with the clinking of glasses and perhaps even toasts to the church and the school that were footing the bill.

With the arrival from England of the six-foot three-inch Charles S. Fosbery, however, the moral tone of the school was much improved. From the moment he assumed joint responsibilities as headmaster of the school and organist and choirmaster for the church, it was plain that Charles ("Fuzzie") Fosbery intended to be The Boss, a name by which he is affectionately remembered to this day by generations of St. John's and Lower Canada College Old Boys. The Honourable Brooke Claxton recalls his first meeting with The Boss as a New Boy at the school in the fall of 1905. "I gained a terror of him which was modified into admiration, respect, friendship and love, but even to the day when thirty years later I was Chairman of the Board and he retired as Headmaster, there was still an element of that terror left. For Dr. Fosbery was not only terrific; he was a bit terrifying."

Fosbery was not the sort of man to be satisfied with the classrooms he found divided into sections by curtains and other such makeshift arrangements. He revived the cadet corps once again, this time with great success, although the drills were sometimes hilarious—if The Boss wasn't there to keep order. In war time, however, former cadets went on to serve with distinction in battle, among them General E.L.M. Burns, later the first commander of the United Nations Emergency Force.

Before The Boss's arrival games had been voluntary, but they now became an integral and compulsory part of the school's program. Dr. Fosbery was convinced that nothing built school spirit more effectively or more quickly than games. In fact it was the sale of the property that St. John's had been using as a playing field, coupled with the undesirable number of taverns and brothels in the neighborhood, that precipitated a move to a new location, and the beginnings of Lower Canada College.

The site Dr. Fosbery chose was on Royal Avenue in the west end of the city, well out of harm's way. It was also well away from the Church of St. John. The limitations of running a school in close association with the church had undoubtedly become onerous and Dr. Fosbery deliberately set out to continue the school independently in a new location. Throughout negotiations with the church Dr. Fosbery had made a point of maintaining good relations, keeping the church and Father Wood fully informed of his plans. It must have come as a painful shock to him to discover that he did not have their enthusiastic support. A number of churchmen, including Father Wood himself, opposed the move and declared their intention to continue the school in connection with the church. This, of course, left Dr. Fosbery's new school disowned and nameless. It was the boys themselves who selected the school's new name, Lower Canada College.

Although the church and the school were later reconciled, relations were strained for many years. The church's attempt to keep the old St. John's School going came to nothing, perhaps because Father Wood died soon after Lower Canada College had opened. A bust of Father Wood was offered to Lower Canada College after his death, but Dr. Fosbery, still smarting from old wounds, adamantly refused to display it (it now has a prominent place in the dining hall).

Lower Canada College was successful from the start, although the building itself would never win any architectural prizes. At best it could be called functional. The first time he tried to find it, V. C. Wansbrough, a teacher at the school and later Dr. Fosbery's successor, mistook it for a factory and got lost in the woods beyond. But though the building might have been called painfully practical, the accent was traditional. Games, good sportsmanship, and scholarship were stressed, possibly at times in that order. Every able-bodied boy was required to participate in team sports, an experience that was meant to reinforce the high standards of manners, conduct and personal integrity demanded both in and out of the classroom. The school was utterly dominated by the personality of The Boss, who was so involved in its operation that he even kept the books and stoked the fires on weekends. He also enforced his own small idiosyncrasies. He especially abominated belts, as a substitute for braces, and umbrellas. The sight of a boy carrying an umbrella was enough to send him into a positive frenzy. So effective was his anti-umbrella campaign that years later grown men—normal in every other way—would rather be thoroughly drenched than be seen carrying a "bumber-shoot".

The Boss always presided over the morning Scripture lesson, and frequently took a regular class. If a boy could not answer one of his questions he would pass on to the next in order, going down the lines of seats from right to left like an auctioneer—"Nex', nex', nex"—and then, if no one could come up with the right answer, he would bellow in triumph, "All 'round, nobody knows!"

His own life was spartan. His bedroom was on the main dormitory floor, and was furnished with an iron cot, varnished dresser, table and chair, and a plain unshielded light hanging on a wire from the centre of the ceiling. There was not even a carpet on the floor, and the heat was kept low. It was good for the health, and economical to boot.

As the years passed, Charles Fosbery began thinking about

the perpetuation of his school. His solution was as simple as it was sensible—he decided to give Lower Canada College lock, stock, and barrel to its Old Boys. Without a word of warning he announced his intentions at an Old Boys' dinner in the fall of 1920. The Old Boys' Association was then in its infancy, having been formed in the post-war years by those who felt a debt not just to the school but to Dr. Fosbery personally. His letters and parcels overseas had not been forgotten.

At a garden party in June of 1935 the school made its farewell to Dr. Fosbery. The day was marked by special games and by speeches and tributes, including a letter from Prime Minister R. B. Bennett promising to recommend Dr. Fosbery for an O.B.E. Fosbery returned to England, where he married a former matron of the school. Characteristically, he had proposed to her by cable from mid-Atlantic on his way home. Shortly after the war the Old Boys invited Dr. and Mrs. Fosbery out to Canada for a visit. After the Old Boys' dinner held in his honour The Boss took off his jacket and greeted 300 of his former students individually, recalling all their names. *Time* magazine wrote,

> Without endowment, Lower Canada has combined a few features of the English Public School (but not the fag system) with distinctly Canadian traits. It is formal without being stuffy; strict without being severe. For all this the grateful boys give the credit to Fuzzy. Asked how he liked being back, he replied: "I'm having a perfectly tip top time, my dear fellow—perfectly tip top!

With Fosbery's retirement Lower Canada College entered a new era. The building was renovated, the property enlarged, a pension plan for the masters was introduced, and women teachers were engaged for the primary grades, although this latter proposal met with the usual resistance from some of the Old Boys on the Board. Hugh Maclennan taught there for a time, writing *Barometer Rising* at night. The school flourished under Fosbery's two distinguished successors, V. C. Wansbrough and Stephen Penton, who weathered the recurrent problems of outmoded buildings, periodic drops in enrolment, and lack of funds. The second decade of Dr. Penton's headship was one of more construction and expansion. The boarding school was discontinued and converted to classrooms. Academically, too, the school improved and broadened its curriculum.

Shortly before his retirement in 1968 Dr. Penton was awarded the Order of Scholastic Merit by the Quebec Ministry of Education, the first headmaster of an independent school to receive such an honour. His distinguished service to education has been widely recognized.

Through the years, first at St. John's School and later at Lower Canada College, men of rare dedication have brought the school a national reputation. Still known for its emphasis on sports and more recently for its undeniable academic superiority, Lower Canada College is today among the most prestigious of Canada's independent day schools for boys.

Miss Edgar's and Miss Cramp's School

Montreal, Quebec

1909

All attempts to update the name of Miss Edgar's and Miss Cramp's School have failed dismally, even though anyone hearing the name for the first time is likely to find it amusing and quaint, especially by comparison with the stately and often sainted names which have been bestowed on most Canadian schools for girls—names with the ring of substance if not divine blessing.

By the time Miss Maude Caroline Edgar and Miss Mary Cramp set about establishing their school they had developed some very strong views on exactly how a school should and should not be run, though not everyone who subsequently taught under them found herself in total agreement with either their methods or their priorities. The idea of starting their own school probably originated in Toronto, where both had been teaching at Havergal College under the legendary Ellen Knox. Their backgrounds were quite different. Miss Edgar's was an old Ontario family and she had attended Bishop Strachan in Toronto; Miss Cramp had grown up in England. In other ways, however, the two found that they had much in common, especially in their ideas about education. After tendering their resignations they first went to New York, where Miss Cramp took a job at Miss Spence's School while Miss Edgar studied current theories of education. A year later they returned to Canada to open their school in a large house with an acre of garden at 507 Guy Street in Montreal. With Trafalgar as their only competition they did well, and within a few years their school had acquired a reputation which extended at least as far west as Toronto. The daughters of many fine old Ontario families were packed off to Miss Edgar's to become educated young ladies of refinement and culture. By the thirties Miss Edgar's, as the name was usually abbreviated, had become a permanent fixture in Montreal.

With twenty years behind them, the co-principals decided to commit some of their annual words of wisdom to print. Their addresses to young girls, entitled *Eternal Youth*, are the essence and embodiment of Miss Edgar's and Miss Cramp's philosophy. A few excerpts can provide only a pale imitation of what it must have been like to sit in one's finest frilly white frock listening to these graduation speeches. "The problems of youth," according to Miss Edgar and Miss Cramp, "with superficial variations due to time, place and circumstance, remain ever essentially the same." The problems they referred to were almost assuredly such vices as lack of diligence, neatness, punctuality, and discipline. From their own experiences they had stumbled upon another eternal truth known to wise headmistresses: "Girls know far more of girls than we teachers can ever know—both good and bad."

As for work, "Work, productive work, is the panacea of all ills." "Only one thing are you bound to do—to accomplish as perfectly as you can the work assigned to you." "Approach your work with system and order." The matter of parental influence also received a few words. "The difference between one child and another in school is not so much a difference in capacity as in home environment and in all the interests that have been stimulated in the little mind, before the child comes to school."

But above all others the role of women in society was the favourite topic. "Professions are now open to women, or rather the door is slightly ajar. But it still requires much courage and determination to face the opposition which exists in many places." "What we want today is women of independent tastes, independent thought and independent action." "Every day the world is casting off its artificialities and insincerities and every year—for your consolation—men are looking for more in their wives. . . . To follow a profession is rapidly ceasing to be equated with spinsterhood."

And finally, "What you are is of far greater value to the world than what you know." "There is scope for individuality in the most trifling affairs of life." "Education that forgets to add mental training, love of truth, beauty and humanity is like a farmer who clears and plows his land but pays no attention to the quality of his soil."

The respect that Miss Edgar and Miss Cramp comanded was not confined to the young. Staff and parents were equally impressed by their bearing, and the story goes that at official gatherings all the other headmistresses would rise when Miss Edgar entered the room.

To meet the demands of changing times the school was eventually incorporated, but like Branksome Hall's Edith Read, the founders were accustomed to absolute autonomy and they chose their Governors with care. Interference would not be brooked and advice need only be given when it was sought. When at last they stepped down after thirty-one years, their choice for a successor was a Canadian from within their own ranks. Miss Maisie MacSporran was to change things very little, and she was to remain almost as long—twenty-five years.

Like The Study and Weston School which followed, Miss Edgar's has had its share of moves and physical changes. The 1971 prospectus drew attention to the school's handsome new building in Westmount. The move to Westmount meant the end of Miss Edgar's as a boarding school because of a local bylaw, but the transition was nonetheless a practical one, since more than half the students lived in Westmount anyway. The internal changes have been even greater. A few years ago the headship of Miss Edgar's was undertaken by a man, a radical enough idea in its own right. An American import, he brought with him many of the innovative ideas that were being implemented at the time in both public and private schools; ideas based on curriculum relevance and the importance of "self-experimentation" and interpersonal relationships. Perhaps Miss Cramp would have approved of the change; after all, she once wrote: "The problem [of education] seems to be forever the same and yet it is forever different, for the substance upon which it works, though always plastic, is forever changing, and new forms emerge under the same old instruments." But the Board of the school was less sure that the changes constituted progress, and after a brief two-year tenure the headmaster was replaced by a woman of more traditional orientation. The problem reflects a very common situation in many independent schools, trapped between the ways of the past and the fashionable (some would say faddish) progressivism that has swept education in the last ten years. Their attempts to reconcile the two are often uneasy.

Appleby College

Oakville, Ontario

1911

Of Ontario's successful independent schools for boys, only a few were established after 1900. Among them was Appleby College, one of many private venture schools but one of the few to survive.

John F. H. "Gimper" Guest, the young Cambridge graduate who was Appleby's founder and first headmaster, had already gained some valuable experience as the first headmaster of Upper Canada College's preparatory Lower School. Upper Canada's Prep has acquired a reputation as the foremost school of its kind, but in Guest's view it was not without its disadvantages. The ideal school, he believed, should be strictly residential and set in open country—isolated and insulated from the more distracting aspects of city life, yet at the same time accessible to cultural advantages. The school he envisaged would be "founded in the tradition of the Old Land—rich in heritage and experience but adaptable to the needs of a new country and the ways of Canadian boys."

Headmasters with dreams of this sort rarely have fathers-in-law who share their enthusiasm, let alone the capital to turn castles in the air into schools with buildings and grounds. In this respect, John Guest was inordinately fortunate. His wife's father was Sir Edmund Walker, a man keenly interested in every aspect of education as well as a wide range of other philanthropic activity. Sir Edmund Walker's interests outside his career as a financier and banker embraced paleontology and geology, art, music, and Canadian history. He was the first chairman of the Royal Ontario Museum, chancellor of the University of Toronto, chairman of the Conservatory of Music, of the Art Gallery of Toronto and of the National Gallery, president of the Royal Canadian Institute and the Mendelssohn Choir, and also a founder of the Champlain Society.

Two years before the college opened Sir Edmund purchased an extensive piece of property in Oakville on the lakeshore, midway between Toronto and Hamilton. It was a place magnificently suited to its future purpose, and, by coincidence the land had been granted originally to a family named Appleby. (This was not discovered, however, until well after Guest had decided on the name of Appleby for reasons of his own, naming it after the ancient grammar school at Appleby Magna in Leicestershire, England, where his ancestors had been educated for generations.)

Appleby School (it did not become Appleby College until after its incorporation in 1918) opened in September, 1911, with twenty-eight boarders. By the end of the second year the number had doubled and in less than twenty years had reached 120 students. During the thirties the original policy of maintaining a strictly residential school was modified to compensate for the shortage of boarders. While the founders envisaged Appleby as a country boarding school in the British tradition, the Hamilton-Toronto urban sprawl has considerably altered the school's position. The demand for independent day schools has never been greater, but even today Appleby insists that every boy in grades eleven through thirteen be a resident student.

Administrative continuity has been one of Appleby's major strengths. Guest stayed with his school for twenty-three years until 1934, and Reverend John A. M. "Rusty" Bell, who took over after the sudden death of Guest's successor, remained headmaster for thirty-one years (1937-1968).

As enrolment increased, and with it the need for expansion and modernization, residences, classroom blocks, gymnasiums and dining halls have all had to be added. In order to compete with the larger and more affluent schools close by, Appleby's facilities—and its academic standards—have had to be comparable or better. An indication of its sensitivity to fresh ideas is the school's Environmental Studies program on Lake Temagami. The first program of its kind in Ontario, it was launched in 1974 under the direction of Winton Noble. The program offers a mandatory one-month off-campus wilderness experience in

grade ten. It is a concept with endless possibilities for experimentation and the development of a whole range of new
skills and attitudes. The success of the project may well influence
the future direction of both public and private education in the
field of wilderness survival training.

Norfolk House

Victoria, B.C.

1913

Victoria's Norfolk House School opened on the eve of World War I, five years after St. Margaret's. A group of women, including the wife of the Anglican Bishop of Victoria, had been growing impatient with the poor educational facilities in the city's Oak Bay area. Taking the matter into their own hands, they decided to import a teacher from England. At Bishop Doull's request, Miss Julia McDermott left her post at Norwich High School (one of the earliest day schools for girls in England) and was joined in Victoria the following year by a former colleague at Norwich, Miss Dora Atkins. Together they decided on the name Norfolk House School, using the same initials as those of their beloved Norwich High School. Just when things had begun to take hold, Miss McDermott left to be married, leaving the school in Miss Atkins' capable hands. Dora Atkins, described as a quiet scholar whose "limpid and lisping voice belied a steel fist in a velvet glove", saw Norfolk House through nearly forty more years of moving, money-raising, and making do in lean years.

Just after World War I Norfolk House began accepting boarders, mainly the daughters of China Families—merchants and missionaries posted in the Orient—and the school grew to include a separate residence for the boarders. In 1928 there arrived an extraordinary addition to Norfolk House in the person of Mrs. Ivy Cheetham, the school's mainstay and assistant headmistress for the next twenty-nine years.

The fates had not dealt kindly with Ivy Cheetham, either in her native England or in post-war Victoria, where she had arrived penniless with a small son in tow. The former actress first turned her hand to teaching "up island" at Strathcona Lodge

School, and from there moved on to St. George's in Victoria, and finally, after the amalgamation of St. George's and St. Margaret's, to Norfolk House and Miss Atkins. She was like a whirlwind, striding up and down the hockey field, lashing out with her favourite epithet, "Cabbage Head!" She always wore a viyella dress, cut in the same pattern, and always had at least one dog at her heels. (If anything exceeded her fondness for tea and the stage, it was her fondness for animals.)

In the early 1930s Norfolk House became a limited company with stockholders and moved from Granite Street to its present site, a new beamed and stuccoed classroom building on Bank Street. Stubbornly, Miss Atkins and Mrs. Cheetham maintained the boarding residence together under increasingly difficult conditions. At last, in 1952, they were persuaded to close the residence and upper school and continue Norfolk House as a junior school only. Soon the choice would have to be made: either Norfolk House would die a quiet and dignified death, or it would have to be incorporated as a non-profit society under a Board of Governors with old traditions and a new headmistress. The latter course was chosen and in 1956 Miss Winifred Scott, an Old Girl of Miss Ganong's Netherwood in New Brunswick, and former head of Miss Matthew's School in London, Ontario, was invited to become Norfolk House's headmistress. In accepting the post, she also became the only Canadian-born headmistress in the entire province. With Norfolk House once more reinstated as a senior school, Winifred Scott has skillfully managed to blend the best of the old with the constantly shifting patterns of the new.

Elmwood School

Rockcliffe Park, Ottawa, Ontario

1915

Once Ashbury College had established itself in Rockcliffe Park in 1910, the need for a junior preparatory school in the Ottawa area quickly became apparent. Since at that time Ashbury confined itself to the education of older boys only, the Rockcliffe Preparatory School, as it was then known, at first included girls as well as small boys. Before it became a girls' school its young pupils included geophysicist, J. Tuzo Wilson.

When Mrs. Hamlet S. Philpot opened her little school in Rockcliffe Park she had four eager pupils all under the age of ten. The school's first home was a rambling old timber and stucco homestead surrounded by fields and the tall elm trees which eventually gave the school its name. The property also bordered on a large marsh, which became a prime breeding ground for mosquitoes in the spring. The school's closing ceremonies were invariably punctuated by loud whacks and swats as the captive audience fended off swarms of unwelcome visitors.

Elmwood's early years could scarcely be termed uneventful. Its first year was marked by a fire that broke out in the school kitchen. Within minutes a rescue squad composed of boys from the nearby Ashbury had arrived on the scene, dashed upstairs, and dumped the contents of Mrs. Philpot's drawers out the window. Fortunately, the fire was brought under control before the boys succeeded in disposing of Mrs. Philpot's entire wardrobe.

Within two years Mrs. Philpot's school acquired a substantial red barn which was moved to the site and later joined to the original house. But although the future of her little school looked promising, Mrs. Philpot decided to return to England when her health began to fail. She sold the school in 1919 to two well-to-do Ottawa women, Mrs. Harry Southam and Mrs. Edward Fauquier along with the Honourable Thomas Ahearn. They, in turn, appointed another Englishwoman, Mrs. Clement H. Buck, as headmistress in 1920, and with Mrs. Buck's arrival the present Elmwood School took shape. By 1922 it had become incorporated under the patronage of Her Royal Highness Princess Alice. Among the impressive array of co-patrons were the Duchess of Devonshire, the Lady Byng of Vimy, the Lady Tweedsmuir, the Countess of Willingdon, and the Countess of Bessborough.

These illustrious names, however, did not guarantee aristocratic premises. When a teacher's foot went right through the floorboards of her classroom, it became clear that something had to be done before anything truly disastrous occurred. The old barn was replaced and its loss mourned by girls, who had grown fond of dropping pencils through the enormous cracks and holes in the floor on unsuspecting heads beneath. Soon the original homestead too was torn down. The present school building, also beamed and stuccoed, was erected in 1925, largely through the generosity of the Honourable Thomas Ahearn, pioneer of the electric streetcar and one of Elmwood's chief benefactors. It is certain that Elmwood's singularly generous and supportive benefactors made all the difference between success and failure for the school. For many years Mrs. Southam, Mrs. Fauquier and later, Senator Cairine Wilson, all Old Girls, formed the backbone of Elmwood's Board of Governors.

Mrs. Buck was of one accord with the philosophy of her predecessor, Mrs. Philpot, who in spite of a badly constructed and ill-equipped building had implanted many worthwhile traditions. Under Mrs. Buck "the spirit of Service, Fellowship, Freedom and Fair Play" was emphasized. To her, it seemed that a school should be a place where children, like the daffodil, the school emblem, might "grow in merry companies and open spaces—joyous, strong, companionable and free".

Joyous companionship was certainly what Elmwood meant to the girls of Mrs. Buck's day—especially those in boarding. There were never more than forty and family feeling was very strong, even during endless waits for the single telephone set aside for their use. To Rockcliffe dwellers Mrs. Buck became a familiar sight enthroned duchess-style in the back seat of her car, with her husband at the wheel. Elmwood has, in fact, been unique in its succession of married headmistresses and in the unusual number of women on its Board of Governors.

When Mrs. Buck retired and returned to England in 1957 she left behind an exceptionally happy school. In the intervening years, however, city boarding schools have often become both uneconomical and fraught with problems. It is increasingly difficult to find competent staff to live in, and it is less and less possible (or even desirable) to regulate the girls' personal behaviour. In the 1960s Elmwood became a day school. Gone were the Sunday walks and the closely chaperoned entourages which trooped off to dances at Ashbury, shepherded into the headmaster's house to await the arrival of their dates and afterwards pairing up to walk back to Elmwood hand in hand—always with an Ashbury master at the end of the parade to ensure that the young ladies were returned safely to the fold. Gone also were the headaches that have forced many boarding schools to close altogether.

As a concession to the past the original names on the doors of the boarders' rooms have never been removed, and in fact very few of Elmwood's traditions have been set aside. The houses, the prefect system, the honours and awards have all been retained, and there is little to suggest that there will be any profound change in the direction and philosophy of the school. Change for the sake of change is not in the Elmwood tradition.

To at least two generations of Old Girls it is impossible to think of Elmwood without thinking of Mrs. Buck. She was a woman of great courage, wisdom and flexibility of mind. She is remembered more fondly than many headmistresses because of the close relationship she maintained with her girls. Mrs. Buck was not merely a good headmistress, she was an extraordinarily beloved one. "The worth of a school," she said, "is measured not by its numbers but by the spirit which animates each and every one of us who have the privilege of being part of it."

The Study

Westmount, Quebec
1915

It is an unusual name for a school, but then The Study has never been a usual sort of school. Nor was its founder, Miss Margaret Gascoigne, an ordinary sort of woman. At the turn of the century she was among a tiny minority of well-educated women in the English-speaking world. Her account of her own education in England gives an insight into the sort of headmistress she would become.

> At the age of seven [in 1881] I was sent to a school near home kept by an old Scottish lady and her three daughters. All were cultured, intelligent gentlewomen of the Old School. They were musical and read aloud in a very pleasant way and all wrote a beautiful hand. As I look back, I feel that they must have had quite modern ideas on education. There was no superficiality about the school. The teaching of Literature was sound and thorough and we were all happy. Then some Aunts insisted on a change of school to something more stylish—one that was kept by a lady, who was a typical example of the Victorian headmistress and the possessor of a very variable temper. The staff were the very poorest types of teacher one could imagine. The craze for examinations was just beginning and from that time, my education was just a cramming for the Oxford local examinations. How I hated the text books, and lessons and papers on Literature and Shakespeare and History. They were enough to create a life-long distaste! . . . As I happened to pass what was not a very stiff examination, the first women's examination for Oxford, to Oxford I went.

She was sixteen years old when she entered Lady Margaret Hall, the first of the Oxford colleges for women, and here she found her "spiritual home and the strongest influence of my life".

235

Lady Margaret Hall was a place of rigid economy, stressing plain living and high thinking. These were to become ingrained characteristics of Margaret Gascoigne's own school, The Study. Indeed, her high-minded, pinch-every-penny-three-times-round approach was common to more than one Canadian girls' school of the same era, an approach that often succeeded in turning penury into a virtue.

After a series of teaching positions in various girls' schools in England Margaret Gascoigne grew disenchanted. She felt she was not fulfilling her potential, and in 1912 she decided to come out to Canada to join the staff of Miss Edgar's and Miss Cramp's. Anyone who knew the personalities involved could have foreseen that things would not work out well for her there. Miss Gascoigne was not impressed with the way things were done and did not hesitate to say so. Miss Edgar and Miss Cramp, for their part, felt that she had let down the side badly. Miss Gascoigne and her equally strong-minded employers agreed to disagree at the end of her teaching contract. Fortunately, lack of money did not deter Miss Gascoigne from setting up her own school, and from time to time in her career she found it expedient to borrow money. It was always promptly and meticulously repaid. In her diary Margaret Gascoigne describes the beginnings of The Study:

> One morning in September, 1915, six children came to school for the first time. We had a very cheerful room with two large windows and blue home-spun curtains with carpet and coverings to match. There were six little folding tables and every morning the children used to come very early. Often, I was still in the dining room of the boarding house on Drummond Street when they arrived. They'd come in to say good morning and then run upstairs to get the room ready for school. The tables and chairs were placed in two rows and the books were placed neatly on the tables, and when all was ready, one girl or boy would come down to fetch me. The little children's lessons ended before noon and then six big girls came in to have lessons in History, English and Latin. By 1916, we had moved into a nice little apartment on Durocher Street, which I thought was just the right size for two classes—but, during the summer holidays, there were so many applications for the next year that we had to move into a larger apartment in the same building. There we stayed for two terms and had

three classes, one for big girls preparing for Matric and two for younger children. The older girls used to go to McGill for Maths and Physics. After Christmas some of the parents advised me to look for a house that would be better fitted for a school. We looked at several and at last decided that the most suitable was one on Sherbrooke Street.

Although she had to borrow the first month's rent on the new house, Miss Gascoigne had every confidence that she would be able to repay it in due course—as she always did. The Study, to that point, had been a purely private venture with a staff of two, Miss Gascoigne and Mlle Boucher (who remained at the school from 1916 to 1959). But by September 1917 the little school had expanded to such an extent that several more teachers were taken on. With fifty-six girls and a couple of little boys, Miss Gascoigne was able to say with a broad grin, "Now I have a real school!"

It was a "real school"—but not like other schools. There was a wonderful fluidity built into the timetable. The emphasis was on spontaneity and stimulus. Margaret Gascoigne was almost compulsive about trying new ideas. Anything might happen at any time. Music usually happened on Wednesday afternoons and Miss Gascoigne, who was a very accomplished pianist, would sit and play to the children by the hour, letting them choose what they wanted to hear. She was ahead of her time again when it came to the idea of student government. She discussed everything with her head girls. One of them remembers how exciting and creative it was—having come from a conventional school —to be really involved with the running of the school.

By 1929 the house was getting too crowded and the parents were beginning to urge her to find some place with more elbow-room. Already there was an overflow to Miss Gascoigne's own quarters next door to the school, where the Juniors met for lessons with two teachers, a dog, and two cats named Marmalade and Café au Lait. It may have been this parental interest and concern for the school and its future that prompted Miss Gascoigne to agree to incorporate the school. The formation of The Study Corporation made possible the acquisition of a large house on Seaforth Avenue. The terms of the agreement guaranteed her a twenty-year appointment, complete internal control of the school, a salary that depended on enrolment, and living quarters within the school. "There were very good men on the board," recalls Katharine Lamont, a later headmistress. "Miss Gascoigne kept having ideas—often quite grandiose—and they kept bringing her feet back on the ground again." Marked by mutual concern and respect, the relationship between Board and principal was one other schools could envy. Things seemed almost too good to be true through the school's second decade. In 1928 a gymnasium was built, and in 1929 the house next door was annexed. There was even talk of a pension scheme for the staff when the Crash came.

For The Study it meant the end of expansion for quite a long period. The first year or so things were relatively good, but by 1931 enrolment had begun to fall off sharply. According to her nephew, who came out from England to be with her, Margaret Gascoigne spent that summer at a tiny cottage in the country waiting for the letters of withdrawal which arrived with disheartening regularity. The next year, to add to her burden, there were cuts in salary for the staff. Her health as well as her spirits began to falter. By the next fall, she was seriously ill and the Old Girls and parents sent her to Bermuda to recuperate from an operation. As a parting gesture the whole school knitted her an afghan. Everyone contributed a square, the youngest using dark shades because their hands were bound to be the dirtiest, while the white squares were saved for the Sixth Form. By autumn, Miss Gascoigne was completely bedridden and had moved out of the school into a nursing home. Her death in 1935 was a terrible blow. Hers would be difficult shoes to fill.

Fortunately in those days of financial uncertainty, the next headmistress, a Canadian who had come from Bishop Strachan in Toronto, Miss Mary G. Harvey, had much to recommend her. While she was perhaps less colourful than her predecessor, she had keen business acumen—a sorely needed quality. By 1939 the school was secure again, when the attention of the world turned elsewhere. From then on, it was more a matter of holding things steady than of introducing startlingly progressive new programs. Still, an English war guest recalls it as "the happiest school I was ever in".

By the mid-fifties, another building search was underway. For The Study's headmistress Katharine Lamont, another import from Bishop Strachan, it was an anxious time. "We had hunted high and low. Westmount would not take private schools. By the late fifties we were getting frantic, and I wasn't sleeping much. The main building of Upper Canada College in Toronto had just been condemned and we feared the worst might happen to us at any moment. Our building was literally crumbling."

Finally, in 1960 The Study moved into Westmount after all. A Roman Catholic school had somehow managed to set a rather awkward precedent and The Study's imposing new home on The Boulevard, formerly owned by the Bank of Montreal for the use of its president, was purchased. Miss Lamont began to sleep more soundly.

Katharine Lamont once said, "The most important feature of any school is the ideas on which it was founded and on which it lives." Certainly there is a sense of involvement about The Study today, as well as a tangible warmth and loyalty. Most of the school's activities rotate about its four houses, whose Greek names, after the initials of its first four head girls, are a school tradition. While it has adapted to and absorbed change, the basic theme of The Study remains constant: "To produce well-educated girls with a capacity for maximum contribution to the community." It is a mark of the school that, while it places emphasis on high academic standing, that is not the sole criterion for entrance. A girl's potential to contribute to the life of the school and later to the community at large is also taken into account.

Margaret Gascoigne would have been pleased with the course her school has maintained, for it still reflects her accomplishments. In the later years of her life she was reconciled with those two other strong-minded women, Miss Edgar and Miss Cramp. When she died in 1935, Miss Edgar wrote a moving tribute to her memory: "Miss Gascoigne was devoted to the cause of education. Her vision went out beyond her school, and she saw for the girls' schools in Canada possibilities beyond anything that has yet been reached. She believed in cooperation."

Ovenden

Barrie, Ontario

1915-1950

One of several privately owned schools that opened in the midst of World War I, Ovenden is now just a memory. Yet this small, unique girls' boarding school deserves a note in the history of Canadian private education.

One of Ovenden's three founders, Mlle Raina Shopoff, came to Canada from England almost on the spur of the moment in the autumn of 1912 to fill a sudden vacancy as French Mistress at Havergal College. She was put to the test at once. The girls in her first class greeted her with the welcome, "You won't last long! You're the third teacher we've had since September!" To her credit, she remained longer than the other two, although in her opinion Ellen Knox's administration left much to be desired. "At Havergal it seemed to be a policy that the pupil was always right," she remembers. "A lot of the children were very spoiled and wilful little creatures. A school should back its staff through thick and thin, and when we started our own school we stuck to this policy as best we could. . . . And I certainly didn't think that it was wicked for teachers at the school to go to the theatre. In those days Havergal disapproved of the theatre."

Like Miss Edgar and Miss Cramp before her she decided to strike out on her own, together with another Havergal teacher, Miss E.M. Elgood, and Miss E.J. Ingram, who came out from England to join them. They were determined that their school should have a "country atmosphere" and be more like a second home that a strictly regulated boarding school. The town of Barrie, Ontario, about sixty miles north of Toronto, was a perfect location from many standpoints. A small private day school there was in the process of closing and Ovenden was able to draw on its students, as well as some that followed from Havergal. When Ovenden opened in September 1915 there were twenty-five pupils, both boys and girls. "We hadn't said a word about what we were doing when we left," Mlle Shopoff recalls, "but somehow, people found out anyway. At the time, someone told us we were quite mad to even begin, with the price of coal so high. Of course, it never came down."

"Mam'zelle" recalls her first sight of the old house on Lake Simcoe which was to become Ovenden. "It had once been a lovely place, but it had gone to rack and ruin. The grass was about two feet high when we moved in on the first of July." The handyman, an ex-circus strong man, managed to get the grass mowed down to a reasonable height for the September opening, and to keep the costs down and pay the salary of the cook, paying guests were taken in for the summer months.

> That summer—'15—the clover was particularly fine so we chose purple, white and green for our school colours. We hoped that, like the clover, our girls would be both useful and ornamental, which perhaps sounds silly, but it's true. I believe purple and green were the Suffragette colours but we didn't think of that. Anyway we just believed in equal rights. They were most becoming colours to all those healthy fresh youngsters.

For the next twenty-five years, Ovenden was probably one of the happiest little boarding schools anywhere in Canada. It also operated without benefit of a Board of Governors or official church ties, although all three principals were Anglican. According to "Mam'zelle" it was the only tax-paying independent school in the province. In the end, though, the lack of these two vital elements—a board and a religious affiliation—probably led to the closing of Ovenden. There was simply no one willing to carry on the work of the three founders and shoulder the ever-mounting financial burden. Besides, as "Mam'zelle" put it, "If we'd carried on, we wouldn't have had the type of girl we wanted. We didn't want the nouveau riche."

What was it, then, about Ovenden, that made it different from dozens of other girls' boarding schools that have come and gone? Its general approach towards education was well ahead of its time in Canada. Elements of the Montessori system were adapted for use with the younger children, and while there was

plenty of time set aside for academic work, the school's surroundings were put to good use for games and outings—winter
picnics and hikes to the fishing huts out on Lake Simcoe, a week
of sapping every spring. The school field club often took off on
snowshoeing expeditions in search of nature lore. For many
years, the smaller children were encouraged to plant their own
little gardens. The school museum included over 500 rock sam-
ples and sixty stuffed birds, and had its own student curator.
Tobogganing was always a favourite pastime, too, and later
horseback riding became very popular. Ovenden was one of the
few schools in the province in a position to offer it at the time.
The school's active debating society considered such questions as
whether children should be discouraged from playing warlike
games (carried) and whether conscription should be adopted in
Canada (defeated).

Everything at Ovenden was done with enthusiasm, though
when it came to discipline, there was a purposefulness that
would be difficult to duplicate today. "Unlike most other schools
we never resorted to giving 'order marks'. We always believed
that the punishment should fit the crime. As someone once said:
'Crime may be more devastating—but bad manners are so much
more uncomfortable.' When there was talking after lights out,
"Mam'zelle" would make the talkers get fully dressed and go
down for an hour's work regardless of the time. "They forgive
me now," she muses, "but they haven't forgotten." Miss Elgood,
it seems, was the major strength of the school when it came to
discipline. Certainly none of her girls was in the least surprised
to learn that she had commandeered a lifeboat during the sink-
ing of the *Athenia* and kept all its occupants calm and under
control until they were rescued.

Ovenden's real strength was that it belonged totally to its three
founders, and they, in turn, were totally dedicated to the school.
"We laid stress on the things that really matter: honest effort,
sympathy, honour, right judgment, perseverance, courage,"
Mlle Shopoff recalls. They encouraged their students to develop
"a sense of excellence rather than a spirit of competition". But
Ovenden's strength was in the end its greatest drawback. As the
forties passed, a whole way of life gradually began to disappear,
never to return. This was probably clear to Ovenden's three
owners long before the end of World War II, when so many

boarding schools failed. In 1950 they agreed that Ovenden's usefulness was over. Miss Elgood and Miss Ingram retired to England and only "Mam'zelle" remained in Barrie.

Even today, more than twenty-five years since the school closed, people still speak of it with an extraordinary degree of warmth and affection. As someone once said, "Remembered joys are never past." And so it is with Ovenden.

Shawnigan Lake School

Vancouver Island, B.C.

1915

Many independent schools were established on the rock of financial stability, with a clearly defined organizational structure from the outset. But there are just as many that owe their success more to the will and determination of individual men and women than to benefactors and governing bodies. Shawnigan Lake School belongs in the second category.

Christopher Windley Lonsdale was a worldly and widely travelled young Englishman who, just prior to World War I, took on a milk route in the town of Duncan on Vancouver Island. The job was more a means of keeping body and soul together than a lasting commitment to the dairy industry. During the course of his daily rounds, Lonsdale often paused to discuss the ills of the world with his customers and soon discovered that there were a number of families in the area who were interested in private tuition for their youngsters. To Lonsdale it seemed a promising idea. He was an educated man—young, vigorous, and ripe for challenge. He gave up the milk route when he found an old estate for rent at nearby Shawnigan Like, and in the autumn of 1915 "Mr. Lonsdale's School" was officially launched. It was an immediate success, and Lonsdale instituted many of the traditions of his own revered Westminster School in England. Among these were the annual Shrove Tuesday Pancake Greaze, an ancient British custom designed to tax the staying powers of all participants. It has remained a Shawnigan tradition to this day. He also endowed the school with its motto, "Palman Qui Meruit Perat"—not a mark of great originality, as anyone familiar with Upper Canada College will attest.

Within ten years Lonsdale had built Shawnigan Lake into a

school of close to a hundred boys, in his words, "a going concern". Just as his sense of purpose had carried him through the initial growing pains, it would also see him through disappointment and near-disaster. During the late twenties a fire broke out and completely gutted the main school building. Lonsdale immediately sent telegrams off to the boys' parents; the message was a measure of his faith in the future of his school and in himself. It read, SCHOOL DESTROYED BY FIRE STOP NO ONE HURT STOP WILL RESUME OPERATION NEXT TERM STOP." With a small group of loyal supporters, Lonsdale incorporated his school as a non-profit-making venture and began to rebuild.

By 1929, after only thirteen years of operation, there were over 200 boys in the school and it had acquired something of a name for itself. Then, almost overnight, the enrolment was down by sixty boys. One entire residence had to be closed and remained empty for the next twenty-five years. The war years brought an increase in enrolment but problems of a different sort. Lonsdale's teaching staff was badly decimated and maintenance men at a premium. Shouldering his double-headed axe, he often led the daily woodcutting contingent out to collect a supply of firewood. It was a very necessary exercise, since the school's entire heating system was fired by one gargantuan wood-burning furnace. Nor was Lonsdale, who took great pride in his stationary engineer's papers, above doing his eight-hour stint in the school's power house along with the rest. Those who remember him more as a dictator than an inspiration find it difficult to recall those years with anything faintly resembling affection, but his devotion to the school and its ideals cannot be refuted.

Lonsdale considered one of his main tasks to be "training boys to be less obnoxious". His most important job was to develop leaders, and this could never be achieved by "letting boys do as they damn well please". There were, of course, a few who were always ready to try; but his "new boys' system" helped keep things well in hand. A newcomer to the school would become a "shadow" placed in the charge of an older "substance", and for the first few weeks at the school the "shadow" could do no wrong. The "substance" was punished in his place.

The prefects' record book of the 1930s is a classic of its kind. It itemizes a series of wins and losses in games, and beatings or "lickings" administered for wide variety of sins—"being cheeky, making a nuisance of himself, taking master's food". Stealing was, of course, an offence which warranted a sound thrashing—but so was wearing running shoes at meals or fooling in the dorm or losing one's temper and throwing ink or eating fruit during school or being out of bounds. The list was endless: "not kneeling in chapel, telling lies, unseemly conduct in the lavatories". By the 1940s things had obviously gone from bad to worse. Someone had chopped up a changing room with an axe, another had stolen cigarettes at the local store and run away, and yet another culprit was caught "spitting on the boathouse floor". But the prefects did their best to do their duty and keep order.

Ironically, it was some of Shawnigan Lake School's Old Boys who were responsible for bringing about the founder's retirement. By 1952 the school's fortunes were at their lowest ebb and Mr. Lonsdale's own health had been failing for several years, although he refused to admit it—even to himself. With mixed feelings—personal loyalty on the one hand and concern for the school's future on the other—the Board asked him to relinquish the running of the school to a younger man. It was a mutually painful moment and one which Christopher Lonsdale found impossible to accept. He died a broken and disconsolate man two months after leaving his beloved school.

His successor was a Vancouver chartered accountant, Peter Kaye, whose job was to put the school on a solid financial footing. Within five years, enrolment had doubled and under its next headmaster, E.R. "Ned" Larsen, another hundred boys were added to the school roster. Larsen, a former head prefect, had spent several years at the school under Lonsdale and is reputed to have been Lonsdale's personal choice as his successor. During his nine years as headmaster of Shenanigan Lake School (as it was dubbed by some), the program and facilities were updated and vastly improved. But essentially the school was maintained in the Lonsdale tradition. Like his predecessor, Larsen also had to deal with a fire—a less than frivolous boy's prank which levelled one of the school's boarding houses. It has since been replaced by an attractive group of three-tiered concrete buildings, set in the school's expansive campus of magnificently landscaped gardens and playing fields.

On the surface, at least, Lonsdale's one-man wonder has become a very different school from the one he created. Yet at Shawnigan Lake School, leadership training, character development, and good citizenship continue to be stressed, although with a greater emphasis on self-reliance and self-discipline. After six decades of highs and lows, minor scandals and major fires, Christopher Lonsdale's Shawnigan Lake School is once again "a going concern".

Weston School

Montreal, Quebec

1917

Friendly, non-establishment, and innovative are the words most often used to describe Weston School. It has always been a relatively small school, and has attracted a broader range of students than some of the older and perhaps slightly more fashionable Montreal girls' schools. (As one former staff member explains, "Money goes where money is.") Weston has also always been among the first to institute changes in educational methods and try out new ideas.

The school's lack of rigidity and flexible curriculum reflect the personalities of its two founders, Miss Amy Stone, an artist, and her American partner Miss Mabel Sewell, a musician. Amy Stone had already spent several years teaching at other girls' schools in Quebec, including King's Hall-Compton and Miss Edgar's and Miss Cramp's. Like Margaret Gascoigne, who had earlier left Miss Edgar's to start The Study, Miss Stone had also grown disenchanted with Miss Edgar and Miss Cramp. Since she was not only a teacher but an artist as well, it is hardly surprising that her educational priorities and those of her partner were vastly different from the expectations of headmistresses whose approach to education was more strictly academic.

The two partners in the Weston School began their venture in a rented house on Rosemount Avenue. Within two years they bought a larger house, part of the Trenholm estate on Severn Avenue in Westmount. Because the property was not zoned at the time, they were able to continue operating the school there for many years, to the frustration of local authorities, many of whom sent their children to private schools but certainly did not want such institutions located in the neighbourhood. Through the twenties the school continued to expand but the Depression brought on a crisis familiar to nearly all private schools. Being practical women, the two decided that the only way to recoup their losses was to sell the school. Their attempts to find a prospective buyer were in vain, and eventually they leased the school and departed for England.

The lessee was Jean Nichol, a Canadian and a former vice-principal of Miss Edgar's and Miss Cramp's. She carried the school through the thirties and the war years, making changes as she went along. It was during this period that boys were introduced in the elementary grades, perhaps more to keep the wolf from the door than in the name of progress.

With the post-war sale of the school to Dr. Mary Winspear, Weston underwent its greatest transformation. Mary Winspear is, on the one hand, perhaps the last of a generation of unforgettable characters, but she was as well the first of a new breed of Canadian educators. She had been teaching at McGill during the war and was due to be replaced when the professor of English for whom she had been filling in returned from overseas. "The prospects for a woman academic in the forties looked rather bleak," she says, "so I panicked, pawned everything I could and bought the place." (One of its great attractions, she recalls, was that it did not happen to be named after a saint.) With the post-war baby boom came an unprecedented demand for pre-school education, a field that interested her very much. And running a private venture school, despite the financial perils, allowed her an uncommon autonomy. "You could pick your own staff. You were completely free. I was particularly free because I had no board of governors. I owned the school and the property. It was a matriarchy ... a friendly school, a family school really, with the staff and the older girls and the little ones all thrown in together." Dr. Winspear never wished to trade her independence for financial security. In 1952 she decided to incorporate the school as a non-profit organization, but she made sure that the small hand-picked Board would not interfere.

During the mid-fifties Mary Winspear realized that schools were losing a great opportunity in the field of language teaching, and she introduced language study at the pre-school level. (The grant money for the project came from a Toronto foundation,

Westmount having been found unresponsive.) As well as being academically ahead of its time, the school has always been socially liberal as well, dedicated to religious and racial integration.

Today, Weston continues its philosophy of "change and grow". The school has become completely co-educational. Student involvement is stressed, and at one stage students even advised on the selection of new staff. A small pre-selected committee of students interviewed prospective teachers and then passed on its cryptic but generally astute observations and recommendations to the principal. It is an approach which seems preposterous to those of a more traditional persuasion, but at Weston it appears to have enjoyed moderate if temporary success.

Queen Margaret's School

Duncan, B.C.

1921

St. Margaret's in Victoria had become a substantial school when a second and very different venture opened "up island" in the Cowichan District under the patronage of the same sainted queen of Scotland. The character of this distinctly different school bears the stamp of its two remarkable and indefatigable founders, Norah Cremma Denny and Dorothy Geoghegan. Norah Denny had spent World War I in France as an army nurse, an experience that must have left her prepared to face almost any eventuality. On arriving in Duncan after the war she rolled up her sleeves and took on any and all available work —chopping wood, digging gardens, scrubbing floors, looking after children. All of this experience would be useful in her next enterprise.

A private venture school seemed as if it might provide a steady means of support, and a common interest in the new Girl Guide movement led her into partnership with her friend Dorothy Geoghegan. Their first school was a rented garage; their first class consisted of four pupils. Soon they found an old house with "wonderful possibilities", but with less than wonderful old plumbing, cracked ceilings, and drafty walls. By the following autumn, however, Queen Margaret's had acquired seven boarders, the backbone of a "rag-tag and bob-tail croc". It was typical of these two determined individualists that the existence of St. Margaret's School in Victoria did not deter them from naming their own school Queen Margaret's, despite the inevitable confusion.

When the success of their first term exceeded all expectations they decided to abandon the original building in favour of

251

something more sturdy. With a down payment borrowed from family and friends (they could not obtain credit locally), they moved the school to its present site on six acres of land, which at that time contained a four-room cottage, a vast, crumbling barn, numerous chicken houses, a newly planted orchard, and plenty of old stumps that made it bumpy going on the hockey field. The stumps, the orchard, the barn, and the chicken house have long since disappeared. Only the original cottage has survived fifty years of extensive additions and alterations. Work on a new wing for the school was begun during its second year. At a phenomenal rate Miss Denny sewed curtains and stained floors while Miss Geoghegan and their first staff member painted feverishly. A gymnasium followed, then another new wing, and the school's outdoor swimming pool ("Miss Denny's folly").

In 1934 the school chapel was built, entirely of native woods, and financed by donations and "entertainments". With its needlepoint kneelers worked in the school colours, each with a different design, the chapel symbolizes the founders' enduring faith. The chapel book's first entry in 1934 records, "In work for God there are commonly three stages—first, impossible, then difficult, then done." Since 1956, members of the Queen Margaret School's chapel choir have worn the badge of membership in England's Royal School of Church Music.

Innisfree, a farm complete with chickens, fruit trees, and a vegetable patch, was the next project to be undertaken, and the headmistresses' investment in two cows of mixed heritage eventually produced several prize-winning cattle and a first-class Ayreshire herd. The school's one polo pony was the nucleus of what has since become the most extensive riding facilities offered by any independent school in the country today, including a large, covered indoor ring and instruction by highly trained full-time riding mistresses.

During World War II, the school's Girl Guide companies on their salvage collection rounds became a familiar sight in the streets of Duncan. As a personal contribution to the war effort, the headmistresses gave up the school car, took to their bicycles, and cashed in their life insurance policies to build an air raid shelter. This last move was prompted by the reply they received from the authorities when they asked what they ought to do if the Japanese attacked the coast. "Scatter the children in the woods!" they were advised.

Although their endurance seemed almost boundless, Miss Denny and Miss Geoghegan wanted to assure the future of their school after they had gone. By 1954 they had given the property to the Queen Margaret's School Society under a Board of Governors, so that the school would be in the hands of those committed to perpetuating their work. The Board's first major undertaking was the construction of a new boarding school block in 1961, funded through the sale of Innisfree and another property and bolstered by the time-honoured avails of bake sales, entertainments, and "musical showcases". It would be the last building project in which the founders would actively participate. In 1963 their successor, Margaret Glide, inherited a school with a spirit and identity all its own, and has since become the guardian of Queen Margaret's band of self-appointed "mis-Glided girls".

The history of Queen Margaret's is one of an almost endless process of moving, tearing down, and building up. But in less tangible ways the school has remained as it began, "illumined above all by an idea or purpose, which gives to varied individuals a feeling of belonging to something essentially decent". The school will remain a reflection of the two women who gave it life, love, and laughter.

Brentwood College School

Mill Bay, Vancouver Island, B.C.

1923

Unlike most independent schools that opened after 1900, Brentwood College began not as a single-handed private venture but as a well-organized joint stock company. It was a school designed for profit as well as for education. Prospective investors were, of course, not deluded enough to expect their pockets to be lined with gold overnight, but expectations for Brentwood's money-making potential ran high. A financial prospectus issued by a group of wading Victoria business and professional men outlined the initial purposes and objectives of the proposed school in enticing terms.

> For some time a demand has existed in British Columbia for a school run on the lines of the great English and Scotch Public Schools. Parents who want to send their boys to England to get what is usually called English Public School Education are now faced with serious obstacles—both fees and travelling costs have increased tremendously ... and to a lesser extent the same drawbacks apply to eastern Canadian schools. These obstacles will be overcome by a school founded in B.C. for boys thirteen-eighteen and on English Public School lines.

The promoters envisaged work at the first-year university level with adequate preparation for law, the Royal Military College, and chartered accountancy examination. Although these ambitious plans were to be more modest in the realization, Brentwood had a financial year start such as few private schools could claim.

Although Kryle Symons of St. Michael's School in Victoria had tried to set up a similar school two years earlier, nothing came of the idea until a group of influential people— "with money that talks on such occasions", as Symons put it—met with the same idea and established Brentwood College. (His three sons later attended Brentwood.) When it came to the choice of headmaster, the promoters and Mr. Symons were in agreement. Cambridge-educated H.P. Hope, a former B.C. school inspector and principal of a public high school with an outstanding academic record, was the perfect man for the job. For nearly ten years (1923-1932) he tried to set Brentwood firmly on its feet. He was followed in turn, by M.A. Ellis (1932-1939) and Arthur C. Privett (139-1946), who had been a staff member since 1929.

The old Brentwood Hotel, once described as the finest of its kind along the Pacific coast, was the property selected by the Company of the new school. Its amenities included two launches, a boathouse, and twenty-two acres of land. Once opened, the school grew steadily, and achieved a wide reputation for academic and athletic excellence. Its prospectus boasted that its very low insurance rate "proves the excellence of the existing fire protection".

Then, in the summer of 1947, the school burned to the ground. W. "Chip" Molson, appointed headmaster a year earlier, was left with charred rubble for a school while the Governors attempted to arrange temporary accommodation for the coming term at nearby Shawnigan Lake School. Later in the year, some thirty boys and staff formed the nucleus of Brentwood House at the University School in Victoria, bringing with them the Brentwood cups and shields which had been salvaged from the fire. But there was for a time no indication that the Brentwood school itself would be revived. The devastation was too complete.

Twelve years passed before Brentwood College was re-established, not as a stock-holding company, but as an incorporated society formed by a group of Brentwood Old Boys and friends. The first step was the long and exhaustive search for a new location. The Brentwood Bay site was ruled out as inadequate for redevelopment, although this decision meant that the soul of the old school, a beautiful little chapel built almost entirely by the boys themselves, would have to be abandoned. Across Saanich Inlet the old deserted Alexandra Solarium was chosen as the most promising prospect. Despite a state of disrepair that beggared description, it stood on forty-five secluded acres with a 1,000-foot frontage on Mill Bay and a gradually shelving beach.

The chief source of inspiration in the revitalization of Brentwood College was Lieutenant-Commander David Mackenzie, the product of a Scottish boarding school and a former World War II test pilot and Olympic athlete. He entered with enthusiasm into the task of repairing the decrepit old solarium. The morning of the grand re-opening, in September 1961, has since become a school legend. With ninety-three boys on the roll, there were still no heat, no doors, and no cooks (they had all been fired the night before).

But such difficulties were rapidly overcome. Since 1961 Brentwood has developed into a vibrant school of over 250 students, primarily boarders, and in 1972 it was decided that a limited number of girls should be admitted at the senior level. Discipline, the development of leadership potential, outdoor sports and academic preparation are still important aspects of Brentwood's approach to education, although fine arts and drama are equally emphasized today. The school continues to offer a well-balanced philosophy of excellence that more than justifies the decision to open it once more.

Strathcona Lodge School

Shawnigan Lake, Vancouver Island, B.C.

1927

Like Brentwood College, Strathcona Lodge School began its similarly chequered career in an old hotel. But in the beginning it was a strictly private affair. Its founder, Minna Gildea, had once taught at Miss Edgar's and Miss Cramp's school in Montreal and like her former employers she, too, had definite ideas of her own on exactly how girls should be educated. The thought of being responsible to anyone but herself would have gone against the grain. Strathcona Lodge School was to be hers and hers alone until her death in 1950. Her fierce individualism gave her much in common with a neighbouring "independent", C.W. Lonsdale, whose Shawnigan Lake School just across the lake was in the process of being rebuilt after its first disastrous fire. A cordial entente soon developed between the two heads. Both were staunch Anglicans and both ran a tight ship. As for their students—the usual liaisons of proximity developed without any encouragement on the part of either. Both would most likely have been appalled at the present cooperative arrangement between the two schools at the senior level.

This is not to suggest that "Min" Gildea was old-fashioned in her outlook. "I want Strathcona girls to be thoroughly modern,' she wrote in 1932, "to lead in all sensible and beautiful things away in front of their time!" To this end she chose as the school motto "Cherchons", and the school crest bore a circle, for Truth, surrounding a question mark. Later the question mark was replaced with the provincial emblem, perhaps in the interests of the school's image.

With its superb view over Shawnigan Lake, the rambling old wooden CPR Lodge that would become Strathcona Lodge

School had changed hands several times before Miss Gildea bought it. Constructed by a Shawnigan Lake hotel company in 1900 for $15,000, it later became part of the CPR hotel chain. During World War I, it was booked solidly as a vacation home away from home by British "China families" on holiday from postings in the Orient. Having played host to princes and princesses, dukes and duchesses, in 1927 it received a new breed of guests—seventy schoolgirls, who took over the premises with high-spirited enthusiasm. The main building became Marjorie Pickthall House, and the second house was named after Canada's first educator, Mère Marie, an Ursuline nun.

By 1929, the fleet of rowboats and canoes that had come with the Lodge had lost much of their original enchantment. The age of horsepower had arrived. A boat club was formed and thirty schoolgirl-shareholders became the proud owners of a three-horsepower Johnston outboard motor and a fifteen-foot Peterborough skiff. Miss Gildea held eight shares and supplied the gasoline. Later the school was to acquire the ultimate in high-speed water transport, a seventeen-foot outboard with a magnificent ten-horsepower motor that could carry fifteen.

At Strathcona Lodge School, as elsewhere, the thirties were lean years. But for the girls whose parents could still afford to keep them there—sheltered from the unpleasant truths of breadlines and broken dreams—there were happy times.

Hiking, for instance, was a hearty, healthy pastime that involved little or no expense. Onward, ever onward tramped the girls of Strathcona Lodge in their sturdy nailed boots, their legs encased in long black stockings and the inevitable sweaters wrapped around their waists. The girls spent a great deal of time in the woods building "shacks" from foraged materials, in all shapes and sorts and sizes, on carefully selected home ground. They even built a few on the islands in the lake, perhaps in hope that the boys from Shawnigan would chance to sail by. No refinement was too grand for the shacks, and many boasted glass garnered from a nearby "haunted house". For the Christmas of 1931 the most popular gifts were shiny new hatchets, hammers and saws, and by the end of the term the shacks were enlarged and embellished according to the skill and imagination of their creators.

In 1946 Miss Gildea returned to England and assumed the

role of absentee landlady. It was a short retirement. By 1950 she had returned as headmistress to oversee her cherished investment, but after she died, as has been so often the case with private venture schools, Strathcona closed. For a time it reverted to its earlier role as a hotel but without much success. In 1959 a group of parents, Old Girls and Old Boys from Shawnigan Lake School, formed the working core of a Board of Governors for a newly incorporated Strathcona Lodge School. They appointed Mrs. C.C. "Nonie" Guthrie, a former head girl of the school, as its first headmistress.

It was now clear that the old Lodge would have to be replaced. It was a fire trap, and fire drills were almost a daily necessity. A million-and-a-half-dollar campaign for a seven-building complex to accommodate two hundred girls and staff was mounted in 1967, and by 1968 the old Lodge was replaced. Opinions of the modern architectural style of the new school are mixed (on more than one occasion it has been mistaken for a motel), but it is certainly functional and comfortable.

In recent years the Lodge's approach to education has altered almost as much as its appearance. Since 1972, when its present headmistress Angela Brown took over at a point when financial collapse was imminent, the curriculum has been broadened. Music and sailing in particular are highlighted in the school's highly varied program of extracurricular activities. Yet the school still considers education without a spiritual basis and a well-defined standard of values to be of little worth. As the school attempts to answer new needs, the means of application may have changed, but the philosophy of Strathcona Lodge School is perhaps not so radically different from what it was fifty years ago.

St. George's School

Vancouver, B.C.

1931

Vancouver's only remaining independent school for boys first opened its doors in the midst of the Depression. At the time there were already several other boys' boarding and day schools serving the Vancouver area, among them the now defunct north shore schools of Chesterfield (then the oldest in B.C.), and Kingsley. Yet in spite of the times and the competition the school did well. Captain Danby-Hunter, the first headmaster of St. George's School, helped raise the capital to start St. George's School Limited, though he did not stay in Vancouver long enough to see it grow. Two years after it opened he returned to England, leaving St. George's in the hands of its bursar John Harker.

Harker was an immensely personable and persuasive man, whose two great loves were his boys and his dogs. In his thirty-year rule there was never a term or a year when the number of students did not increase. Within a few weeks of the start of its first term, excavations had already begun on a new wing. Next came dormitories, fire escapes, then a gymnasium, more classrooms, and a chapel. Always, it seemed, the demand for new facilities exceeded the amount of money available, but on the strength of its rapidly rising reputation, the school gained support from wealthy and prominent Vancouver citizens. Lacking endowment, St. George's raised most of its money through private donations and substantial mortgages held by its backers. In 1948, when the original limited company of shareholders was dissolved and St. George's became a non-profit organization, every single investor donated his original stake back to the school.

The key to this loyal and continuing support was, of course, Johny Harker, the man who gave St. George's its essential colour and character. His unbounded sense of humour, immense versatility and pleasant informality went a long way in the business of winning influential friends. His ultimate purpose was the education of "a whole and decent man". His staff, he insisted, must be highly qualified and well paid, right down to the football coach. He considered organized games to be "essential tools" in the task of character building. The school's rallying cry (adapted to western requirements) was Kipling's "Be Fit—Be Fit—in Honour's Name Be Fit!"

Although excellence was the main objective, Harker's approach to academic subjects was far from traditional. Long before such innovations became generally acceptable he established the "Dalton Plan," a system of individualized programing that allowed each child to progress through prepared units of work at his own pace. The system had gradually been gaining popularity in both Europe and the United States since its introduction during World War I, but Harker (and The Study's Miss Harvey in Montreal) were among the first to bring it to Canada. Under the Dalton Plan the old methods of chalk and talk were replaced by "active study", enabling the boy to "Do rather than to Listen". Those interested were invited to visit the school and see the plan in action. Comments and criticisms were welcomed, and there must have been many of both, for the plan was eventually dropped.

St. George's did not neglect the religious component of child development. Mrs. Harker was a Roman Catholic and encouraged her husband to provide for the needs of the Catholic boys, which he did by raising the money for their own separate chapel and introducing Catholic religious instruction into the curriculum. In time the chapel, like the Dalton Plan, was abandoned as the Roman Catholic boarding population at St. George's gradually diminished.

In 1940 St. George's, like many other schools, agreed to become a distribution centre for British public school evacuees. To the dismay of the staff assembled to greet them, the first arrivals turned out to be a large contingent of schoolgirls. Their stay, the first and last permitted to any girls at the school, was brief. St. George's is among the dwindling number of independent schools that have not compromised on the matter of co-education.

Johnny Harker's vice principal and right-hand man was his brother Douglas, who succeeded him as headmaster in 1963. In 1970 St. George's entered a new Harker-less age when Alan C.M. Brown, the son of a school Governor and an Old Boy of fairly recent vintage, was appointed fourth headmaster at St. George's. Since then the school's list of scholastic, athletic and artistic awards has been impressive. In a competitive world, St. George's is still out to compete, and, whenever it can, to excel.

York House School

Vancouver, B.C.

1932

The six determined and versatile women who founded York House were undeterred by either the times or the fact that there were already several girls' schools in Vancouver. In the face of all opposition, they had decided among themselves to leave the private school where they had been teaching and strike out on their own. By pooling their resources, the six teachers-turned-entrepreneurs became joint shareholders in the York House School Company Limited, and invited a group of businessmen to sit on an advisory Board of Governors. Mrs. Lena Cotsworth Clarke, the group's only non-Canadian, was appointed headmistress by acclamation; the school was named after her birthplace in England. She had had extensive teaching experience in British Columbia, beginning at St. Margaret's School in Victoria as a well-loved gym mistress. It was agreed that each of the other partners would have charge over her own bailiwick according to her talent. Policy decisions, however, were to be made democratically; the majority would rule. Janet (MacDonald) Mitchell was delegated as vice principal and second in command to Mrs. Clarke, with Mrs. Grace "Pappa" Faris as treasurer and watchdog of the York House funds. Mrs. Faris' talent for business was augmented by her talent for stopping leaking pipes with wads of chewing gum. Mrs. Virginia (Moore) Mackay, Mrs. Gladys Jopling and Mrs. Marie Gerhardt-Olly rounded out the partnership. "Most of us were rather naive about the ins and outs of running a school," Mrs. Mackay recalls, "but each knew instinctively without question that she could count on the others' loyalty and support through thick and thin and that any differences would alway be resolved in a civilized and agreeable manner."

Even before the school's opening the group ran into problems in their search for a house. Fear of competition, in times that were already difficult, led a rival school to try to prevent York House from settling in the Shaunnessy district. A canvass of the neighbourhood to produce the written consent of all the school's potential neighbours was necessary before York House could begin operations.

With seventeen pupils on the roll, including several boarders, a modest but confident beginning was made in a rented house on Granville Street at Manton. The original six members of the "upstart school" became seven the following year when Mrs. Gretchen Hyland joined the group. By 1935, the autumn of the school's third year, many schools were barely clinging to life, but the enrolment at York House stood at well over 100. A second Granville Street house was leased for the Junior School. Property at King Edward Avenue (Twenty-fifth Street and Granville), the present York House site, was acquired two years later in 1937. Here the school continued to thrive, making the best use of every available inch of space. Mrs. Clarke's kind but firm character-building regimen stressed the vital importance of Deportment, and even among the senior girls any slackness was immediately noticed and a remedy applied.

By 1958, however, two of the original members had reached retirement age and the rest agreed that their interest in the school should be relinquished. It became an educational trust administered by parents and friends. The first headmistress chosen by the newly formed Board to succeed Mrs. Clark was Clare (Harris) Buckland (1958-1964). She laid much of the groundwork for the extensive development that was to come: new classroom blocks, new labs, and a new library. Later the boarding school was closed, and under Peter Tacon (1967-1970), western Canada's first bilingual program at the elementary level was introduced. It is still one of the few in existence.

Since Tacon's departure, York House has been under the direction of its second consecutive headmaster, Bryan Peet, an Englishman and a former principal in the province's public school system. In a little more than forty years the original seventeen girls have become 400. To the obvious pleasure of its founders, the original spirit of adventure, lack of stuffiness, and faith in the future still flourish at York House.

The Strathcona-Tweedsmuir School

Calgary, Alberta

1934

The amalgamation of Strathcona and Tweedsmuir is a recent development, but Strathcona, originally a boarding and day school for boys, opened in Calgary just five years after Ravenscourt made its debut in Winnipeg. Ravenscourt was the first to amalgamate when it joined forces with St. John's College in 1950, setting a precedent for future independent school unions, but Strathcona too acquired a double-barreled name when it formed a partnership with a school for girls in 1971. The two schools, Strathcona and Tweedsmuir, had developed along similar lines and shared many of the same goals, yet both were determined to maintain their own identity and traditions. For a year or so they carried on a coordinate, non co-educational operation under one roof, sharing facilities and interchanging staff. Strathcona, which was a Junior School until the late 1960s, had favoured single-sex education since the beginning. Tweedsmuir, for its part, had championed a girls-only policy passed on to it from its predecessor St. Hilda's College.

St. Hilda's had opened in 1905 under Mrs. Caroline Gerrie-Smith. A new arrival from Toronto, she found no Protestant boarding schools for girls in Calgary and decided to remedy the situation. After combing the city for weeks without finding suitable quarters, she was on the verge of abandoning her plans when the Anglican Dean and the Bishop of Calgary came forward with an offer of assistance. They offered to build her a school on Church of England property and lease it back to her. When the church relinquished its own interest in the school, it became incorporated as St. Hilda's School for Girls, a nondenominational institution with Anglican sympathies from 1924 onwards. After World War II many boarding schools for girls found that the demand for the type of education they had to offer was diminishing almost to the vanishing point. St. Hilda's, under its last headmistress Beatrice Shand, was one of the first to close, in 1949. Another factor in its demise was a ruling by the provincial government that only teachers certified in Alberta would be allowed to recommend pupils for promotion in Grades ten and eleven. As it had always been a practice at St. Hilda's (and most other schools for girls) to hire teachers from across Canada as well as from overseas, this ruling severely diminished any hope for the school's future. Ten years would pass before a renewed demand for private education led to the establishment of Tweedsmuir, an independent day school which was able to attract several of St. Hilda's former board members and financial backers.

Ten years later Strathcona was admitting boys as far as grade nine, and coordination with Tweedsmuir was being discussed. A substantial bequest to Tweedsmuir and the gift to Strathcona of an extensive property in the foothills to the south of the city made for a marriage of convenience. The girls had money—the boys had land—and as both were housed in buildings that were far from modern with facilities to match, it was clear that their resources could be combined to mutual advantage.

The first stage was accomplished by an exchange of teaching duties, while the fund raising committee beat the drums. In the fall of 1971 the new Strathcona-Tweedsmuir School under joint principalship welcomed its first busload of boys and girls (from kindergarten to grade twelve) who had jounced their way over the last mile of potholes to their new school in the country. Whether or not projected plans to expand Strathcona-Tweedsmuir to include a boarding school come to pass, its pupils can look forward to many more years of excitement, change, and expansion under headmaster "Sandy" Heard, a former TCS staff member who was largely instrumental in the creation of the new school.

When the two schools first amalgamated, they were determined to resist co-education. "It has been proven," the fund-raising literature stated emphatically, "that a classroom composed of entirely one sex is more conducive to efficient learning. . . . Students find concentration easier and there is less tendency to show off and use other means of attracting attention. In addition, teachers have more freedom of expression and students have less inhibitions about speaking up." It is a concise statement of the blessings of single-sex education. But as at Hillfield-Strathallan in Hamilton, the concept of coordinate education—equal, but separate—was short-lived. The blessings of single-sex education were soon overriden by financial and practical considerations, and perhaps by increasing pressures for integration on the part of the students and staff.

Balmoral Hall

Winnipeg, Manitoba

1950

When it was established in the autumn of 1950, it was officially declared that Balmoral Hall was "something completely new —not a merger". Perhaps; but its creation involved the students and staff of two existing church-affiliated girls' schools: Rupert's Land School, which had close ties with the Anglican Church and Riverbend School, which had been operated under the auspices of the United Church of Canada. The Riverbend premises were also acquired by Balmoral Hall, so even though 1950 may be considered its founding date, Balmoral Hall has a considerable prehistory.

Rupert's Land's immediate predecessor, in turn, was a school called Havergal College, established in 1901. Havergal eventually changed its name when it was taken over as an Anglican school, but at first it maintained close contact with the Presbyterians as well. The staff and boarders were encouraged to attend Holy Trinity, the Anglican church, on Sunday mornings, and the Presbyterian church on Sunday evenings. At the time Reverend R. Gordon, better known as Ralph Connor, author of *Glengarry School Days* and *Sky Pilot*, presided over St. Stephen's Presbyterian Church and was a familiar figure to many Havergal girls.

The name Havergal later created a certain inevitable confusion. The name was probably chosen as a gesture of gratitude to Havergal College in Toronto, which had given the new school a great deal of advice and encouragement. In the late 1890's the Toronto school was popular with Winnipeg families, and it was logical that the Toronto Havergal should be the most likely source of information when a school was set up along similar lines in Winnipeg. In fact, Havergal Toronto's vice principal, Mary Jane Dalton, was lured away to become the first headmistress of Havergal, Winnipeg.

By August, 1901, Miss Dalton was able to move into 122 Carlton Street and receive her first pupils. She was accompanied by Brigit, a faithful Irish cook who at once adopted a stray black kitten as a good-luck token for the new enterprise. Perhaps it worked. Just three days before opening, the school was overwhelmed with applicants. People who had been away all summer appeared in droves at the school to register their daughters. This meant that more staff and more accommodation had to be found quickly.

Miss Dalton's reminiscences of Havergal life in the first years of the century depict a long-departed and much less complex way of life. In young Winnipeg, a city with no movies and very few automobiles and far away from other centres of culture, the school had to depend on its own resources for diversion. There were charades, concerts, gym displays, "occasional talks" and expedition to various places. On Sports Day parents and friends came to watch the girls run the hurdles, put the shot, run races and compete in high and broad jumping. There were tennis and basketball courts on the grounds and skating in the winter. There were walks when the Winnipeg mud was not too bad. Occasionally, when riding horses could be hired, a few girls had wonderful rides across the prairie that began, in those days, at the top of Broadway by the Osborne Barracks near All Saints Church. In the winter the girls who were left in the school on Saturdays often a tobogganed on the banks of the Assiniboine River. When there was a good moon and crisp frost, the staff and boarders went for a prairie bobsleigh ride with buffalo robes, jingle bells and horns—all complete. This was very popular, especially if a friend living on the prairie invited the party in for hot coffee and buns.

Miss Dalton's successor, Miss Eva L. Jones, was also lured away from Havergal Toronto, and carried on the school in much the same fashion. But she found some of the newer distractions of the growing city increasingly frustrating. In her 1907 report to parents she despaired:

I have come to the regretful conclusion that there is no

place in which I have yet lived which offers so many distractions and hindrances to a girl during her learning years. . . . When her best and most earnest work should begin, when thought and feeling need most direction and development, she is swept away by a flood of social engagements, household duties and small excitements. . . . I am no fanatic on the subject of theatre-going, but I am sure that the weekly visit to a hot and crowded building at a time when a growing girl should be using a free afternoon in the air must, in the end, do more harm than good.

She went on, "It is too much, I suppose, in this land of telephones, to hope for the peaceful silence to be found in most English and Scotch homes where schoolchildren are preparing their work. I wish it were possible to institute a Winnipeg curfew by 6:00, after which it would not be lawful for any child with evening work to use or approach the telephone." She bemoaned as well "the restless craving for excitement, the round of visiting, afternoon or evening, or of shop gazing, and small gossip. The telephone and the matinee are far more exhausting to girls' nerves than anything in the classroom. . . . There is grave moral effect in allowing a child habitually to put pleasure before duty and responsibility."

In 1917, when St. John's Anglican College assumed responsibility for the school's operation, the name Havergal was relinquished in favour of Rupert's Land School for Girls. There was little change, however, in the general direction of the school until the formation of Balmoral Hall in 1950. During the Rupert's Land era, however, there was one ironic twist involving Havergal Toronto, which was at last repaid in kind when the principal of Rupert's Land, Miss Gladys Millard, left Winnipeg to become headmistress of Havergal Toronto in 1937.

The Riverbend half of Balmoral Hall's history is closely tied to the beginnings of the United Church of Canada, and to a benefactor with strong convictions about the importance of educating young women. Sir James Aikins, the driving force in the move to establish Riverbend, felt that far too many people were sending their daughters to convents or to boarding schools in Toronto or Montreal "at great expense and inconvenience". Riverbend was to be an "up-to-date" school for girls under church direction, designed to "provide an education of sound academic standing in an atmosphere conducive to the development of a fine Canadian womanhood". Miss Joan Foster, a Canadian and daughter of a former premier of New Brunswick, was selected as the person most likely to accomplish these objectives. Riverbend was soon under way in its magnificent new home on eighteen acres of parkland on the Assiniboine River.

The founding of Riverbend in 1929 coincided with that of Ravenscourt School for Boys, and not unexpectedly a good many of the same men were involved with the affairs of both schools. Riverbend, however, operated under the auspices of the United Church, whereas Ravenscourt operated independently of any church. Each amalgamated with other schools in 1950 as a response to that most prevalent of independent school diseases, deficititis. The amalgamation of St. John's and Ravenscourt and the creation of Balmoral Hall on the Riverbend premises alleviated the crisis, but at Balmoral Hall in particular there were wrinkles which only time could iron out. Divided by old loyalties, the new school was a hotbed of rivalry among girls and staff members alike. The school's chief source of strength during this unsettled period was "G.M.W."—Miss Gwendolyn Murrell-Wright, its devoted headmistress. Hers was no easy task, for not only was she faced with the full range of problems that usually beset a new school, but she had to contend with a divided camp as well.

Her successor, Dr. Harriet Perry, introduced a "child-centred" approach to education at the school that involved a minimum of formality and structure. A further departure from tradition was made in 1973 with the appointment of Balmoral Hall's first male principal, R. Martin Kenney. He was the fourth man appointed to head an all-girl school in as many years and yet one more symptom of a growing trend in girls' independent schools across Canada. One suspects, however, that it will be many years before any boys' school displays enough daring (or desperation) to invite applications from qualified female candidates.

Postscript

It has not been within the scope of this book to discuss the many other types of alternative schools that have emerged within the last few years across Canada, and not even all of the independent schools themselves have been considered. Two Quebec schools which have not been dealt with in depth are St. George's School, Montreal, established in 1930 and Sedbergh School, which opened in 1939 just north of Montebello. The former is a highly successful non-traditional experiment in co-education, the latter a one-man wonder built from scratch by its founder, Tom Wood, in partnership with a former fellow-master at Lakefield. Both St. George's and Sedbergh remain unique among Canadian schools. St. George's is now a member school of both the CHA and CAPISG and has expanded substantially. Its enrolment stands at roughly 400, while Sedbergh has held its enrolment to about 70 boys between the ages of eight and eighteen, maintaining its traditions as a small country boarding school based on hard work, participation and physical fitness. Operated almost single-handedly by the founder's son, it has only recently become an incorporated school, in compliance with provincial requirements for private schools operating in the province of Quebec.

Then there is UTS—the University of Toronto Schools, set up in 1910 as a Lab school for the Ontario College of Education (now the Faculty of Education, University of Toronto). Originally it was intended that the school should provide a first-class academic program for both sexes. This explains the fact that its official title is in the plural, although it operated as a boys' school for over sixty years. It was not until 1971 that the University Senate was persuaded that an equal number of girls should also be admitted to the school. Since UTS remains a subsidized affiliate of U of T its fee structure is substantially lower than that of independent schools and the competition for entrance has never been stiffer.

Dozens of other private schools have opened since 1950, both unstructured and traditional. Among those which have managed to remain afloat are the Halifax Grammar School and Dartmouth Academy in Nova Scotia; and in the Toronto area the Toronto French school (which now operates in five different locations), St. George's College School, the Hawthorne School, the Montcrest School (formerly the January School), the Waldorf School (which has a pre-school branch in Vancouver), and the King City Country Day School. In the Muskoka district, the Rosseau School has persevered through four devastating fires since it opened in 1967 and St. John's and St. Margaret's Schools have recently opened in Elora, Ontario. Further west are St. John's Cathedral School in Selkirk, Manitoba, with a branch school near Edmonton and St. David's in Squamish, B.C. near Whistler Mountain.

In a category all its own is the National Ballet School in Toronto. Now in its eighteenth year, it is funded both publicly and privately, a combination that makes it possible for the school to offer an academic program (grades five-twelve) and professional ballet training as well as a scholarship and bursary system that is without equal. Virtually no talented applicant is turned away for lack of ability to pay the tuition fees. Even its normal fee structure has been deliberately kept well within the bounds of reason, through the determined efforts of its founder and principal, Betty Oliphant. It is a school which enjoys a unique and enviable position in this regard and its uncompromising standards of excellence should continue to serve it as well in the future as they have in the past.

EPILOGUE

The Price of Excellence:
The Independent School Today

Institutions are born, grow and prosper or wilt and die in relationship to the quality of the human beings who serve them.

Richard B. Howard
Headmaster, Upper Canada College
Preparatory School

It is not improbable that the historians of the future might explain many of the social movements of this third quarter of the twentieth century as prompted by one last great surge of optimism about the perfectability of mankind, an optimism that was born in the great social reform movements of the nineteenth century. It is among the most fondly cherished beliefs of Western society that social justice will prevail if only the means of advancement and access to opportunity are equally open to all. With the application of money and expertise (resources that we have possessed in abundance), we have believed that we could eradicate those two great impediments to equality of opportunity, poverty and prejudice. And what was the fundamental source of poverty and prejudice if it was not ignorance itself?

The nineteenth century saw the birth of the dream of universal equality through universal education. Education would raise the masses not only materially but spiritually: with learning would come piety, industriousness, and respect for the values of church and state. Yet, as education became an instrument of social policy it was found that there was a price to be paid for egalitarianism. According to historian W.L. Morton, the trend was already evident in the 1920s:

The public schools were becoming steadily less concerned

with academic training and more and more involved as agents of social policy. It was becoming their prime function, undeclared but imperative, to diminish the distinctions caused by home and class among their pupils and to produce from diversity of background and national origin the social conformity a democratic society required. In the process, academic excellence suffered before the hand of social mediocrity.

The Canadians, 1867-1967

Yet at the same time, the educators have always argued their duty to make the system not less but more accessible to as many people as possible. Laments about the appalling failure rates of students in the schools are nearly as old as the schools themselves. To examine the possibility that education through the secondary level, and today even beyond, might not be apr o-priate for every child would have been undemocratic in the extreme. Instead, the proffered solution was to minimize the possibility of failure, by offering something for everyone.

It was a brave idea, although from the first there have been a few people who were uncertain about the results. Among the hundreds of studies on the philosophy of Canadian education that have appeared during the last twenty-five years, perhaps one of the most significant, even today, is the late Dr. Hilda Neatby's *So Little for the Mind*. It raised uncomfortable questions about the quality of education within the state system, questions that for growing numbers of people are more urgently in need of answers now than ever before. Expressing similar sentiments, in 1969 Professor James Daly of McMaster University wrote a brilliant and witty critique of Ontario's Hall-Dennis Report entitled *Education or Molasses?* "There is something like a bandwagon psychosis sweeping through Ontario education today.... Many of the Report's suggestions are being attempted without the proper preparations. It is being quoted as the Holy Writ without anything like the necessary reflection.... At its best the Report is good clear water but at its frequent worst it is a bucket of molasses, sticky sentiment couched in wretched prose." Daly's book was dismissed at the time as the ravings of a reactionary. Today, only a few years later, many people would fervently second him. Ontario's Ministry of Education is retreating cautiously, promising to re-institute some mandatory courses in the high schools and to re-examine the idea of provincial examinations. Newspapers from Vancouver to St. John's are full of reports of high school students ignorant of their own country's history, geography, and literature; of first year university students who can neither read nor write. According to a recent survey by the CTV network television show *W-5*, forty-five per cent of parents rate the quality of public school teaching mediocre or worse. Thirty-one per cent of those parents said they would send their children to private schools if they could afford it.

But few parents can afford to pay twice over. Since the 1950s the so-called "massification" of public education has required more and more money. Admittedly, it was money that few were unwilling to spend. Education was, after all, a noble and necessary investment in the technocratic, highly specialized society we envisioned for the future, and educational spending by provincial governments was hardly less popular than motherhood. The spirit of "spend now and worry about it later" has prevailed for a good twenty years. Only recently, like motherhood, has it found its detractors.

In order to contend with their state-subsidized competition, many independent schools were faced with a hard choice. They must either admit their inability to match those resources and close their doors, or face a future fraught with uncertainty. The majority, of course, opted for modernization and expansion of facilities, which led them into a series of frenetic fund-raising campaigns. But they found that all the proceeds of dinners, dances, raffles, lotteries, bazaars and Theatre Nights were but a tiny drop in a very large bucket. Only through substantial individual contributions could these schools even begin to meet the costs of rejuvenating old buildings and adding new ones. By the late sixties a number of the larger schools had begun to retain the services of a full-time fund-raiser, known variously as an Old Boys' (or Girls') secretary, campaign manager, or bagman, whose job it was to coordinate the affairs of a newly created school corporation or "family" (a body that includes everyone who has ever been involved with the school in any capacity, as student, parent, teacher, governor, or simply casual acquaintance). The method has proved to be fairly effective, at least as a means of promoting interest in the school. The money donated out of loyalty, obligation, gratitude, or self-interest has generally been invested wisely, though on occasion with a large measure of hope and a minimum of foresight. The fates of both St. Helen's and King's Hall serve as good examples of the latter.

Gradually, almost imperceptibly at first, the climate of the independent schools became more variable. Most of them, in keeping with a basic conservatism, were content to hold the line as best they could for as long as they could, planning for physical expansion without committing themselves to wholesale ideological turnabouts. A certain amount of well-planned experimentation might cautiously be introduced, or a slightly more flexible approach to the curriculum. But these were almost the only indications of an awareness that survival often depends on adaptability. The old value systems, the existing framework of traditions, and the well-established patterns of organization often remained unchanged.

But little by little the atmosphere in the independent schools has grown less rarefied, and there is today a clearer distinction between matters of mere appearance and those of substance. The length of hair and the shortness of tunics or skirts, once major moral issues, have become the responsibility of the individual student in many schools. The student population, too, is far less homogeneous. Sometimes this brings new strains, such as the problems of communication that have been encountered at some West Coast schools where large numbers of Chinese students, mainly from Hong Kong, have been accepted as boarders.

In urban schools particularly, cadet corps and after-school games are no longer mandatory. Increasingly the choice is left to the student. There is, instead, a renewed emphasis on fitness and "lifetime" sports such as tennis, squash, badminton, and cross-country skiing, as opposed to those character-building team sports that created pleasure for the few and anguish for the many. All of these changes are part of a movement away from rigidity, compulsory activities, and the imposition of too many do's and don't's.

But while expectations in dress, behaviour, and extra-curricular activity have become less demanding, academic expectations have often increased, especially among the day schools. The competition for entrance has never been keener despite fewer course options and heavier workloads than in the public schools, and despite all the social risks of separation from former friends and classmates.

Some independent schools, on the other hand, have flung themselves wholeheartedly into the vanguard of experimental education. Often, however, the avant-garde headmasters or headmistresses who had been ushered in to the sound of trumpets soon found themselves in a double if not triple bind, caught between students, staff, and parents—to say nothing of the Board. It was a bind that, more often than not, resulted in a tenure as brief as it was stormy. Perhaps because the head of a private school is constantly accountable to these several vitally concerned and generally conservative groups and individuals, most heads prefer to let the mills of the gods grind slowly and finely. As the inimitable Johnny Harker of St. George's School in Vancouver once remarked, "There are two kinds of fool. One says, 'This is old, therefore it is good,' and the other insists, 'This is new, therefore it is better.' "

For the head of a school, however, the selection of staff is as crucial as the selection of an educational philosophy, and in the final analysis the former probably has a good deal more influence on the tenor and quality of a school. No doubt many heads occasionally wish there still existed the diligent, middle-aged mentors of unsurpassed devotion, such as encountered by the writer Marian Engel during her brief tenure as a teacher at one of the schools in Montreal's Square Mile:

> They actually felt that it was some kind of honour and privilege to be able to teach the daughters of Montreal's First Families. Their reward was their work, I suppose, because the salaries they were getting were hardly enough to subsist on . . . yet none of them would have dreamed of complaining about it. Perhaps they thought it was too demeaning or that it was unbecoming for a "lady" to discuss money. . . . Perhaps they were too proud . . . or too frightened for their jobs.

But this breed has all but disappeared. After World War II a whole new generation of teachers began to drift in and out of the independent schools. The halcyon days of "lifetime" staff were coming to an end, especially in the girls' schools that acceded to the times by hiring well-educated married women, whose husbands and children demanded equal time outside the classroom.

It was, however, a change that brought advantages as well as disadvantages. The involvement of this new generation of men and women with their schools is seldom so absolute, yet there is no doubt that their more varied lives lead to a more balanced and realistic approach towards their work, and their students.

Both the administration and the staff of these schools face a major obstacle in coming to grips with inevitable change. The delicate business of sorting out the lasting trends from the passing fancies ultimately falls to the head of the school. Traditions, teaching techniques, and even teachers that once served a school well at one stage may become an impediment at another. Furthermore, the head must justify and defend his policies to a Board of Governors, occasionally fickle bodies that cannot always be relied upon to back him to the finish. (The Board of one independent school is reputed to have fired all of its headmasters, right down to the founder himself.) By the late sixties virtually every private venture independent school had become a non-profit corporation managed by a Board, and increasingly it is the Board which has become the ultimate source of policy. While it is vigorously contended that a Board's primary function is to involve itself with the school's financial well-being, that well-being is largely dependent on the general reputation of the school. And, in turn, the reputation of the school directly reflects the policies and personality of the man or woman who heads that school, a man or woman hired—and also fired—by the Board.

In effect, then, both the principal and to a lesser degree the staff of an independent school are at the mercy of a group of individuals who may or may not have the faintest notion of what they are about—and although competence, business acumen and an interest in the school are purported to be major considerations in the selection of board members, a healthy bank balance and social connections are hardly disqualifications. Paupers, unless otherwise qualified, need not apply.

Today as never before the composition of the Board of an independent school is the key to that school's finances and reputation, and thus to its success or failure. The extent of its members' commitment and their ability to make wise and responsible judgments concerning the school's future are as vital as they are variable. Yet in spite of the increased complexity of its task, the status of most school governing bodies has remained essentially unaltered. To most students, board members are more or less invisible beings (a collection of "fine-feathered foofs",* one student has called them) who materialize a few times a year for school plays, prizegivings, and other ritual events. To the staff, the members of the Board are too powerful to be popular, and their qualifications are often suspect. Yet without the individual efforts of many of these same board members, there would probably be even fewer independent schools in Canada today.

Despite the continuing problem of financial resources on the one hand, and anti-elitist sentiment on the other, more and more parents are seeking out educational alternatives for their children and are willing to pay the price. The waiting lists for entrance into private schools are less a sign of a return to snobbery than they are of a growing disenchantment with the public school product. Yet when it comes to government subsidies and grants, many independent schools, if given the choice, would prefer to maintain their current unsubsidized status—poorer but prouder. The spectre of government interference, whether real or imagined, no doubt plays a part in this reluctance to accept handouts from the public purse (the hand that feeds might also bite). There are other schools, however, as well as, one can be sure, a great many parents, who would welcome a system of grants or vouchers and who are less concerned about the distant future than they are about the fact that they are currently paying twice for their children's education, once as taxpayers and a second time to exercise their freedom of choice. More and more would support the view of Professor Robert Stamp:

> Machinery must exist so parents and students may choose teachers within a school, schools within a system, and even among competing systems. Parents, along with teachers and students, must also have the right to propose and initiate alternative or experimental schools of their own. This right should exist both within and without public school systems and must not entail an economic burden on those individuals.

It has become clear to all those concerned with education in Canada that in the course of the last century the state has achieved its goal of offering a place in its schools to all—at the

*Fine Old Ontario Families

price of offering true learning to fewer and fewer. If we have learned anything, it is that no one formula or method or system, structured or open, traditional or progressive, is best for every child. We will not have truly child-centred education until we are able to provide our children with many possibilities, with many kinds of "alternative schools". Whether the huge, inevitably bureaucratic public school systems will be able to accommodate such flexibility remains to be seen. In the meantime, there is no doubt that the independent schools will continue to be the choice of those increasing numbers of people who are, privately, searching for alternatives.

APPENDIX

Member Schools of the Canadian Headmasters' Association and the Canadian Association of Principals of Independent Schools for Girls

D = Day students   R = Residents

Albert College
Belleville, Ontario K8P 1A6
(613) 968-5726
Headmaster: Lorne L. Shewfelt, M.A.; Registration: Boys—15 D, 86 R (ages 12-19), Girls—5 D, 52 R (ages 12-19); Fees: $2,200 (D), $4,500-$4,800 (R).

Alma College
96 Moore Street
St. Thomas, Ontario N5R 5B6
Principal: Miss M.E. Bone, B.A.; Registration: Girls—140 R (grades 9-13); Fees: $2,600 (R).

Appleby College
Oakville, Ontario L6K 3P1
(416) 845-4681
Headmaster: Edward R. Larsen, M.A. (Oxon); Registration: Boys—189 D, 203 R (ages 8-18); Fees $2,700-$3,000 + $300 extras (D), $4,900-$5,200 (R).

Ashbury College
Rockcliffe Park
Ottawa, Ontario K1M 0T3
(613) 749-5954
Headmaster: W.A. Joyce, D.S.O., E.D., B.Sc.; Registration: Boys—254 D, 111 R (ages 10-18); Fees: $2,550-$2,600 + $500 extras (D), $4,750-$4,800 + $500 extras (R).

Balmoral Hall School
630 Westminster Avenue
Winnipeg, Manitoba R3C 3S1
(204) 786-8643
Principal: N. Thomas Russell, B.Ed., Dip.Eng.; Registration: Girls—300 D & R (grades K-12); Fees: $2,000 (D), $4,000-$4,200 (R).

Bishop's College School
Lennoxville, Quebec J1M 1Z8
(819) 569-0657
Principal: John D. Cowans, B.A., M.A.; Registration: Girls—15 D, 80 R (grades 7-12), Boys—25 D, 165 R (grades 7-12); Fees: $2,800 + $600 extras (D), $5,300 + $600 extras (R).

The Bishop Strachan School
Lonsdale Road
Toronto, Ontario M4V 1X2
Principal: Miss Katherine E. Wicks, M.A., M.S.; Registration: Girls—550 D, 120 R (grades N-13), Boys—30 D (grades N-4); Fees: $1,800-$2,100 (D), $4,900 (R).

Branksome Hall
10 Elm Avenue
Toronto, Ontario   M4W 1N4
(416) 920-9741
Principal: Miss Allison Roach, B.A., M.Ed.; Registration: Girls—555 D (grades K-13), 130 R (grades 5-13), Boys—10 D (grades K-4); Fees: $650-$2,150 (D), $4,450 (R).

Brentwood College School
Mill Bay, B.C.   V0R 2P0
(604) 743-5521
Principal: W.T. Ross, B.A.; Registration: Boys—30 D, 235 R (grades 8-12), Girls—5 D, 55 R (grades 11, 12); Fees: $1,850 + $300 (D), $4,750 + $200 (R).

Convent of the Sacred Heart
5820 Spring Garden Road
Halifax, N.S.   B3H 1X8
(902) 422-4459
Principal: Miss Pauline Scott; Registration: Girls—254 D (grades 1-12), Boys—16 D (grades 1-8); Fees: $600-$1,050 (D).

Convent of the Sacred Heart
3635 Atwater Avenue
Montreal, Quebec H3H 1Y4
(514) 937-2845
Principal: Sister Margaret Johnson, R.S.C.J., B.A.; Registration: Girls—335 D, 55 R (grades 7-11); Fees: Government grant + fee determined by Ministry of Education (D), same + $1,500 (R).

Crescent School
2365 Bayview Avenue
Willowdale, Ontario M2L 1A2
(416) 449-2556
Headmaster: Christopher B. Gordon, A.B., B.Ed.; Registration: Boys—335 D (ages 9-18); Fees: $2,325-$2,475 (all-inclusive) (D).

Crofton House School
3200 West 41st Avenue
Vancouver, B.C.   V6N 3E1
(604) 263-3255
Principal: Miss Rosalind W. Addison, B.Sc. (Hons.), Dip.Ed.; Registration: Girls—370 D, 50 R (grades 1-12); Fees: $1,150-$1,950 (D), $4,115-$4,700 (R).

Elmwood School
231 Buena Vista Road
Rockcliffe Park
Ottawa, Ontario K1M 0V9
(613) 749-6761
Principal: Mrs. J.C. Whitwill, M.A. (Hons.); Registration: Girls—170 D (grades 4-13); Fees: $1,800   (D).

Halifax Grammar School
5750 Atlantic Street
Halifax, N.S.   B3H 1G9
(902) 422-6497-8
Principal: Douglas J. Williams, M.A. (Oxon); Registration: Boys—160 D (grades 1-12), Girls—100 D (grades 1-12); Fees: $1,100-$1,430 (D).

Halifax Ladies' College
1400 Oxford Street
Halifax, N.S. B3H 3Y8
(902) 432-7920
Principal: Miss Carol F. Salton, M.A.; Registration: Girls—160 D (grades N-12), Boys—35 D (grades N-2); Fees: $530-$900 (D).

Havergal College
1451 Avenue Road
Toronto, Ontario M5N 2H9
(416) 483-3519
Principal: Miss Mary Dennys, B.A.; Registration: Girls—550 D, 105 R (grades N-13), Boys—20 D (grades N-2); Fees: $950-$2,240 (D), $4,660 (R) (grades 8-13).

Hillfield-Strathallan College
299 Fennell Avenue West
Hamilton, Ontario L9C 1G3
(416) 389-1367
Principal: M.B. Wansbrough, B.A.; Dean of Women: Mrs. J.C. Callaghan, B.A.; Registration: Boys—435 D, Girls—300 D (grades K-13; Montessori ages 3-5); Fees: $2,100-$2,560 (incl. transportation and lunch).

King's-Edgehill School
Windsor, N.S. B0N 2T0
(902) 798-2278
Principal: T.T. Menzies, M.A. (Cantab); Registration: Boys—42 D, 64 R (ages 12-18), Girls—18 D, 52 R (ages 12-18); Fees: $1,000 + $200 extras (D), $4,000 + $500 extras (Boys) (R), $3,600 (Girls) (R).

Lakefield College School
Lakefield, Ontario K0L 2H0
(705) 652-3112
Headmaster: J.T.M. Guest, B.A.; Registration: Boys—31 D, 208 R (ages 10-18); Fees: $2,300 + $80 extras + books + $1.25/lunch (D), $5,150-$5,175 + $200 extras (R).

Lower Canada College
4090 Royal Avenue
Montreal, Quebec H4A 2M5
(514) 482-9916
Headmaster: G.H. Merrill, M.A.; Registration: Boys—595 D (ages 8-17); Fees: $1,645-$2,370 + $280 lunches + books (D).

Miss Edgar's and Miss Cramp's School
525 Mount Pleasant Avenue
Montreal, Quebec H3Y 3H6
(514) 935-6357
Principal: Miss Jean C. Murray, M.A., Dip.Ed., Cert. Soc.Sc.; Registration: Girls—300 D (grades 1-11); Fees: $1,300-$1,600 (grades 1-6), govt. grant + fee determined by Ministry of Education (grades 7-11) (D).

Netherwood—The Rothesay School for Girls
Box 160
Rothesay, N.B. E0G 2W0
(506) 847-7496

Principal: Miss Lynda A. Heffernan, B.Sc., B.Ed.; Registration: Girls—25 D, 50 R (grades 7-12); Fees: $1,600 (D), $3,850 (R). (Netherwood is affiliated with Rothesay Collegiate School for Boys. (Girls live on the Netherwood campus, but all classes are held at RCS.)

Norfolk House
801 Bank Street
Victoria, B.C. V8S 4A8
(604) 598-2621
Principal: Miss A. Winifred Scott, B.Sc.; Registration: Girls—270 D (grades 1-12); Fees: $1,190-$1,695.

Ontario Ladies' College
401 Reynolds Street
Whitby, Ontario L1N 3W9
(416) 668-3358
Principal: Dr. Reginald C. Davis, M.A., M.Mus., M.Ed., PR.D.; Registration: Girls—20 D, 110 R (grades 7-13); Fees: $1,560 (D), $3,900 (R).

Pickering College
Newmarket, Ontario L3Y 4X2
(416) 895-1700
Headmaster: Harry M. Beer, B.A.; Registration: Boys—163 R (ages 10-19); Fees: $5,100 + $300-$400 extras (R)

Queen Margaret's School
1031 Government Street
Duncan, B.C. V9L 1C2
(604) 746-4185
Principal: Miss Margaret Glide, A.C.P., Dip. Teach.; Registration: Girls—60D, 85 R (grades 5-12); Fees: $1,500 (D), $4,350 (R).

Queen of Angels Academy
100 Bouchard Blvd.
Dorval, Quebec H9S 1A7
(514) 636-0900
Principal: Sister Rose D. Beauvais, S.S.A., B.Ed., M.A.; Registration: Girls—205 D, 40 R (grades 7-11); Fees: $400.

Ridley College
Box 3013
St. Catharines, Ontario L2R 7C3
(416) 684-8193
Headmaster: Richard A. Bradley, M.A. (Oxon); Registration: Boys—139 D, 330 R (ages 10-13), Girls—23 D (ages 10-13); Fees: $2,250-$2,550 + $500-$800 extras (incl. meals) (D), $5,000-$5,250 + $300-$400 extras (R).

Rothesay Collegiate School
Rothesay, N.B. E0G 2W0
(506) 847-8224
Headmaster: Clifford J. Inns, B.A.; Registration: Boys—22 D, 89 R (ages 12-18), Girls—23 D, 47 R (ages 12-18); Fees: $1,600 + $200 extras (D), $3,850 + $200 extras (R). (RCS is affiliated with Netherwood School for Girls.)

St. Andrew's College
Aurora, Ontario L4G 3H7
(416) 727-3178

Headmaster: T.A. Hockin, M.P.A., Ph.D.; Registration: Boys—90 D, 280 R (ages 11-19); Fees: $2,975 + $200 lunches (D), $5,275 + $700 extras (R).

St. Clement's School
21 St. Clement's Avenue
Toronto, Ontario M4R 1G8
(416) 483-4835
Principal: Miss Hazel W. Perkin, M.A.; Registration: Girls—340 D (grades 1-13); Fees: $875-$1,575 (D).

St. George's College
120 Howland Avenue
Toronto, Ontario M5R 3B5
(416) 533-9481
Headmaster: John L. Wright, E.D., B.A.; Registration: Boys—375 D (ages 9-18); Fees: $1,675-$1,925 + $55 books + $40-$50 athletic charges (D).

St. George's School
4175 West 29th Avenue
Vancouver, B.C. V6S 1V6
(604) 224-1304
Headmaster: Alan C.M. Brown, B.Sc., M.A.T., Dip.Ed.; Registration: Boys—521 D, 102 R (ages 7-17); Fees: $1,200-$2,040 + $150-$300 extras (D), $2,930 + $225-$450 extras (R).

St. George's School of Montreal
3100 The Boulevard
Montreal, Quebec H3Y 1R9
(514) 937-9289
Headmaster: Vincent P. Skinner, M.A., M.Ed., C.A.G.S.; Registration: Boys—277 D (ages 5-18), Girls—204 D (ages 5-18); Fees: $630-$1,630 (all-inclusive) (D).

St. John's-Ravenscourt School
400 South Drive
Winnipeg, Manitoba R3T 3K5
(204) 452-3572
Registration: Boys—340 D, 90 R (grades 1-12), Girls—30 D (grades 10-12); Fees: $1,295-$2,360 + $150 extras (D), $4,080-$4,540 + $150-$200 extras (R).

St. Margaret's School
1080 Lucas Avenue
Victoria, B.C. V8X 3P7
(604) 479-7171
Principal: Mrs. M.R. Sendall, B.A. (Hons.); Registration: Girls—220 D (grades K-12); 70 R (grades 5-12), Boys—10 D (grades K-3); Fees: $900-$4,600.

St. Michael's University School
3400 Richmond Road
Victoria, B.C. V8P 4P5
(604) 592-4022/1322
Headmaster: P.A. Caleb, LL.B. (London); Registration: Boys—365 D, 195 R (ages 7-18); Fees: $1,080-$1,710 (D), $3,900-$4,450 + $300 extras (R).

St. Mildred's-Lightbourn School
1080 Linbrook Road
Oakville, Ontario L6J 2L1
(416) 845-2386
Principal: Mrs. Doris L. Bull, B.A.; Registration: Girls—355 D (grades K-13);
Fees: $1,100-$1,500 ($550 for K) (D).

Sedbergh School
Montebello, Quebec J0V 1L0
(819) 423-5523
Headmaster: Tom Wood; Registration: Boys—73 R (ages 8-17); Fees: $4,400 +
$250 (approx.) extras (R).

Selwyn House School
95 Côte St. Antoine Road
Westmount, Quebec H3Y 2H8
(514) 931-9481-2-3-4
Headmaster: Alexis S. Troubetzkoy, B.A.; Registration: Boys—431 D (ages
6-18); Fees: $1,240-$1,700 + $375-$405 extras (D).

Shawnigan Lake School
Shawnigan Lake, B.C. V0R 2W0
(604) 743-5516
Headmaster: The Rev. Horace McClelland, M.B.E., M.A.; Registration: Boys—
13 D, 221 R (ages 13-18); Fees: $2,860 (D), $4,950 (R) (all-inclusive).

Stanstead College
Stanstead, Quebec J0B 3E0
(819) 876-2702
Headmaster: Jeremy M. Riley; Registration: Boys—32 D, 158 R (ages 12-20);
Fees: $600 + $40 extras (D), $4,700 + $180 extras (R).

Strathcona Lodge School
Shawnigan Lake, B.C. V0R 2W0
(604) 743-5582
Principal: Miss Angela J.V. Brown, B.A. (Hons.), Dip.Ed.; Registration: Girls—
135 R (grades 6-12); Fees: $4,400 (R).

Strathcona-Tweedsmuir School
R.R. #2
Okotoks, Alberta T0L 1T0
(403) 938-4431
Principal: W.A. Heard, B.Ed.; Registration: Girls—150 D (grades 1-12), Boys—
200 D (grades 1-12); Fees: $1,320-$1,785 (D).

The Study
3233 The Boulevard
Montreal, Quebec H3Y 1S4
(514) 935-9352
Principal: Mrs. Haldane (Jean C.) Scott, B.A., M.A.T.; Registration: Girls—
245 D (grades K-11), Boys—12 D (grades K-2); Fees: $1,200-$1,750 (grades
K-6), government grant + fee determined by Ministry of Education (grades
7-11) (D).

Trafalgar
3495 Simpson Street
Montreal, Quebec H3G 2J7
(514) 935-2644
Principal: Mrs. Janette Doupe, M.Ed.; Registration: Girls—250 D (grades 7-11);
Fees: Government grant + fee determined by Ministry of Education (D).

Trinity College School
Port Hope, Ontario L1A 3W2
(416) 885-4072
Headmaster: Angus C. Scott, B.A., M.A.; Registration: Boys—12 D, 323 R
(ages 12-18); Fees: $2,900 (D), $4,950-$5,100 (R).

Upper Canada College
200 Lonsdale Road
Toronto, Ontario M4V 1W6
(416) 488-1125
Headmaster: Richard H. Sadleir, M.A.; Registration: Boys—744 D, 170 R
(ages 8-18); Fees: $2,750 (D) + extras, $5,250 (R) + extras.

Weston School
124 Ballantyne Avenue S.
Montreal, Quebec H4X 2B3
(514) 486-6339
Principal: Mrs. Elizabeth A. Goddard; Registration: Girls and Boys—100 D
(grades 1-11); Fees: $1,150-$1,650 (D).

York House School
1500 West King Edward Avenue
Vancouver, B.C. V6J 2V6
(604) 736-6551
Principal: Bryan Peet, A.D.Ed., M.Ed.; Registration: Girls—320 D (grades
K-12), Boys—80 D (grades K-6); Fees: $580-$2,150.

BIBLIOGRAPHY

Beattie, Kim. *Ridley: The Story of a School,* 2 vols. St. Catharines, Ont., 1963.

Bell, Murray. "Sir Edmund Walker". Address given at the Royal Ontario Museum, May 1974. Toronto: ROM, 1974.

Benent, C.L.; Filion, Gérard; Clark, Gregory; Campbell, Manjone Wilkins; Haig-Brown, Roderick. *The Face of Canada.* Toronto: Clarke, Irwin, 1959.

Bell, Walter N. *The Development of the Ontario High School.* Toronto: University of Toronto Press, 1918.

Birmingham, Stephen. *The Right People: A Portrait of the American Social Establishment.* Boston: Little, Brown, 1958.

Bishop, Susan O. "Where Have All the Headmistresses Gone?" *The Independent School Bulletin,* October 1974.

Campbell, Archibal Hamilton. *Archibal Hamilton Campbell (1819-1909) and His Family (A History).* Toronto, 1959.

Cambell, Marjorie F. *A Mountain and a City: The Story of Hamilton.* Toronto: McClelland & Stewart, 1966.

Canadian Headmasters' Association. *Directory of Canadian Independent Schools for Boys.* CHA, 1950.

Careless, J.M.S., and Brown, R. Craig. *The Canadians 1867-1967.* Toronto: Macmillan of Canada, 1967.

Clarke, Sheila, and Linton, Marilyn. "A Better School for Your Money". *Toronto Life,* August 1975.

Clement, Wallace. *The Canadian Corporate Elite: An Analysis of Economic Power.* Toronto: McClelland & Stewart, 1975.

Collard, Edgar Andrew. "The Story of St. Helen's School". *The Montreal Gazette,* 6 May 1972.

Cramp, Mary, and Edgar, Maud C. *Eternal Youth: Addresses to Girls 1913-1930.* Toronto: Macmillan's of Canada, 1931.

Cran, Mrs. George. *A Woman in Canada.* Toronto: Musson, 1910.

Cunningham, John. "Rothesay Collegiate School: Where Boys Still Thrive on Discipline and Supervision". *The Telegraph Journal* (St. John, N.B.), 16 November 1974.

Daly, James. *Education or Molasses? : A Critical Look at the Hall-Dennis Report.* Ancaster, Ont.: Cromlech Press, 1969.

Davies, D.I., and Herman, Kathleen. *Social Space: Canadian Perspectives.* Toronto: New Press, 1971.

de Wolf, Mark, and File, George. *All the King's Men: The Story of a Colonial University.* Halifax, 1972.

Dickman, Thelma. "Well Fed, Well Bred, Well Read . . ." *The Canadian Magazine,* 13 June 1970.

Dickson, George, and Adam, G. Mercer. *A History of Upper Canada College (1829-1892).* Toronto, 1893.

Donald, George. Address given on the occasion of the closing of St. Helen's School, Dunham, P.Q., June 1972.

Eaton, Flora. *Memory's Wall.* Toronto: Clarke, Irwin, 1956.

Edwards, Rev. Edwin Wesley. *The History of Alma College.* St. Thomas, Ont., 1927.

Ellis, W.K. "A Feasibility Study on an Experimental School". Richmond Hill, Ont.: Bayview Secondary School, 1970.

Ganong, Susan B. *A Sketch of Life at Netherwood 1903-1944.* The Rothesay School for Girls, 1952.

Gidney, R.D. "Elementary Education in Upper Canada: A Reassessment". *Ontario History*, vol. 65, no. 3 (September 1973).

Grant, W.L., and Young, A.H. *Upper Canada College 1829-1929: A Short History.* Toronto, 1929.

Green, H. Gordon. "The Dehumanized Pedagogue and the Uneducated Student". *Weekend Magazine,* 22 September 1973.

Halifax, N.S. Public Archives of Nova Scotia. Announcement of the opening of the Halifax Grammar School, 1789. *Royal Gazette and Nova Scotia Advertiser,* 16 June 1789.

Halifax, N.S. Public Archives of Nova Scotia. "The Years of Growth at the Halifax Grammar School (1958-1969)".

Hall, Emmet, and Dennis, Lloyd A. *Living and Learning.* Report of the Provincial Committee on Aims and Objectives of Education in the Schools of Ontario, 1968.

Hardy, E.H., and Cochrane, Honora M. *Centennial Story: The Board of Education for the City of Toronto 1859-1950.* Toronto: Thomas Nelson & Sons, 1950.

Harris, Jean S. "Let's Hear It for Coeducation, Folks". *The Independent School Bulletin* (Boston), vol. 33, no. 2 (December 1973).

Harris, Reginald V. *History of King's Collegiate School (1788-1939).* Windsor, N.S., 1939.

Harris, Robin S. *Quiet Evolution: A Study of the Educational System of Ontario.* Toronto: University of Toronto Press, 1968.

Hodgetts, A.B. *What Culture? What Heritage? : A Study of Civic Education in Canada.* Toronto: The Ontario Institute for Studies in Education, 1968.

Hodgins, J. George. *The Establishment of Schools and Colleges in Ontario 1792-1910.* Vol. 2, Parts 2-11. Part 10: "Classical Colleges and Preparatory Schools for Boys", pp. 188-230. Part 11: "Ladies' Colleges and Preparatory Schools for Girls", pp. 232-267. Toronto: L.K. Cameron Printers and Publishers, 1910.

Holly, Douglas. *Schools, Society and Humanity . . . The Changing World of Secondary Education.* London, Eng.: Paladin Press, 1972.

Houston, Susan E. "Politics, Schools and Social Change in Upper Canada". *The Canadian Historical Review*, vol. 53, no. 3 (September 1972).

Humble, A.H. *The School on the Hill: A History of Trinity College School,*

Port Hope. Privately printed, 1966.

Huxley, Julian. *A Collection of Essays: Knowledge, Morality and Destiny.* (Original title: *New Bottles for New Wine*). New York: The New American Library, 1957.

Johnson, Valerie Miner. "Bringing Schools and People Together". *Saturday Night*, November 1973.

Kamm, Josephine. *How Different from Us, Miss Beale and Miss Buss.* London, Eng.: Bodley Head, 1958.

Ketchum, Anthony. "Independent Schools". Unpublished paper. Toronto: Ontario Institute for Studies in Education, 1971.

King's College School. "The Collegiate School, Windsor". *The Canadian Church Magazine*, March 1890.

_____. "The Education of Commonwealth Youth". *London Illustrated News*, 1 April, 1961.

Kittson, Arthur. *Berthier Yesterday and Today.* Brockville, Ont.: St. Alban's School, 1953.

Kraushaar, Otto F. *American Nonpublic Schools: Patterns of Diversity.* Baltimore, Md.: The Johns Hopkins University Press, 1972.

Lambert, Toyson. *The Hothouse Society.* London, Eng.: Weidenfeld & Nicolson, 1968.

Lamont, Katharine. *The Canadian Association of Headmistresses . . . A History (1931-1972).* Montreal, 1972.

_____. *The Study . . . A Chronicle.* Montreal, 1974.

Ludwig, Johann Bartholdt. "Control and Financing of Private Education in Alberta: The Roles of Parents, the Church and the State". Master's thesis, University of Alberta, 1970.

Macleod, Sandra. "A History of Halifax Ladies' College". Unpublished paper. Halifax, 1971.

Mair, Shirley E. "Edith Read's Ungentle Formula for Raising Young Ladies". *Maclean's*, 2 March, 1957.

Massey, Vincent, Rt. Hon. C.H. *What's Past is Prologue.* Toronto: Macmillan's of Canada, 1963.

Maxwell, Mary Percival. "Social Structure, Socialization and Social Class in a Canadian Private School for Girls". Ph.D. thesis, Cornell University, 1970.

McCulley, Joseph. "The Role of the Private School". Printed address, n.d.

McGilton, Gordon L. "Stanstead College in Relation to the Border Communities During the Past One Hundred Years". Address to the Stanstead Historical Society, May 1973.

McGregor, Alex. "Egerton Ryerson, Albert Carman and the Founding of Albert College, Belleville". *Ontario History*, vol. 63, no. 4 (December 1971).

McIntyre, Hugh. "Why the Private School Lives On". *The Financial Post*, August 1972.

McLachlan, James. *American Boarding Schools: A Historical Study.* New York: Charles Scribners Sons, 1970.

Memories of Edgehill 1891-1966. Privately printed, Windsor, N.S.

National Association of Independent Schools. *The Role of the Business Manager in the Independent School.* Boston: NAIS, 1967.

———————. *Financing the Independent School of the Future.* Boston: NAIS, 1968.

———————. *The Selection and Appointment of School Heads: A Manual of Suggestions.* Boston: NAIS, 1971.

———————. *To Change the Climate.* NAIS Report no. 46. Boston: NAIS, 1973.

———————. *Annual Statistics.* NAIS Report no. 49. Boston: NAIS, 1974.

———————. *Pluralism in Education.* NAIS Report no. 50. Boston: NAIS, 1974.

Neatby, Hilda. *So Little for the Mind.* Toronto: Clarke, Irwin, 1953.

Newman, Peter. *The Canadian Establishment.* Toronto: McClelland & Stewart, 1975. (See "The Private School Fraternity", Appendix K.)

Northway, Mary L. *William Emet Blatz, M.S., M.B., Ph.D. (1895-1964).* Toronto: Institute of Child Study, University of Toronto, 1965.

Parkman, Francis, and Springer, E. Laurence. *The Independent School Trustee Handbook.* Boston: National Association of Independent Schools, 1970.

Penton, D. Stephen. *"Non Nobis Solum": The History of Lower Canada College and its Predecessor, St. John's School.* Montreal: The Corporation of LCC, 1972.

Porter, John. *The Vertical Mosaic.* Toronto: University of Toronto Press, 1965.

Prentice, Alison L. *John Strachan and Early Upper Canada (1799-1814).* Toronto, 1960.

Preparatory School. New York: Coward-McCann Inc., 1970.

Private Independent Schools (A Directory). Wallingford, Conn.: Bunting & Lyon, 1973.

Purdy, J.D. "John Strachan's Educational Policies (1815-1841)". *Ontario History,* vol. 64, no. 1 (March 1972).

Ridley, H.M. "Famous Schools of Canada" Series. *Willison's Monthly,* 1927-28. Articles on TCS, Woodstock College, BSS, Glen Mawr, Mount Royal College.

Robertson, John Ross. "The Founding of Upper Canada College". *The Evening Telegram,* November 24, 1888.

Rourke, R.E.K. "The Independent Schools . . . A Needed Contribution". *Saturday Night,* vol. 70 (1954).

Scarfe, N.V. "It's Impossible to Teach Hostile Students". *The Vancouver Sun,* 19 March, 1974.

Seeley, John; Sim, R. Alexander; Loosley, Elizabeth W. *Crestwood Heights.* Toronto: University of Toronto Press, 1956.

Shack, Sybil. *The Two-Thirds Minority: Women in Canadian Education.* Faculty of Education, Guidance Centre. University of Toronto, 1973.

Shukyn, Beverley, and Shukyn, Murray. *A Personal History of SEED: A New Approach to Secondary School Education.* Toronto: Holt Rinehard & Winston, 1973.

Simmons, Ted. "A Place to Stand and a Place to Grow: Independent Schools in Ontario". Unpublished paper. Peterborough, Ont.: Trent University, 1972.

Smith, Waldo E.L. *Albert College (1857-1957): A History.* Belleville, Ont., 1957.

Sowby, Cedric W. *A Family Writ Large: Memoirs of a Former Headmaster.* Toronto: Longman, 1971.

Stamp, Robert. "The Right to Choose". *Weekend Magazine,* 13 September 1975.

Stanstead College. "The Story of Stanstead College". *Stanstead County Historical Society Journal,* vol. 3 (1969).

_____. *One Hundred Years After.* Stanstead, P.Q., 1973.

Steele, Catherine. *Havergal College: A Brief Historical Sketch.* Toronto: The York Pioneer and Historical Society, 1971.

Stephen, Alan G.A., ed. *Private Schools in Canada: A Handbook of Boys' Schools Which are Members of the Canadian Headmasters' Association.* Toronto: Clarke, Irwin, 1938.

Symons, Kyrle C. *That Amazing Institution.* Victoria, B.C.: St. Michael's School, 1947.

"To Let Some Air in the Hothouse". *The New York Times,* 1 October, 1972.

University of Toronto Schools. *The First Fifty Years.* Toronto, 1960.

Upper Canada College. *A Short History and Documents.* Toronto, 1967.

Vasey, Paul. "Private Schools: There's a New Air in the Old Place. *The Hamilton Spectator,* 29 September, 1973.

Watson, Geoffrey G. "Sports and Games in Ontario Private Schools (1830-1930)". Master's thesis, University of Alberta, 1970.

Weinzweig, Paul. "Socialization and Subculture in Elite Education". Ph.D. thesis, University of Toronto, 1970.

Wigney, Trevor. *Education of Women and Girls.* Toronto: College of Education, University of Toronto, 1963.

Wilson, J.D.; Stamp, R.M.; Audet, L.P. *Canadian Education: A History.* Toronto: Prentice-Hall, 1970.

Winter, Brian. "From Castle to College". *The Whitby Argosy,* 28 May, 1970.

Wober, Mallory. *English Girls' Boarding Schools.* London, Eng.: The Penguin Press, 1971.

Young, Phyllis Brett. *The Torontonians.* Toronto: Longman, 1960.

INDEX